THE ETHICS OF EMMANUEL LEVINAS

Cultural Memory

in

the

Present

Mieke Bal and Hent de Vries, Editors

THE ETHICS OF EMMANUEL LEVINAS

Diane Perpich

STANFORD UNIVERSITY PRESS

STANFORD, CALIFORNIA

2008

Stanford University Press
Stanford, California

Printed in the United States of America on acid-free, archival-quality paper

Library of Congress Cataloging-in-Publication Data

Perpich, Diane.
  The ethics of Emmanuel Levinas / Diane Perpich.
    p.   cm.—(Cultural memory in the present)
  Includes bibliographical references and index.
  ISBN 978-0-8047-5942-7 (cloth : alk. paper)
  ISBN 978-0-8047-5943-4 (pbk. : alk. paper)
    1. Levinas, Emmanuel—Ethics.   2. Responsibility.   3. Other (Philosophy)
I. Title. II. Series.
B2430.L484P465 2008
170.92—dc22

                                                          2007051703

Contents

Abbreviations

WORKS BY LEVINAS

AT   *Alterité et transcendence.* Paris: Fata Morgana, 1995.
BPW   *Emmanuel Levinas: Basic Philosophical Writings.* Edited by
        Adriaan T. Peperzak, Simon Critchley, and Robert Bernas-
        coni. Bloomington: Indiana University Press, 1996.
CPP   *Collected Philosophical Papers.* Translated by Alphonso Lingis.
        Dordrecht: Martinus Nijhoff, 1987.
DE   *Discovering Existence with Husserl.* Translated and edited
        by Richard A. Cohen and Michael B. Smith. Evanston, IL:
        Northwestern University Press, 1998.
DF   *Difficult Freedom: Essays on Judaism.* Translated by Seán Hand.
        Baltimore: Johns Hopkins University Press, 1990.
EDE   *En découvrant l'existence avec Husserl et Heidegger.* Paris: J.
        Vrin, 1988.
EE   *Existence and Existents.* Translated by Alphonso Lingis. The
        Hague: Nijhoff Press, 1978.
EI   *Ethics and Infinity: Conversations with Philippe Nemo.* Trans-
        lated by Richard A. Cohen. Pittsburgh: Duquesne University
        Press, 1985.
EN   *Entre Nous: Thinking-of-the-Other.* Translated by Michael B.
        Smith and Barbara Harshav. New York: Columbia University
        Press, 1998.
GCM   *Of God Who Comes to Mind.* Translated by Bettina Bergo.
        Stanford, CA: Stanford University Press, 1998.
IR   *Is It Righteous to Be? Interviews with Emmanuel Levinas.* Edited
        by Jill Robbins. Stanford, CA: Stanford University Press,
        2001.

LR   *The Levinas Reader.* Edited by Seán Hand. Oxford: Blackwell
          Publishers, 1989.
NTR   *Nine Talmudic Readings.* Translated with an introduction by
          Annette Aronowicz. Bloomington: Indiana University Press,
          1990.
OB   *Otherwise Than Being, or Beyond Essence.* Translated by Al-
          phonso Lingis. Pittsburgh: Duquesne University Press, 1998.
OE   *On Escape.* Translated by Bettina Bergo. Stanford, CA: Stan-
          ford University Press, 2003.
OS   *Outside the Subject.* Translated by Michael B. Smith. Stanford,
          CA: Stanford University Press, 1993.
RPH   "Reflections on the Philosophy of Hitlerism" (translated by
          Seán Hand). *Critical Inquiry* 17, no. 1 (Autumn 1990): 62–71.
TI   *Totality and Infinity.* Translated by Alphonso Lingis. Pitts-
          burgh: Duquesne University Press, 1969.
TIHP   *The Theory of Intuition in Husserl's Phenomenology.* Translated
          by André Orianne. Evanston, IL: Northwestern University
          Press, 1973.
TO   *Time and the Other.* Translated by Alphonso Lingis. Pitts-
          burgh: Duquesne University Press, 1987.
"Trace"   "The Trace of the Other." In *Deconstruction in Context,* edited
          by Mark C. Taylor. Chicago: University of Chicago Press,
          1986.

OTHER WORKS

BPP   Martin Heidegger. *The Basic Problems of Phenomenology.*
          Translation, introduction, and lexicon by Albert Hofstadter.
          Rev. ed. Bloomington: Indiana University Press, 1988.
BT   Martin Heidegger. *Being and Time.* Translated by John Mac-
          quarrie and Edward Robinson. New York: Harper Collins,
          1962.
BW   *Martin Heidegger: Basic Writings.* Edited by David Farrell
          Krell. New York: Harper & Row, 1977.
HCT   Martin Heidegger. *History of the Concept of Time: Prolegom-
          ena.* Translated by Theodore Kisiel. Bloomington: Indiana
          University Press, 1985.

IP   Edmund Husserl. *The Idea of Phenomenology.* Translated by
        William P. Alston and George Nakhnikian; introduction by
        George Nakhnikian. The Hague: Nijhoff Publishers, 1964.
LI   Edmund Husserl. *Logical Investigations,* vol. 1. Translated by J.
        N. Findlay. London: Routledge & Kegan Paul, 1970.
MFL   Heidegger, Martin. *The Metaphysical Foundations of Logic.*
        Translated by Michael Heim. Bloomington: Indiana Univer-
        sity Press, 1984.
VM   Jacques Derrida. "Violence and Metaphysics." In *Writing and
        Difference,* translated with an introduction and additional
        notes by Alan Bass. Chicago: University of Chicago Press,
        1978.

Preface and Acknowledgments

This book grew out of questions that have puzzled me from my earliest reading of Levinas. Like others, I was attracted to Levinas's writings by their simultaneous sobriety and excess. Never in the history of Western philosophy has there been an ethical responsibility so severe: a responsibility that increases with my every attempt to discharge it; that does not depend on choice or voluntary action; that is a responsibility not just for the other but for all of his responsibility as well. In this picture of responsible subjectivity, there seems to be no place for the complacencies of ordinary moral life, where obligations are met, duties attended to, and the ego has time afterward to attend to his own cares and concerns. The Levinasian subject is a hostage to the other, impaled by responsibility, never allowed to say this or that is none of her own doing or affair. The picture is at once utterly preposterous and deeply moving. Can we even imagine what it would be like to live as if one were responsible in this way? Is such a life practically possible? The existential and practical problems raised by Levinas's account run in tandem with the conceptual problems his work generates. First and foremost among these, for me, is the problem of how to understand the notion of an *infinite* responsibility. Does responsibility retain a coherent meaning when its scope is extended in this way, or when obligation in every way surpasses what it is possible for the agent to do? If I am responsible for everything, isn't that just the same as being responsible for nothing? What becomes of the other's autonomy in such an ethics? And what of duties I might be said to have to myself? A related set of questions concerns the status of Levinas's claims about responsibility. Are such claims descriptive, phenomenological, normative, something else altogether? Similar questions, of course, have long been addressed to Levinas's notion of the "face" and to its role in the provocation of responsibility. Using the face to represent the unrepresentable other, Levinas says that this face calls me to responsibility but also that there is never any certainty of my having been called. What are we to make of this? In what sense have I been called? In what sense am I uncertain? In what sense is the other unrepresentable?

I suspect that the questions asked here are, in a sense, unpopular ones. Levinas's readers tend to think either that it is obvious that he is not "doing ethics" in the usual sense, or that it is obvious that he is. Neither position rings true, since, at the least, almost nothing about Levinas's relation to more traditional and familiar forms of ethical inquiry is straightforward or obvious. He himself said relatively little that is helpful on the subject, and possibly with good reason. The interest of this book is not in sorting through Levinas's relation to traditional forms of philosophical ethics, nor is the principal idea to put Levinas's thought in conversation with Anglo-American forms of moral theory—far from it. But at the same time, this book rejects the idea that we must at all costs retain the separation of Levinas's thought from such discourses.

I argue in what follows that it is essential to raise anew the question of "Levinas and ethics." The book begins from the notion of alterity, a natural starting place for any discussion of Levinas (though not the only one), and follows the movement of his thought from its initial concern with the problem of transcendence, through the analysis of the face-to-face relation, to the elaboration of responsibility, and then to questions of normativity and the ethical relationship. In the final chapters, I turn in a limited way to politics and consider two sets of questions that have arisen in relation to Levinas's thought: the ethics of animals and the environment, on the one hand, and of gender and identity-based politics, on the other. With respect to three key notions—alterity, the face, and responsibility—the book reads them against the grain, with an eye more interested in the tensions they generate than in the problems they are meant to solve. For many years I counted myself among Levinas's apologists, interpreting him primarily with the aim of weaving the strands of his thought into a single cloth. It wasn't until I began reading Levinas's work *for* the failures of his texts, and for the positive work done by those failures, that I arrived at the full interpretation developed here. This doesn't mean I've given up the idea that Levinas makes sense. I'm as wary of the idea that his work is "beyond" sense as he is about the possibility of getting "beyond" being. But when his texts, especially *Totality and Infinity*, are read *for the sake of* the tensions they harbor rather than with the goal of eliminating them, a much richer landscape and a more complex sense of what he means by ethics or the ethical ultimately emerges. Indeed, it is one of the central theses of the present work that ethical life, as Levinas portrays and imagines it, is a life constituted by its tensions. Ethics, on this view, is not a matter of living up to one's responsibilities, but neither is it a matter of seeing that such an attempt will always be futile. Ethics is lived and understood, on the interpretation of Levinas developed here, as the demand for ethics in the face of the failure of ethics. An analysis of what this demand is and its relation to subjectivity is central to the present work.

I have had the generous help and support of numerous friends, mentors, and colleagues as I worked through the issues that became this book. My oldest debts are to my teachers: to Richard Bernstein, who encouraged my earliest attempts at philosophical writing and whose continued support has been invaluable; to Arnold Davidson, who first introduced me to Levinas and whose probing questions nurtured my skepticism; and to Adriaan Peperzak, whose immeasurable knowledge and generosity showed me what a life of Levinasian responsibility might look like. I also count Robert Bernasconi among those who have most generously shared their understanding of Levinas with me over the years while encouraging and challenging my own interpretation.

This book has benefited greatly from discussions with various academic audiences and I thank them for their careful criticisms and helpful suggestions. An early draft of Chapter 1 was presented at the Collegium Phaenomenologicum in Città di Castella. A talk given to the Levinas Research Seminar when it met at Penn State during the blizzard of 2003 was the seed for the arguments in Chapter 2. This same group provided much welcome feedback on the penultimate version of Chapter 4. An earlier version of Chapter 4 was given at the "Centennial Conference on Levinas and Law" at McGill University Law School. I am thankful to Desmond Manderson for extensive comments on this chapter, which improved it considerably. Parts of Chapter 5 were presented at the University of Toledo, and at Purdue University at the inaugural meeting of the North American Levinas Society, and benefited from those discussions. Chapter 6 was improved by lively and informed discussions at Loyola University Baltimore and at the Society for Phenomenology and Existential Philosophy. Two further places figured prominently in the writing of this book. For giving me a room of my own during a fellowship year and for a year beyond that I owe a special debt of gratitude to Mona Frederick and Galyn Martin at the Robert Penn Warren Center for the Humanities at Vanderbilt University. Their friendship, infectious laughter, and ability to brew a great cup of coffee sustained me during the early phases of writing this book. The International Philosophical Colloquium Evian has been a most genial place to test the ideas in several later chapters. I am grateful for the friendship of Georg Bertram, who was always ready to discuss the question of Levinas and normativity and who encouraged this project when it most needed it. David Lauer and Robin Celikates made *La Sapinière* a philosophical home away from home for several summers, and I thank them for their friendship, intellectual prowess, and late-night camaraderie.

Friends old and new have given generously of their time to respond to the arguments of this book or to lend their support during the writing of it. Thanks are due to Brooke Ackerly, Ellen Armour, Peter Atterton, Silvia Benso, Debra Bergoffen, Paul Blum, Matt Calarco, Lynne Clark, Scott Davidson, Rosalyn Diprose, Penelope Deutscher, William Edelglass, Matt Eshleman, Dana Hollander, Claire Katz, Len Lawlor, Joseph Mai, William Maker, Lee Morrisey, Eric Nelson, Ben Pryor, François Raffoul, Lucius Outlaw, Alan Schrift, J. Aaron Simmons, Daniel Smith, Jill Stauffer, John Thatamanil, David Wood, Ben Yost, Ewa Ziarek, and Krzysztof Ziarek. I owe a special debt to Todd May, whose philosophical acumen and sheer good sense I have relied on tremendously in the final phases of this project. Very special thanks are due to Hent de Vries, who encouraged me to submit the manuscript to Stanford and whose work on Levinas has often inspired and formed my own. I also owe a debt of gratitude to Richard Cohen, who read this manuscript for Stanford University Press and provided encouraging and helpful comments. Levinas studies would not be what it is without Richard's early and continued engagements in the field. My sincere thanks are also due to Emily-Jane Cohen and Tim Robbins for their superb work and reassuring presence at different stages of the publication process. My family has been my greatest and most constant source of support, and what I owe them cannot be put into words. This book is dedicated to them.

THE ETHICS OF EMMANUEL LEVINAS

Introduction: But Is It *Ethics*?

Whether shamefully, gloriously, mistakenly, or by default, we are all philosophers; especially when we submit whatever seems philosophical . . . to a questioning so radical that the entire tradition would have to be called forth in its support.

—MAURICE BLANCHOT

When Levinas speaks of ethics . . . ethics is wholly other; and yet it is the same word indeed.

—JACQUES DERRIDA

Though the name Emmanuel Levinas has become synonymous with the phrase "ethics as first philosophy,"[1] is it certain what we mean when we speak of *ethics* (or *philosophy*) in relation to his work? There is the famous concern for the alterity of the other, to be sure. Likewise the rich descriptions of the face-to-face encounter, of a responsibility that deepens with every attempt to discharge it, of subjectivity itself as a being-*for*-the other. But is it obvious why alterity should be thought of as making ethical demands on me? Or why otherness rather than sameness should serve as the basis for ethical relationships? Further, what does it mean to "encounter" a face if the principal feature of the face, as Levinas understands it, is that it cannot be seen, known, or represented? And how does this face-to-face encounter put me under an obligation or make me responsible? Finally, what can it mean to have a responsibility that cannot be discharged or fulfilled?

Let's begin with the question of
in an undifferentiated way as othern
has most often been sameness rathe
ters for ethical inquiry: it is a sha
that matters to thinkers like Ari
pleasure and pain that interest early a
sentiments, habits, and dispositions that ta
theory, in virtue ethics, and in phenomenologicai
philosophical tradition, it has been our *likeness* to one a
crucial respect, that has served as the basis for estimating what w
one another in moral or ethical terms. For that tradition, the scope of i
sponsibility as well as its targets are established by considering the expectations and possibilities created by our *shared* inheritance—whether that inheritance be rational, affective, dispositional, or of some other kind.

Levinas, by contrast, insists that it is the alterity of the other which
commands my responsibility. A large part of the appeal of Levinas's thought
derives, no doubt, from its contestation of the logic and dominance of
sameness within Western moral philosophy. The social and political climate of the late twentieth century, in both academic and popular culture,
is marked deeply by a concern with diversity, otherness, and difference. It
is in this climate, moreover, that Levinas's philosophy has risen to prominence, becoming an "obligatory reference point" in a range of disciplines
from philosophy and theology to psychology, sociology, literary theory,
communications studies, psychotherapy, pedagogy, nursing, international relations, and, most recently, legal theory and jurisprudence (Critchley and Bernasconi 2002, 5). But in sorting out the question of Levinas
and ethics, it should be noted first of all that alterity in Levinas's sense
must be distinguished from relative or specific forms of difference. Alterity is not the difference of people who live in different times and places
or who inhabit different cultural *milieux*. With the phrase "the alterity of
the Other," Levinas indicates an unbridgeable otherness, an *absolute* alterity, that is not merely *other than me*. He suggests, further, that this sort of
alterity puts me under an infinite obligation to the other, binds me to the
other—but only me. In everyday contexts, we speak of responsibility in a
limited way—as accountability and responsibility for what one has done
oneself, for what is one's own doing or one's own affair. Levinas writes of
a responsibility that goes beyond what I do, beyond my actions and their

4

Introduction: But Is It Ethics?

ethics or to claim that he simply is
sense at all. Likewise, critics have b
seen it as part and parcel of a discr
porters herald it as one of the mo
late twentieth century.
In the remainder
trum of views conc
ing some of the
thought ab
ethica

Introduction: But Is It *Ethics?*

Whether shamefully, gloriously, mistakenly, or by default, we are all philosophers;
especially when we submit whatever seems philosophical . . . to a questioning so
radical that the entire tradition would have to be called forth in its support.

—MAURICE BLANCHOT

When Levinas speaks of ethics . . . ethics is wholly other; and yet it is the same
word indeed.

—JACQUES DERRIDA

Though the name Emmanuel Levinas has become synonymous with
the phrase "ethics as first philosophy,"[1] is it certain what we mean when we
speak of *ethics* (or *philosophy*) in relation to his work? There is the famous
concern for the alterity of the other, to be sure. Likewise the rich descriptions of the face-to-face encounter, of a responsibility that deepens with
every attempt to discharge it, of subjectivity itself as a being-*for*-the other.
But is it obvious why alterity should be thought of as making ethical demands on me? Or why otherness rather than sameness should serve as the
basis for ethical relationships? Further, what does it mean to "encounter" a
face if the principal feature of the face, as Levinas understands it, is that it
cannot be seen, known, or represented? And how does this face-to-face encounter put me under an obligation or make me responsible? Finally, what
can it mean to have a responsibility that cannot be discharged or fulfilled?

Let's begin with the question of alterity, understood for the moment in an undifferentiated way as otherness. For the Western moral tradition, it has most often been sameness rather than otherness or difference that matters for ethical inquiry: it is a shared capacity for reason or rational willing that matters to thinkers like Aristotle and Kant; it is shared capacities for pleasure and pain that interest early and late utilitarians; and it is common sentiments, habits, and dispositions that take center stage in moral sense theory, in virtue ethics, and in phenomenological ethics. For the Western philosophical tradition, it has been our *likeness* to one another, in some crucial respect, that has served as the basis for estimating what we owe to one another in moral or ethical terms. For that tradition, the scope of responsibility as well as its targets are established by considering the expectations and possibilities created by our *shared* inheritance—whether that inheritance be rational, affective, dispositional, or of some other kind.

Levinas, by contrast, insists that it is the alterity of the other which commands my responsibility. A large part of the appeal of Levinas's thought derives, no doubt, from its contestation of the logic and dominance of sameness within Western moral philosophy. The social and political climate of the late twentieth century, in both academic and popular culture, is marked deeply by a concern with diversity, otherness, and difference. It is in this climate, moreover, that Levinas's philosophy has risen to prominence, becoming an "obligatory reference point" in a range of disciplines from philosophy and theology to psychology, sociology, literary theory, communications studies, psychotherapy, pedagogy, nursing, international relations, and, most recently, legal theory and jurisprudence (Critchley and Bernasconi 2002, 5). But in sorting out the question of Levinas and ethics, it should be noted first of all that alterity in Levinas's sense must be distinguished from relative or specific forms of difference. Alterity is not the difference of people who live in different times and places or who inhabit different cultural *milieux*. With the phrase "the alterity of the Other," Levinas indicates an unbridgeable otherness, an *absolute* alterity, that is not merely *other than me*. He suggests, further, that this sort of alterity puts me under an infinite obligation to the other, binds me to the other—but only me. In everyday contexts, we speak of responsibility in a limited way—as accountability and responsibility for what one has done oneself, for what is one's own doing or one's own affair. Levinas writes of a responsibility that goes beyond what I do, beyond my actions and their consequences, to an infinite, irrefusable responsibility for the other. I am responsible to the point of being responsible for the other's responsibility. Responsibility "is not a debt that can be limited by the extent of one's active commitment, for one can acquit oneself of a debt of that sort, whereas, unless we compromise our thought, we can never be clear of our debts to the Other. It is an infinite responsibility, a responsibility which does not suit my wishes: the responsibility of a hostage" (*LR* 206)!

Enlightenment morality is often portrayed as being concerned with the question, "What ought I do?" Ancient ethics, on the other hand, is credited with asking the broader questions, "How should one live?" or "What is the best life for human beings?"[2] These questions are sometimes depicted as marking the end points of a continuum along which normative ethical inquiry may run, depending on whether it is individual actions or the shape of a whole life that is most at issue. Levinas's notion of an infinite responsibility does not clearly answer to either sort of question, nor can it be comfortably located anywhere along such a continuum. Indeed, the notion of an infinite responsibility is puzzling and troubling if it is understood straightforwardly as an answer to either the Socratic or the Kantian question. If I am responsible for everything and everyone, can I really be held responsible for anything or anyone? If it is a given that I will fail to carry out or live up to my responsibilities, in what sense are they really obligatory or even mine? And why mine alone? Readers have found this notion of responsibility and the absolute alterity from which it issues by turns unthinkable, ridiculous, scandalous, and sublime. Thus, though it seems strange indeed to say it, there remains a question about how to relate the term "ethics" to the signature "Emmanuel Levinas."

In the secondary literature on Levinas's thought, there appear to be two main responses to this quandary: at one end of the spectrum are those for whom it is obvious that Levinas's thought has ethical import or contains an ethical address, even if his philosophical writings depart from more familiar forms of ethical inquiry. At the opposite end are those for whom it is not apparent at all that Levinas's thought shares more than a name with ethics as it usually understood. Contrary to expectations, Levinas's supporters do not cluster at one end of this continuum, nor do his critics alone crowd the other pole. Sympathizers are as likely as detractors to distance Levinas's thought from mainstream forms of philosophical ethics or to claim that he simply is not engaged in ethics in any familiar sense at all. Likewise, critics have branded his thought an ethics and have seen it as part and parcel of a discredited humanism just as often as supporters herald it as one of the most significant ethical contributions of the late twentieth century.

In the remainder of this Introduction, I first canvas the broad spectrum of views concerning the question of "Levinas and Ethics," illuminating some of the confusions that arise from the attempt to distance Levinas's thought altogether from questions of normativity (or the binding force of ethical claims). Second, I glance briefly at one of the most important historical sources for this confusion, namely, Heidegger's dismissal of ethics in his famous "Letter on Humanism." And finally, I outline the path that the current work will take as it attempts to reinterpret the central ethical categories of Levinas's thought in a manner that is at once mindful of the ways in which his work departs substantively and formally from traditional ethical inquiries and attentive to possible bridges that permit us to move with greater ease and fluency toward an understanding of the nature of Levinasian responsibility and the claims it makes on us.

Conflicting Views and Normative Confusions

There have been strident denials that Levinas is engaged in anything recognizable as an ethics. In an exchange with Simon Critchley about the ethical and political dimensions of Derrida's work, Richard Rorty remarks, quoting Critchley, "I . . . agree with Critchley that if 'one understands ethics in the particular and radical sense given to that word' by Levinas, then Derrida's practice may well have 'an overriding ethical significance.' But I don't understand the word 'ethics' that way, and I don't think it useful to give that word that sense" (Mouffe 1996, 41). Rorty confesses that he simply does not find Levinas's "Other" a useful tool for ethical deliberation, quite apart from any question of whether what Levinas says about the other is right or edifying. In an earlier phase of the exchange, Rorty unabashedly admits being "unable to connect Levinas's pathos of the infinite with ethics or politics," since the latter have to do with "reaching accommodation between competing interests" and it simply is not clear how Levinas's descriptions of the other contribute to that project (17). Elsewhere,

Rorty remarks that Levinas's notion of an infinite responsibility "may be useful to some of us in our individual quests for private perfection. [But w]hen we take up our public responsibilities . . . the infinite and the unrepresentable are merely nuisances. Thinking of our responsibilities in these terms is as much of a stumbling-block to effective political organization as is the sense of sin" (Rorty 1998, 97). Rorty's comments vacillate between the claim that there is no recognizable sense of ethics in Levinas's thought and the insinuation that the ethics found there is of an entirely too familiar type. It may not matter to the pragmatist which view is correct, since the criteria for preserving certain kinds of discourse is not truth-value but usefulness. For Rorty, whatever the use of Levinas's thought in the private life of an individual, it is not a discourse that can command broad allegiance in the public sphere, and thus its use there is extremely limited and possibly counterproductive.

If it is tempting to dismiss Rorty's critique as the uncharitable reading of someone who works far outside the phenomenological tradition from which Levinas's thought emerges, it is worth considering a similar criticism made from within that tradition and in explicit defense of it. Dominique Janicaud's (1991) dismissal of Levinas's thought as a turn from a justified descriptive phenomenology to an unjustified theological metaphysics shares Rorty's suspicion that Levinas's thought can be convincing only to those committed to a positive religious tradition. For Janicaud, Levinas uses the tools or language of phenomenological description but turns them to the service of that which cannot appear, and the move seems to him no more and no less than a theological turn to the invisible. Other readers have been equally explicit, though often more approving, in suggesting that Levinas's thought is best construed as a religious ethics (Blum 1983) or as having theological commitments without which his ethics cannot get off the ground (Visker 1997; Newman 2000). To say this is to agree with Rorty that the readership for Levinas's work will be limited to those with similar religious leanings—those, in other words, who will not demand a nonreligious justification of the major claims of his thought.

Supporters, perhaps not surprisingly, have sometimes pursued a similar line, seeing in it a strength rather than a weakness of Levinas's work. In *Driven Back to the Text*, which argues for the essentially Jewish character of Levinas's thought, Oona Ajzenstat intentionally forgoes the attempt to adduce evidence or justification for Levinas's ethical claims, being "content" to pronounce herself "persuaded by the ethical address" of his work (Ajzenstat 2001, 6). There is a subtle logic to Ajzenstat's position, since Levinas's thought explicitly attempts to render problematic any demand for arguments that would prove the "truth" of ethical responsibility. Nonetheless, insofar as such a view appears to set aside altogether the requirement to provide a defense of the ethical claims, it risks conceding that Levinas's thought can have a legitimate place in our religious or ethico-religious lives (understood as regions of private codes or beliefs) but denies Levinas a place in our public, philosophical lives—that is, in that sphere where justification is rightly demanded. In this respect, Ajzenstat's reading is fully concordant with Rorty's and Janicaud's, though in no other way, I imagine, would she find herself their fellow traveler. And this in itself is significant.

As varied as these interpretations are, their effect is the same: Levinas's thought is relegated to the sphere of private reflection (if there is such a thing) or personal belief, meaning belief that one is not called upon to justify to another. This privatization of Levinas's thought, with its implicit invocation of subjectivity as an inward and isolated possession, would be a strange fate for a body of work literally obsessed by the other and by a responsibility constitutive of subjectivity itself. To be responsible for the other, I will argue in what follows, does not only or even primarily mean taking over for the other or doing for the other what he would not or could not do for himself. Responsibility in the Levinasian sense requires an apology in the Greek sense of the term: it means giving a defense of oneself, justifying oneself before the other. To be called to an ethical life, on the interpretation to be developed here, is not to be called to a life of pious thoughts or religious sentiments—no matter how other-regarding or generous they may be; it is to be called to justify one's life and one's construal of the world before another whose body is vulnerable to hunger, thirst, pain, and misery. Feeding the hungry will be my responsibility on the Levinasian view, to be sure, but justifying my means in doing so will be no less an ethical task. To relegate Levinas's thought to the realm of one's private religious or moral concern is to miss the sense in which it is, despite everything, a *philosophy* with philosophy's concern for justification and critique. It is also, not incidentally, to misunderstand the sense that Levinas gives to the word "religion" when he does use it and to miss its connection to the political and public sphere.

Turning to those who read Levinas's thought as ethical in some broadly philosophical sense, we nonetheless find a second effort to distance his work from ethics as traditionally understood and from normative questions in particular. Commentators routinely point out, for example, that for Levinas ethics is not one branch of philosophy among others; it is not a superstructure whose questions are logically or conceptually dependent on a more primary region of philosophy (e.g., logic, epistemology, or ontology). Such readings note that ethics for Levinas is foundational; it is *prima philosophia*.[3] But unlike Kant, for whom practical philosophy also claims a certain primacy, Levinas is not engaged in a constructive enterprise; he does not articulate and defend a set of normative principles meant to guide action. Indeed, it is often remarked that Levinas's thought stands to traditional normative ethics as Heidegger's fundamental ontology stands to traditional ontological inquiries: it undertakes a radical rethinking of the question of the meaning of the ethical, but it is not *an ethics* per se.[4]

So, much of the story of "Levinas and ethics" is well known and retailed everywhere in the secondary literature. Broad agreement is harder to come by, however, when commentators leave off saying what Levinas's thought is not and attempt to describe what sort of enterprise he *is* engaged in. When pressed, descriptions of the positive project put a decisive strain on the forgoing consensus that Levinas's thought has little or nothing to do with normative ethics. Some have seen Levinas as engaged in a descriptive (phenomenological or existential) enterprise. The sociologist Zygmunt Bauman, for example, takes this view in his well-known text *Modernity and the Holocaust.* For Bauman, Levinas's analyses of the face of the other as that which calls me to responsibility are to be read as offering a "description of the existential condition of 'being with others,'" in which this "primary and irremovable attribute of human existence" is understood in terms of responsibility (Bauman 1989, 182). As Bauman presents the essentials of Levinas's view, "being with others" simply *means* being responsible. Bauman's characterization is not entirely out of keeping with Levinas's own presentation of his work—especially in *Ethics and Infinity,* from which Bauman draws heavily. But the sociologist appears relatively untroubled by the problem of how Levinas could be giving a description of what, strictly speaking, does not appear. For Levinas, neither the face which commands my responsibility nor the ethical character of the encounter with another can be made evident from a third-person or impersonal perspective, so the description, in any case, is not like ordinary descriptions that purport to show something that anyone with the right sort of eyes or method could verify for him- or herself.

More attuned to this problem, others have characterized Levinas's ethics (again as Levinas does himself) as messianic (Chalier 1993; Abensour 1998), as an ethics of prophecy (Ciaramelli 1991), and as engaged in witnessing (Scott 1995; Hatley 2000; Oliver 2001). What each of these terms suggests is an attestation to that which cannot be made an object of knowledge but which is not thereby to be deemed an unreal, illusory, or merely subjective experience. For these readers, the ethical character of the relation to the other is not impressed upon me like a sense-datum or a fact (though somewhat like both, it is something over which I exercise little control). It appears rather in the moment of my *response* to an other whom I do not "know" is there; it consists in a "response-ability," or a response given before I am called and before I could know myself to be called. As Oliver among others emphasizes, witnessing is not something the ego *does* but is that which constitutes the subject itself and constitutes it as always already subjected to ethical obligation (Oliver 2001, 11, 15, 183, and passim). Characterizing this same aspect of Levinas's thought in a different idiom, Hilary Putnam suggests that Levinas fits the mold of a moral perfectionist, in the sense given to this term in recent work by Stanley Cavell. While some ethicists are legislators, interested in the production of detailed social and political rules, Levinas, like others that Cavell calls perfectionists, believes there is something *prior* to rules or principles without which the latter would be worthless. "Such a philosopher is a 'perfectionist' because s/he always describes the commitment we ought to have in ways that seem impossibly demanding; but such a philosopher is also a realist, because s/he realizes that it is only by keeping an 'impossible' demand in view that one can strive for one's 'unattained but attainable self'" (Critchley and Bernasconi 2002, 36).[5]

These accounts all begin from a recognition that Levinas finds the meaning of ethics in the relation to the other and in the singular demand placed on me in this encounter; likewise, almost all perform the seemingly obligatory move of distancing Levinas's thought from traditional constructive normative enterprises. But it is noteworthy that normative language and, even more importantly, normative considerations and reflections are part and parcel of all of these approaches. Bauman, for example, clearly seeks a vantage point from which to understand and denounce the moral indifference generated by bureaucratic forms of human organization. Many of those who use the language of witness, messianism, and prophecy similarly do so in the name of bringing to light and condemning the violence suffered by those who are victims of hatred and oppression of all kinds. Putnam's characterization of Levinas is explicit in seeing a normative dimension to Levinas's thought and cites approvingly the idea that ethics is the name for "the emphasis on alleviating suffering regardless of the class or gender of the sufferer" (Putnam 2004, 23).[6] These discourses most certainly do not lack grounds or reasons for the denunciations and condemnations they urge on our attention; that is, they are neither amoral nor anti-normative in their broader aims. Indeed, *all are in the business of employing Levinas's thought to bolster a normative claim or point of view.* It is as if there is a dilemma at the heart of Levinas scholarship. It is clear that Levinas is not in the business of constructing normative moral principles meant to tell us how to live rightly or virtuously or well, so it seems quite right to distance his thought from what we normally mean by normative ethics. But when we deny that Levinas's thought has anything to do with normative ethics, it then appears contradictory to use his work to do exactly the sort of work that normative ethics is usually employed to do.

Historical Source of the Dilemma

No doubt, the deep reticence some readers feel at the suggestion that Levinas's thought might have something to do with ethical normativity can be traced back to Heidegger's "Letter on Humanism" and the influence it exerted on a whole generation of thinkers who came of age between the end of the Second World War and the political unrest in the spring of 1968. In November 1946, Sorbonne Professor Jean Beaufret wrote to Heidegger saying that for some time he had been trying to "determine precisely the relation of [Heideggerian] ontology to a possible ethics" and asking whether the philosopher had plans to develop an ethics on the basis established

by the existential analytic of *Being and Time* (*BW* 195). In his letter, Beaufret wondered explicitly how to restore meaning to the word "humanism,"
given the loss of meaning suffered by ethics and value theory more generally in the wake of two world wars and the growing secularization of European society. Heidegger's response, expanded and published in 1947 as the
"Letter on Humanism," famously suggests that perhaps the demise of such
terms as "humanism" and "ethics" would not be such a great loss after all:
"[Your] question proceeds from your intention to retain the word 'humanism'. I wonder whether that is really necessary. Or is the damage caused by
all such terms still not sufficiently obvious?" (*BW* 195). Heidegger speculates that the desire for an ethics reflects an understandable though ultimately misguided nostalgia "for a peremptory directive and for rules that
say how man . . . ought to live in a fitting manner" (*BW* 231). Such directives belong to the ontical framework of a philosophical anthropology but
not to Heidegger's own fundamental ontological inquiry into the meaning
of Being. Names, such as *ethics*, he suggests, "begin to flourish only when
original thinking comes to an end" (*BW* 195).

   Heidegger assures the reader that the critique of humanism is not
meant to imply "a defense of the inhuman," but only to open "other vis-
tas" (*BW* 227); nonetheless, the effect of the "Letter" was to chill the climate for anything going under the name "ethics." In this respect, Heidegger's thought was in accord with other figures—notably Nietzsche, Marx,
and Freud—whose work was being employed in France to the end of cre-
ating an extraordinarily rich and varied critique of normativity. The rise
of Lacanian psychoanalysis with its quite different account of the motives of human action and the formation of social norms, the Marxist and
Nietzschean critiques of value, the influence of French structuralism and
post-structuralism, thrived within the climate created by Heidegger's anti-
humanism.[7]

   As contemporary European thought became a distinct tradition
within Anglo-American philosophy departments, Heidegger's admonition
against ethics found a new foothold, and certainly shaped Continental
philosophy's English-speaking face. David Wood reports that, "Readers of
Sartre, Heidegger, and Derrida had become accustomed to having their
hopes for ethical illumination disappointed. Ethics was either deferred,
linked to a discredited humanism, or celebrated by its absence. The best

we could hope for was some sort of affirmative Nietzschean amoralism." Levinas came to that scene, Wood recalls, "as rain to the cracked earth of a parched landscape" (Bernasconi and Wood 1988, 2). Here, at last, was an ethics for those who had taken the point of Heidegger's critique of modern subjectivity and of the liberal bourgeois forms of ethics that accompanied it! But what sort of ethics was it (and is it)? Does Levinas offer us an ethics after Heidegger or an ethics despite Heidegger or, as seems to be the case, an impertinent combination of the two?

No doubt mindful of the influence of Heidegger's "Letter," Levinas himself expressed hesitation about the "moralistic resonances"[8] that might cling to his use of the term "ethics," and he sometimes tried to insulate his work from a moralist tone by distinguishing ethics in his sense from morality as traditionally understood.[9] As might be expected, however, the scant protections afforded by this sort of terminological move do not hold up for long and Levinas's discourse is thick with normative-sounding considerations: the face of the other *calls me into question*; it demands *justification* and *critique*; it arouses my *goodness* and awakens my *moral conscience* (*conscience morale*), making me aware of my own *injustice*. What sort of statements are these? Surely they are claims with a normative dimension, even if Levinas does not offer us a practical philosophy that generates the sorts of specific norms that can be formalized as rules or principles.

In one of the most oft-quoted lines of his entire corpus, Levinas says, "My task does not consist in constructing ethics; I only try to find its meaning" (*EI* 90). Less often repeated, perhaps because it is hard to see how it could be so, is his remark, "One can without doubt construct an ethics in function of what I have just said, but this is not my own theme" (*EI* 90). It is *not* the aim of this book to construct a Levinasian ethics where that means constructing a system of justified rules for right conduct based on his rethinking of the meaning of the ethical. Indeed, this book stands firmly with those who think that a system of moral prescriptions is precisely what a Levinasian ethics cannot and should not generate (which is not to imply that his work has nothing important or concrete to say about human action). But if Levinas's thought refuses us ethical certainties, neither does it teach us the necessity of living without them in a terrain of permanent undecidability. Levinas's thought is not a deconstructive ethics any more than it is a post-humanist or postmodern ethics. Though it shares important suspicions with proponents of the latter sort of views, and though it can contribute in important ways to such discourses, it is not synonymous with any of them and cannot be assimilated without remainder within their discursive borders.[10] Neither providing us with rules nor denying us their comfort, Levinas's work is not about the specifics of our moral life so much as it is a struggle to say how we come to find ourselves within a moral life at all.

It is this recognition that permits a way out of the dilemma sketched earlier. There is an account to be had from Levinas's thought about what it means to find ourselves bound by demands whose force is ethical (rather than physical or causal). But that account of a constitutive non-indifference to the other's claims need not and does not issue in specific directives or rules of the sort that Heidegger equates with a sterile and puerile moral philosophy. Eschewing both theological and naturalist/non-cognitivist answers to the question of how the other's demands command me, Levinas's thought, it will be argued here, struggles to articulate an ethics that never leaves terrestrial existence behind even as it shows what meaning transcendence can have within earthly and human limits.

Outline of the Present Work

The reading developed here grows out of a series of questions about "Levinas and ethics" that seem to me to have no easy answers, despite the genuinely illuminating work and important advances effected in a generation or more of Levinas scholarship. First and foremost among such questions is why alterity should be thought of as the sort of thing that can make a demand on one or put one under an obligation. What, after all, do otherness or difference have to do with responsibility? And are "otherness" and "difference" even adequate approximations for what Levinas means by *altérité*? Chapter 1 traces the roots of Levinas's use of "alterity" to his early concern to find a way "out" of being and the categories appropriate to it; we find that by looking at alterity in this context it becomes clear that the term is used less to indicate the other's otherness or difference than her *singularity*. Levinas turns to the other who presents herself somehow in person (*DF* 8; *CPP* 20), apart from descriptive categories of either identity or difference, in order to effect an "ex-cendence" (*EE* 15) from Being. Even if we understand alterity in terms of singularity, however, this does not yet answer the original question. Phrased now in terms of singularity rather than alterity, we can simply ask anew why singularity should be thought to bring ethical responsibilities along in its train? If singularity is understood first of all in an ethically neutral way as uniqueness, then it is not clear that it can take us far enough into ethical territory to generate something like a responsibility, let alone responsibility that is *infinite* in some way. And if singularity is thought of from the outset as an ethical category indicating something like the ethical standing of the other, then Levinas's thought seems guilty of a certain circularity, building into the I-Other relationship an ethical dimension it later purports to find there. Chapter 2 tackles this difficulty through a reappraisal of the notion of the face. Admittedly, "the face of the other" is one of the most overused terms in discussions of Levinas's thought, and it hardly seems profitable, let alone necessary, to tread this well-beaten path once more. But it is precisely our familiarity with the notion of the face that threatens to rob it of its force as a central concept or notion in Levinas's thought. Chapter 2 tries to restore to Levinas's notion of "the face of the other" all the strangeness and difficulty that it presented to us at first reading. The chapter focuses on the tensions in Levinas's conception of the face, especially as they surface in *Totality and Infinity* and especially as they concern the contradiction between the representation of the other in the figure of the face and the stated claim of this representation according to which the other is unrepresentable. (Chapter 5 extends this reading of the face, ultimately offering an interpretation that is at variance with the usual understandings of it in much of the current secondary literature.)

It is an interpretive principle of the work undertaken throughout the book that tensions such as the one besetting the notion of the face are doubly constitutive for Levinas's project. They are tensions that remain irresolvable within the terms of his thought; that is, they cannot be decided in favor of one pole or another, despite Levinas's own insistence at times that they can be or his stated preference for one side over another. As such, they constitute moments that threaten to undermine key theses of his work. Even so, when we attend carefully to the manner in which two meanings or two senses struggle against one another in these tensions, we discover that the tension itself, the friction or conflict, is constitutive of the very meaning of the ethical developed in Levinas's major writings. For example, if Levinas's ethics is an inquiry into the "meaning of the ethical," it is the contention of this book that the meaning he finds lies precisely in the tension between the necessity and demand for representation and the equal impossibility and inadequacy of every such representation.

On the basis of the readings of singularity and the face produced in the first two chapters, Chapters 3 and 4 tackle most directly the heart of Levinasian ethics, namely, the question of the meaning of responsibility and the question of its normative or binding force. Chapter 3 explores the differences in Levinas's notion of responsibility as it developed, from *Totality and Infinity* to *Otherwise Than Being, or Beyond Essence*. Hypothesizing that the earlier book failed to make the case for an infinite responsibility, despite heroic efforts, Chapter 3 argues that it is precisely this failure that becomes the content of the later, more developed notion of responsibility. In the later work especially, responsibility issues neither in the certainty of a principle nor in the certainty of a face, but in the forever uncertain, unguaranteed desire for ethical and moral certainty. In effect, whereas *Totality and Infinity* sought a kind of certainty about responsibility—and often reads as if there *is* such a certainty—the later writings emphasize that it is the *uncertainty* of responsibility that is constitutive of ethical life. Chapter 4 asks how such an uncertain responsibility can have binding force. Constructing an argument that departs from the idiom of Levinas's writing (though it is arguably and recognizably Levinasian), this chapter suggests that Levinas's thought is driven by normative concerns and offers an account of normative *force* even where it is not in the business of producing normative principles or norms *as such*. Ethical responsibility is lived, it is here argued, not as the certainty of an infinite debt to the other, but in the tenuous space where this debt is by turns urgent and lost from view. "Goodness," Levinas has said, "consists in going where no clarifying—that is, panoramic—thought precedes, in going without knowing where. An absolute adventure, in a primal imprudence, goodness is transcendence itself" (*TI* 305). It is this imprudent adventure of a goodness without certainties that is the hallmark of Levinasian ethics.

The final two chapters of the book pursue this reading of Levinasian responsibility in two concrete contexts. Chapter 5 considers the prospects for developing an environmental ethics on a Levinasian basis, and Chapter 6 takes up the possibility of extending his analyses of the other to current questions about multiculturalism and, specifically, gender politics. In both cases, significant questions have been raised about whether Levinas is truly an ally of progressive ethical and political concerns. Rather than arguing straightforwardly that he is (or is not), both chapters analyze the broader framework within which such questions are posed. The question of whether Levinas's notion of the face of the other can be extended to animals, plants, or ecosystems in such a way as to generate an infinite responsibility to these non-humans is, I argue, indicative of a mistaken view of the face as a causal force. Correcting this view in favor of a reading of the face as that which opens the space in which ethical demands can be posed and heard precisely as *demands*, that is, as requiring justificatory discourse, leads to the suggestion that obligations to animals and other non-humans are, for Levinas, *political* questions rather than ethical ones. They are akin, effectively, to questions about how to adjudicate between the claims of two or more others.

Chapter 6 is even more explicitly concerned with the political implications of Levinas's thought, especially as regards what is known alternately as identity-based politics or the politics of difference. Here I concur with the obvious fact that, for all his concern with the other, Levinas was more often than not insensitive in his treatment of women, of non-Western and non-monotheist religions, and of political and ethnic minorities. But rather than condemn Levinas's notion of the other for being of little use in the emancipatory political struggles of oppressed and minoritized groups, I argue that it is possible to condemn certain of Levinas's own statements, on the grounds that in making them he fails to adhere to the best insights of his own thinking. In addition, Chapter 6 argues there are considerable resources in those best insights for addressing the problems of such groups and the individuals within them.

In *De l'ideé de transcendence à la question du langage*, Etienne Feron suggests that we make a mistake in thinking of ethics as the central rubric or guiding thread of Levinas's philosophy. Such approaches, he warns, inevitably focus too narrowly on the notion of "the Other" and thereby fail to see that Levinas's philosophy is not a thinking of alterity, but of the *relation* no less than the difference between the Same and the Other. In Feron's view, Levinas offers us a philosophy of subjectivity and language as much or more than a "philosophy of the other," and neglecting these poles of his thought has produced what he describes as a one-sided and truncated reading (Feron 1992, 5). This may well be true of the readings of Levinas that have become standard fare in French and Anglophone contexts, but need it be the case? Indeed, there is good reason to be cautious about Feron's caution. For if we forgo thinking about Levinas's writings as an ethics, it is no longer clear how to estimate the main lines or major contribution of his thought. To the extent that he offers a defense of subjectivity, an arguably original analysis of the performative dimension of language, or a rethinking of the overwhelming semantic event expressed by the word "God," it is in the name of thinking subjectivity as constituted within an ethical response, thinking language as providing the formal structure of the possibility of such a response, and thinking the relation to God as consisting in the extraordinary event of the face-to-face ethical encounter. If ethics is too often invoked and too rarely critically engaged by Levinas's readers, and if this results in his work being "at once too much and too little known" (ibid.)—a point on which it is easy to agree with Feron—the right approach may not be to find an alternate route into Levinas's thought that avoids the question of his "ethics" or replaces the privilege of this term with some other. The best approach may be to tackle the problem of his ethics head-on. This is the approach that informs the present work and the task that guides its analyses.

Alterity: The Problem of Transcendence

> The theme of alterity has become an obsession in Europe today.
>
> —MARC GUILLAUME

> Perhaps the greatest transcendence consists in transcending transcendence, that is to say, in falling back into immanence.
>
> —JEAN WAHL

Relative and Absolute Alterity

Marc Guillaume's words have the force of prediction when one considers that more than forty books with the word "*alterité*" in the title have appeared in French since Guillaume and Baudrillard's co-authored work *Figures de l'alterité*—compared to only a handful of such works in the twenty years preceding it (Baudrillard and Guillaume 1994).[1] The *Encyclopédie philosophiques universelle* defines *alterité* as "a simple difference between determinations posited solely in their diversity, exteriority, and reciprocal independence" (Jacob 1989, 1:66). Understood in this way, alterity or otherness is not a part of the "proper determination" of an object but a function of its position in a set of relationships construed by the subject or knower (ibid.). François Mies notes that definitions which make *alterité* broadly synonymous with the abstract noun "otherness" tend to ignore the distinction in Latin between *alius* and *alter*, both of which can be trans-lated "other" (or *autre*). But while *alius* indicates one other among many, *alter* refers more narrowly to the other within a pairing, thus the "other" of some specified "one." In accord with its Latin root, Mies suggests restrict-ing "*alterité*" to this more starkly contrastive sort of otherness where each term mutually and reciprocally determines its opposite (Mies 1994, 9).

Levinas's notion of alterity is altogether different from this subject-relative and contrastive sense of the term. For Levinas, the alterity of the other is not encompassed by logical or dialectical difference. It is "not the simple reverse of identity, and is not formed out of resistance to the same" (*TI* 38). Levinas calls this sort of alterity "formal" alterity (*EN* 189) and ex-plains that it is alterity within a system, as when *a* is other than *b* and *b* is other than *a* (Levinas 1989, 10). Indeed, Levinas is at such pains to distin-guish his notion of alterity from any kind of merely formal or relative dif-ference that he says that the I and the Other are so little in relation that they cannot be said to share a concept in common, not even that of num-ber (*EE* 95; *TI* 39). The other in this sense is not another like me, an *alter ego*, whose difference is produced by space and time or by the difference of accidental attributes (*EE* 95; *TO* 83). Rather, the other is other with an alterity "constitutive" of its very content (*TI* 39; see also *TO* 36). The at-tempt to think alterity in a *positive* manner, as a kind of "alterity-content" (*TO* 36), is present from Levinas's earliest uses of the notion and, most sig-nificantly, it is this conception of alterity that is at issue in the face-to-face relationship that Levinas identifies with ethics. Whereas the I and the Oth-er, or the Other and the Same, are traditionally thought of as correlates, Levinas attempts to break with this tradition as insufficient to a thinking of ethical transcendence (Bailhache 1994, 71).

The central task of this chapter is to trace absolute alterity back to its roots in Levinas's early preoccupation with the problem of transcendence. Pursuing this line of thought will involve returning to the way transcen-dence was employed by Husserl and Heidegger, though an understanding of Levinas's relation to phenomenology is not the fundamental aim here and has been treated extensively elsewhere in the secondary literature.[2] Here it is a matter of clarifying the original problem to which alterity an-swers and of showing, as a result, that Levinas's conception of alterity is better captured by the idea of *singularity* than by the notion of *difference* or even *otherness*. It is not the other's difference from me, but his or her immediate and concrete presence, here and now, in an absolutely unique bit of skin that interests Levinas in this early period and that appears to him to effect a possible "break" with the all-encompassing and horrifying immanence of Being.

That this break must be "accomplished" without leaving the sphere of immanence—that is, without pretending to transcend this world for some other—is central to Levinas's account and guards against a tendency to interpret the adjective *absolute* in the phrase "absolute alterity" in a way that equates alterity or the other with something remote, distant, inaccessible, and in every respect unswayable—like the God of negative theologies. Now, to be sure, there is much in Levinas's writings that suggests this sort of reading. There is talk of the other as the "Most High" and of the face as totally exterior and as coming from a dimension of height (*TI* 215). But by attending to the early writings in which alterity emerges it becomes apparent that the move to the abstract and remote is at most only half the story. When allowed to stand in for the whole of Levinas's account, moreover, this kind of reading creates distinct problems. Most significantly, it makes it unclear how this other who is infinitely remote from me nonetheless commands my responsibility. Or, rather, it makes it far too tempting to suppose that this other imposes ethical commandments by fiat, like a suprasensible authority or God. This is the worry of critics like Dominique Janicaud and Giorgio Agamben, to whom I now turn.

Two Recent Criticisms

In his small but influential treatise, *Le Tournant théologique de la phénoménologie française* (1991), Dominique Janicaud describes the development of phenomenology in France in the previous thirty years as marked by a "rupture" with immanent phenomenality and as subsequently dominated by various openings toward the transcendent, whether it be the "invisible" invoked in the later work of Maurice Merleau-Ponty, the absolute alterity appealed to by Levinas, Jean-Luc Marion's "pure donation," or the "archi-revelation" of Michel Henry (Janicaud et al. 2000, 17). Janicaud argues with respect to Levinas in particular that despite the latter's explicit denials that his aim is to construct a theology or reach ethical conclusions by means of a theological discourse, his work nonetheless exhibits a "quest for divine transcendence" and must be read as an attempt to restore theology, and more specifically "the God of the biblical tradition," to a place of preeminence within a purportedly phenomenological philosophy (27). Janicaud titles his chapter on Levinas "The Swerve," evoking that contradictory and wholly arbitrary doctrine of Stoic thought that claimed that the swerve of a single atom, the cause of which cannot be accounted for, set off the series of ordered and systematic causal collisions which produced the material world as we know it. The implication is that the face of the other, like this swerve, is a kind of philosophical aberration, in that it founds a purportedly philosophical thesis without being itself open to philosophical argumentation or critique.

Two intertwining criticisms are at the center of Janicaud's discussion of Levinas: first, he argues that there is a deep incoherence in Levinas's project from a phenomenological perspective because "he reintroduces a phenomenology after having challenged the phenomenological method" (39). Janicaud is referring here to the sections on eros and fecundity at the end of *Totality and Infinity*, and he is severe in his judgment of these analyses as existentially naïve, phenomenologically impoverished, and literally meaningless, since they propose to be a phenomenological account of an evanescence that does not, properly speaking, appear (see especially 39–43). Second, Janicaud suggests that the "double game" (*double jeu*) Levinas plays by appealing to phenomenology after having dispensed with its method—"two-timing" phenomenology, in the translator's apt expression—is not mere self-contradiction but belies "a more artful strategy" by means of which Levinas's philosophy effects a "*captatio benevolentiae*" that makes phenomenology a hostage to theology (42–43). Janicaud suggests that if Levinas's descriptions of the face, the other, and metaphysical desire are not phenomenological, then their justification can only be "metaphysico-theological" and that the reader of Levinas's work thus "finds himself in the position of a catechumen who has no other choice than to be firmly convinced by saintly speeches and lofty dogmas" (27; translation modified). Urging the reader not to be "intimidated" (27) by this covert theology which refuses to "say its name" (43), Janicaud concludes that the "incantory force with which he [Levinas] infuses altruism is undeniable, but conceals on its dark side—and in the name of a dogmatic conception of transcendence—a kind of violation of critical consciousness" (46).

Though Giorgio Agamben is ultimately more sympathetic to Levinas's project, his characterization of contemporary French philosophy as a contest between philosophies of transcendence and philosophies of immanence lends further support to the suspicion that the former rely on questionable metaphysical presuppositions that the latter are able to do without (Agamben 1999, 239). Agamben's thesis in the essay in *Potentialities* entitled "Absolute Immanence" is that the concept of "life" bequeathed to us in the last essays of Foucault and Deleuze and understood as an "immanence . . . that does not once again produce transcendence, must constitute the subject of the coming philosophy" (238). In the service of this future philosophy, Agamben counsels that it will be necessary to reconstruct a genealogy of contemporary thought that "clearly" distinguishes, on the one hand, an unfruitful lineage of transcendence, or at best transcendence in immanence, which runs from Husserl, mediated by Heidegger, to the philosophies of Levinas and Derrida and, on the other hand, a lineage of "pure" (228), "absolute" (234) immanence, which passes from Spinoza, through Nietzsche and Heidegger, to Deleuze and Foucault (239). Agamben describes Deleuzean immanence as a "postconscious," "postsubjective," "impersonal and non-individual transcendental field" (225), as having "neither a fixed point nor a horizon that can orient thought," and thus as "what must be thought and as what cannot be thought" (228). As Deleuze explains no less paradoxically in *What Is Philosophy?*: "Immanence is immanent only to itself and consequently captures everything, absorbs All-One, and leaves nothing remaining to which it could be immanent" (227). As such, Agamben notes that immanence becomes "a principle of virtual indetermination" which leaves thought no definite direction or fixed point of departure. Agamben concludes that "the only possible point of orientation is the vertigo in which outside and inside, immanence and transcendence, are absolutely indistinguishable" (228).

While both Janicaud and Agamben write in favor of immanence, there is an odd conflict between their respective criticisms. Janicaud in effect takes Levinas to task for giving up the touchstone of phenomenology—namely, reflection on experience or "the things themselves"—leaving his theory vulnerable to charges that its main claims are philosophically and phenomenologically ungrounded. This is one reason why Levinas's thought seems to Janicaud more theological than philosophical. Moreover, it reveals that immanence for Janicaud is allied to the desire to retain Husserl's view of phenomenology as a "rigorous science." Agamben, by contrast, celebrates the vertiginous groundlessness of Foucault's and Deleuze's theories of immanence, and classes Levinas with a tradition that still seeks in some way a transcendent, fixed point (whether ground or telos) that would provide a point of departure or orientation for thought. Setting aside the contradictory conceptions of immanence at work in these two criticisms—an interesting problem in its own right—the more immediately important point is that both critics take Levinas's philosophy to task for purporting to provide a guaranteed foundation, a kind of unshakeable ground that grants to the human other an unbreachable ethical status. While Janicaud sees both the form and the content of this ground as theological, Agamben's position suggests that it may be theological only in form and still do damage enough.

Now, there can be no doubt that Levinas *is* a philosopher of transcendence. Transcendence is a significant theme in Levinas's writings as early as his 1947 monograph *De l'existence à l'existent*; it is absolutely central to his polemic with the phenomenologies of Husserl and Heidegger; and it is the primary means in his later works to express the possibility of an ethical relationship that is "otherwise than being." Transcendence is invoked on almost every major occasion where Levinas gives an accounting of his work as a whole: "Transcendence and Height" is the title given to Levinas's defense of the main themes of *Totality and Infinity*, as put forward in a session of the Société Française de Philosophie in 1962 and subsequently published in the *Bulletin* of that society. "Transcendence and Intelligibility" is the title of a paper given by Levinas in 1983 as a synopsis of his work and subsequently published along with a long interview. *Alterity and Transcendence* is the title chosen by Levinas himself for one of the last collections of his essays. But even if we acknowledge that transcendence is one of the most deeply entrenched and important terms of Levinas's thought, it remains to be asked, transcendence in what sense?

The remainder of this chapter is devoted to showing that transcendence develops in Levinas's thought as a response to phenomenology. In the final section, I return to Janicaud's and Agamben's criticisms and suggest that far from expressing a theological or foundationalist motivation, Levinas's notion of alterity is developed in the service of restoring a meaning to the concrete other whereby it cannot be reduced either to a dumb materialism or absorbed within an overarching and all-encompassing totality or system. Thus, what we have in Levinas is that greatest transcendence, spoken of by Jean Wahl: a transcendence that transcends transcendence for the sake of saving the immanent from (mere) immanence.

Transcendence in the Phenomenological Tradition

The word "transcendence" was used by Husserl and Heidegger in the first half of the twentieth century in a non-theological sense to refer to the epistemological problem of how a subject transcends the world of mental phenomena in order to reach a world of extra-mental or "real" objects. In his dissertation on *The Theory of Intuition in Husserl's Phenomenology*, Levinas explains that Husserl's famous thesis of the intentionality of consciousness, expressed in the claim that "consciousness is always consciousness *of something*," indicates neither a realist nor idealist thesis about mind, but a reorientation of the theory of knowledge away from the problematic manner in which modern epistemology had posed the problem of transcendence—that is, of the subject's relation to extra-mental objects—and toward the development of an adequate description of lived conscious experience and the modes of evidence proper to its various spheres.

Husserl maintained that the critique of cognition was philosophy's first and most fundamental problem, but he believed that the sense in which cognition constitutes a theoretical problem had been largely misunderstood. In the *Logical Investigations* he criticizes Herbart for his "complete inability" to recognize that the "apparently profound problem of the harmony of the subjective course of logical thinking with the real course of external actuality" is "a pseudo-problem bred by unclarity" (*LI* 218). Other early works, such as *The Idea of Phenomenology* (1901), express a similar view, emphasizing that although transcendence is the genuinely mysterious or enigmatic feature of cognition, the problem is not *whether* cognition of transcendent objects is possible (for Husserl, it patently *is* and this cannot be denied without self-contradiction), but *how* it is possible. How does cognition achieve what we manifestly know it achieves? This, according to Husserl, is the problem that the critique of cognition is meant to address once it has a proper understanding of its own task.

For Husserl, certain metaphysical views that keep company with skepticism in its modern variants are at the root of the misunderstanding of the problem of cognition. The skeptical problem of how cognition transcends its subjective sphere in order to reach a world of objects inevitably entangles itself in unsolvable difficulties because it rests on an untenable metaphysics that begins from a dogmatic separation between cognition and its objects and then, Humpty-Dumpty style, fails ever to put them together again. The first task of a phenomenological theory of knowledge is thus the critical and negative one of disabusing us of the temptation to see the subject in itself as isolated from or without access to the objects it knows.[3] For Husserl, rationalism and empiricism share the same problematic picture, and though they respond to it differently, they fail equally to attend descriptively or phenomenologically to lived conscious experience. The phenomenological epoché, the first in a series of methodological "reductions," puts out of play this unjustified metaphysical picture of an immanent subjective sphere isolated from and standing over against a world of transcendent objects. The point of "turning off" or "bracketing" questions about whether something really exists or really has such and such extant qualities is not, in Cartesian fashion, to remain agnostic about questions of existence until one has developed guaranteed tools by which to produce true judgments on this score. The phenomenological reductions are never lifted as long as one is philosophizing, because they do not represent a provisional or instrumental attitude but are more akin to the Wittgensteinian position, which says that what we need in the face of certain seemingly intractable philosophical problems is not a solution but a therapy aimed at breaking the hold of the problem on the way we think. Once the picture of an isolated, "un-worlded" subject holds no attraction for us and is steadfastly held at bay, the theory of knowledge can proceed to a positive inquiry into the essence of cognition, involving an inquiry into the meaning of claims to "validity and correctness," or, more generally, to an investigation and clarification of the nature of the relations pertaining between acts of cognition, the meanings intended in them, and the objectivities thereby given (*IP* 20).

Under the old picture, then, transcendence is primarily a problem about how to ascertain whether our representations of objects match "reality" or are adequate to objects as they are "in themselves."[4]

As Levinas understands Husserl's critique of skepticism, the problem of whether consciousness falsifies its objects in presenting or representing them is "exposed as fictitious once we understand that . . . a subject is not a substance in need of a bridge, namely, knowledge, in order to reach an object, but that the secret of its subjectivity is its being present in front of objects" (*TIHP* 25).[5] The same point is made by Heidegger in a discussion of intentionality in his 1927 lecture course, *The Basic Problems of Phenomenology*: "The idea of a subject which has intentional experiences merely inside its own sphere and is not yet outside it but encapsulated within itself is an absurdity which misconstrues the basic ontological structure of the being that we ourselves are" (*BPP* 64). Intentionality is one of the decisive discoveries of phenomenology, for Levinas and Heidegger both, because it recognizes the profoundly important fact that the "subject" is intentionally structured in and of itself.[6]

Heidegger's departure from the strict letter of Husserlian phenomenology is motivated in part by his consideration that intentionality, though an important advance in the understanding of lived conscious experience, does not yet account for our most fundamental modes of existing.[7] For Heidegger, working through the Husserlian problem of intentionality is "preparatory" to a more fundamental inquiry into the mode of being of the "subject" (this now discredited term replaced by "existing" or "*Dasein*"). Every intentional relating-to is "founded in the Dasein's transcendence and is possible solely for this reason" (*BPP* 162). If we see intentionality as a feature not just of theoretical (or doxical) comportments that have to do with the positing of things or objects generally, and see it as the relatedness-to of all human comporting, then we need to go back and re-describe our everyday or "natural" way of existing. We need an accurate picture of *who* we are and of our mode of *being*. Thus, Heidegger calls for a fundamental ontological inquiry into the *transcendence* of Dasein: "The transcendence of Dasein is the central problem, not for the purpose of explaining 'knowledge,' but for clarifying Dasein and its existence as such" (*MFL* 135).

This claim marks a shift from Husserl's preoccupation with the critique of cognition (and his aim of breaking the grip of skepticism in the formulation of this critique) to a new investigation into the basic structures by means of which an intentional relating-to or comportment toward things within the world first becomes possible. Heidegger's philosophy does not, however, present the logical conditions for the possibility of any experience whatsoever and is not a transcendental philosophy in either the Kantian or Husserlian senses. The task of *Being and Time* and of the lecture courses from this period concerns instead an existential analytic of Dasein. "Heidegger breaks with Husserl and the Cartesian tradition by substituting for *epistemological* questions concerning the relation of the knower and the known *ontological* questions concerning what sort of beings we are and how our being is bound up with the intelligibility of the world" (Dreyfus 1991, 3).[8]

The only significant appearance of the term "transcendence" in the published portions of *Being and Time* comes toward the end, in section 69, where Heidegger alludes to a new way of understanding the problem of transcendence that would be distinct from traditional epistemological understandings: "The problem of transcendence cannot be brought round to the question of how a subject comes out to an Object where the aggregate of Objects is identified with the idea of the world. Rather we must ask: what makes it ontologically possible for entities to be encountered within-in-the-world and Objectified as so encountered? This can be answered by recourse to the transcendence of the world" (*BT* 417–18). The *Basic Problems of Phenomenology* distinguishes transcendence in this new sense from past theological and epistemological uses of the term, proposing to follow the "original pattern" of the Latin word: "Transcendere signifies literally to step over, pass over, go though, and occasionally also to surpass" (*BPP* 298). Presented schematically, Heidegger distinguishes three components of transcendence: *that which transcends* is Dasein; *that which gets transcended* (i.e., that which is stepped over) are entities within the world; and *that toward which* Dasein transcends is the world in the ontological sense (*BPP* 299). In modern epistemological accounts and equally in Husserl's phenomenology, there is no distinction between the latter two designations: objects are the transcendent *x* toward which knowledge aims. Likewise, modern epistemologies, especially those on the idealist end of the spectrum, tend to make a mystery of the transcending itself, taking the subject to be the sort of thing that considered in and of itself is *without* transcendence—an isolated subject shut up with its mental images in a subjective sphere.

Heidegger's account of transcendence invokes, first, the Husserlian insight that Dasein is always already there among things in the world, not in the crude realist sense of being a thing among things, but in the sense that "relating-to" belongs intrinsically to the structure of the sort of being that we are:

> Transcendence is . . . the primordial constitution of the *subjectivity* of a subject. The subject transcends qua subject; it would not be a subject if it did not transcend. To be a subject means to transcend. This means that Dasein does not sort of exist and then occasionally achieve a crossing over outside itself, but existence originally means to cross over. Dasein is itself the passage across. And this implies that transcendence is not just one possible comportment (among others) of Dasein toward other beings, but it is the basic constitution of its being, on the basis of which Dasein can at all relate to beings in the first place. (*MFL*, 165)

Similarly, we read: "Only a being with the mode of being of the Dasein transcends, in such a way in fact that transcendence is precisely what essentially characterizes its being" (*BPP* 299). However, entities within the world (things or objects) are not the end point aimed at in Dasein's transcendence, as they are for narrowly epistemological accounts. Rather, it is Dasein's transcending toward a *world* which makes it ontologically possible for entities to be encountered within the world in the modes of readiness-to-hand or presence-at-hand: "Transcendence means *to understand oneself from a world*" (*BPP*, 300; emphasis in original). For Heidegger, the Dasein is not an ego or self (an "ego-self," as he says) that first of all exists and then steps over to the things or moves toward them in knowledge. Selfhood *presupposes* and is founded on transcendence (*BPP* 300).[9]

The ontological problem of transcendence is thus effectively a question about our relation to the world (in the Heideggerian sense). To be sure, it no longer has the same form or content as its epistemological predecessor, but it remains within the provenance of epistemology and philosophy of mind broadly conceived (Olafson 1987). Heidegger's philosophy no longer asks how the subject "reaches" objects within the world, since this problem has been exposed as based on a false and misleading picture of subjectivity. Nor does it consist in a narrow description of the relation between intentional act and intentional object, grasped essentially as an act of positing (Husserl's approach). Instead, Heidegger's analysis begins from a rich description of the affective, practical, and ultimately historical and temporal structures which condition our experience of an intelligible, meaningful world. Heidegger's account of transcendence is an account of how we are situated in the world. Like Husserl, he does not set out to explain cognition or prove its possibility. The aim is to describe *how it is with us* and to disclose the often hidden structures that frame our experience. For Heidegger, as Jean Wahl rightly notes, our transcendence consists in the "fact that man is outside of himself"—that is, that we always already exist in the midst of and from a world (Wahl 1944, 13). Thus, to say, as Heidegger does, that transcendence is the basic mode of being of Dasein is not to identify some special property or activity of human beings; rather it is a description of human understanding and human consciousness at the broadest level: this is what it is like to be the sort of beings that we are. Moreover, the description offered may not be our everyday commonsense self-understanding, but it is a picture that begins from that self-understanding and one in which we can come to recognize our own mode of life.

Jean Wahl's independent reflections on the problem of transcendence in *Existence humaine et transcendance* are perhaps the most reliable guide to Levinas's formulation of the problem. Wahl largely accepts Heidegger's account of Being-in-the-world and the idea that we are thrown into or immersed in an environment or surrounding world, but transcendence nonetheless remains a problem for him, and it is specifically our transcendence of our facticity that interests him. For Wahl, the problem is how to characterize the immanence of the subject *within* a world and its simultaneous transcendence. Wahl represents the immanence of the environing world in various ways: as the irrecoverability of the past, as the facticity of the material world, as the opacity of the motives or personalities of other people and of society (which, in the spirit of Heidegger's *das Man* he calls *le vous*). In each of these cases, Wahl suggests, our relation to the immanence of the world is equal parts dependence and control, passivity and activity. In each instance, there is room for action that directly shapes our environment and gives it meaning, but at the same time there are numerous constraints on our meaning-bestowing activities. For Wahl, as for Levinas in his own early works, our relationship to food becomes emblematic of the manner in which we are immersed in the surrounding world: we are dependent on the things we eat even as we incorporate them into our own being. Wahl says of this relation that it exemplifies alterity but not yet transcendence (Wahl 1944, 35). Not incidentally, this is exactly how Levinas describes our relation to relative alterities (*EE* 37–45; *TI* 33).

This absorption in the midst of dependence is characterized by Wahl as a negation of negation: the world on which we depend and which we initially experience as a resistance or obstacle to our will (and as a potential threat to or negation of our being) is also the world from which we nourish and enrich ourselves. In the appropriation of the world through perception, knowing, and action, we carry out a negation of negation. This movement, Wahl says, is proper to the unfolding of thought and belongs to its internal development; but it is not yet transcendence. Transcendence is said to concern another kind of negativity, one that cannot be reabsorbed in the internal movement of thought or in the life of the ego. Wahl claims that in the idea of transcendence—which is something more than our being-in-the-world—thought "thinks" another limit or negativity without being able to fully appropriate that limit or claim it as of its own making. Such a thought, Wahl speculates, is not properly speaking a thought, but something more. The idea of transcendence thus destroys "the belief in a thought that knows only itself" (Wahl 1944, 38).

It must be noted that transcendence as Wahl understands it is not a movement that leaves the world behind. Wahl begins his discussion of transcendence by remarking that he will heed the warnings of Hegel, Nietzsche, and others about various "false" forms of transcendence. Transcendence as he uses the term will not indicate an "*arrière-monde*," or a world behind the world or behind the scenes that is then conceived as the final arbiter or justification for a moral code enforced in this world (Wahl 1944, 34). Rather, for Wahl as for Heidegger transcendence is the name of a problem about how we are situated epistemologically, ontologically, existentially, and ethically in the world. But unlike Heidegger, for Wahl transcendence is that dimension of our existing in which we bump up against the limits of thought, though differently from the way in which we bump up against the facticity of things in our environment. Wahl notes that, paradoxically, to the extent that the idea of transcendence destroys the self-sufficiency of thought, it must ultimately be turned on itself, like a snake that bites its own tail or a skepticism that destroys both sides of an argument and then destroys itself. In the case of transcendence, Wahl says, the idea of transcendence is itself never completely destroyed, never completely transcended, but has the status of something like "a paradise lost, the hoped for, regretted presence of which, and the loss of which constitute the value of our attachment to the here-below" (38).

The question of Wahl's influence on Levinas would be worthy of a study in its own right. Levinas dedicates *Totality and Infinity* to Marcelle and Jean Wahl and this trope of a thought that thinks more than it thinks or that does more and better than think is one of the principal ways in which he describes the relation to the infinity (*CPP* 54; *TI* 49, inter alia). Likewise, Levinas's formulation of the problem of transcendence as a problem about how the two terms in the transcendence relation can be *in relation* without thereby being assimilated one to the other finds an earlier expression in Wahl's thought. For Wahl there is an irreconcilable tension between the movement of transcendence and the term toward which it moves. If the movement is explained in terms of the end point or *telos*, then the movement is no longer something that exists in its own right. It is swallowed up or absorbed into that toward which it moves. But, likewise, if the transcendence-term is explained in light of the movement toward it, then it ceases to be anything itself and becomes nothing more than a projection of the movement or the subject who undertakes the movement. It is thus no longer transcendent to that subject. This is exactly how Levinas explains the problem of transcendence in 1949 and again in 1961.[10] Moreover, the problem is exactly that of whether an I and an Other can be in relationship without one of the terms absorbing or determining the meaning of the other. The task remaining in this chapter is to see how the themes of transcendence and of absolute alterity emerge from Levinas's early writings.[11] It will belong to later chapters to mine the ethical significance of this relationship.

Transcendence as "Escape" in Levinas's Early Work

Levinas's earliest original works characterize the philosophical itinerary of the West in terms of a conflict between human freedom and the brute fact of being (*OE* 49) or between the rational order of human consciousness and the determined order of natural events (*EE* 21). For this tradition, ego and world are opposed to one another and the ego is understood and valorized principally in terms of its quest for self-unity and self-determination in opposition to the world which would determine or disperse it. In important respects, the accounts of transcendence in Husserl and Heidegger are consistent with this tradition. For Husserl, the absolute freedom of consciousness in self-reflection is a freedom that is never abrogated. This freedom, moreover, accounts for the advances of the natural sciences and for human learning generally, and also, more specifically, makes possible the phenomenological critique of cognition. Though Heidegger is more attuned to the facticity of human existence and to our "throwness" into a world of meanings not of our own making, he nonetheless emphasizes the possibility of taking up our thrown being explicitly in an authentic self-understanding and thus confirming the primacy of freedom once again. Within the tradition then, as Levinas reads it, the ego is pictured as struggling against heteronomous determination by being or nature and as winning the struggle in such a manner as to preserve itself in its self-sufficiency and autonomy (*OE* 49). Beginning from the idea of a schism between human being and being as such, Western philosophy largely urges us to struggle for "a better being, for a harmony between us and the world, or for the perfection of our own being" (*OE* 51). Levinas notes that for the tradition the "insufficiency" of the human condition is understood as a deficiency due to our limited or finite being, and that the "transcendence of these limits . . . remained philosophy's sole preoccupation" (*OE* 51).[12]

In "On Escape," Levinas heralds a modern sensibility that seems ready to abandon this quest for transcendence (*OE* 51). But the same preoccupation with escape—a term Levinas describes as not merely *à la mode* but as a veritable *mal du siècle*—is also likely to miss its own significance if interpreted in ways that make of the need for escape a false transcendence that does not break with being but only seeks to *be* somewhere else, somewhere better, thus reinstating the notion of transcendence already present in the tradition. Escape, Levinas says, is not necessarily identical with "the dreams of the poet who sought to evade 'lower realities,'"[13] or with a desire to break with social conventions and constraints that are seen as deforming human nature or alienating us from ourselves; nor does it necessarily coincide with the desire to flee the supposedly "degrading types of servitude" imposed on us by the materiality of our bodies (*OE* 53). Each of these flights out of being may represent only the attempt to go elsewhere, to leave our ordinary selves momentarily behind, as we do when we travel to find a change of scenery or climate (*OE* 53; cf. *EE* 25 and *TI* 33). Such flights from being, Levinas claims, approach the theme of escape but still "obey the need to transcend the limits of finite being" (*OE* 53), and as such do not yet put being itself into question. "They translate the horror of a certain *definition* of our being but not [the horror] of being as such" (*OE* 53).[14] The transcendence Levinas seeks in this early text is not a matter of "getting out" of being to *go* somewhere else; it is already an *otherwise than being* not a *being otherwise*—to borrow terms that Levinas will not use until almost forty years later.

The radicality of this idea is easily overlooked, but it is absolutely crucial to a proper understanding of the roots of Levinas's later thought. Levinas seeks a transcendence of being *that does not go "outside" the limits of our finite being*. The transcendence portrayed in these early works by the motif of escape (*l'évasion*—the opposite, etymologically, of *invasion*) will be described in *Totality and Infinity* as "an aspiration to radical exteriority" (*TI* 29) and as a "desire" for that which is "other in an eminent sense" (*TI* 33), but even there it is an aspiration or desire that must find its termination *within* the finitude of finite being. To the extent that this early essay "announces a decisive break with any philosophy of finitude" (de Vries 2005, 382), it nonetheless does not cast the notion of finitude aside or reject the finitude of human beings. Indeed, it is initially the notion of finitude, and not the notion of infinity, as is more often assumed, that undergoes a radical transformation in Levinas's thought. The transcendence of being takes place *in* being, in the finitude of a finite being, and never leaves this finitude behind. It is in this sense that Jean Wahl's comment is appropriately applied to Levinas: "The greatest transcendence consists in transcending transcendence, that is to say, in falling back into immanence" (Wahl 1944, 38)—except, for Levinas, it is not a matter of "falling back" into immanence, but of seeing in immanence a mode of existing that is already beyond immanence.

Guiding Levinas's analysis in his early writings is the possibility that a horror before the very fact of being might be just as fundamentally part of our human situation as anxiety about our own finitude or death:

Does Being contain no other vice than its limitation and nothingness? Is there some sort of underlying evil in its very positivity? Is not anxiety over Being—horror of Being—just as primal as anxiety over death? Is not the fear of Being just as originary as the fear for Being? . . . The fear of nothingness is but the measure of our involvement in Being. Existence of itself harbors something tragic which is not only there because of its finitude. (*EE* 20)

Heidegger, of course, famously gives an analysis of anxiety as qualitatively different from fear (which always has an object, where anxiety does not) and as having the unique ontological function of disclosing to us the fact of our throwness into being and our attempts to flee from our finitude. Levinas maintains that certain philosophically neglected experiences, such as insomnia, fatigue, and suffering, are also uniquely disclosive, though what they reveal is not our finitude but the "elementary truth" (*OE* 52) that being *is* and that there is no escaping it. In physical suffering, for example, life is said to lose its aspect of being a game, not just because it becomes painful or displeasing but "because the ground of suffering consists of the impossibility of interrupting it, and of an acute feeling of being held fast [*rivé*]" (*OE* 52). This sense of being riveted within being and to one's own being shapes Levinas's early descriptions of the self as a "solitude" and an "enchainment" within being. Moreover, the need to escape is described specifically as "the need to get out of oneself, that is, *to break that most radical and unalterably binding of chains, the fact that the I is oneself*" (*OE* 55; emphasis in original). Of course, this longed-for break with being seems to be a contradiction in terms, since what is desired is precisely a self that would no longer be itself, a self who would *be* while breaking with being. The problem of transcendence, then, is experienced as this desire and its seemingly inevitable frustration. In the words of Robert Bernasconi, Levinasian transcendence seems to cry, "I must get out and I can't get out."[15]

Through an analysis of need, the essay on escape makes the case for understanding being as a plenitude that is not a source of contentment and satisfaction but an oppressively brutal weight that we cannot shake off. Idealism is introduced at the end of this essay as having the right aspiration—viz., toward escape—but as taking the wrong path insofar as it reassigns the ideal realms it discovers to being which is thereby enlarged rather than broken up or shaken off. Levinas suggests that the only path open to a thought that genuinely aspires to break with being is "to measure without fear all the weight of being and its universality," and thus to recognize that action and thought (the two realms of human spontaneity and freedom) are equally "incapable of taking the place of an event that breaks up existence in the very accomplishment of its existence" (*OE* 73).

Action, in particular, which the tradition has represented as a kind of descent of thought into being, does not break with being (nor break it up) but enmeshes us in it further. For Levinas, action enacts the comedy of being: in doing something that it intends to do (and through which it perhaps sees itself as a sovereign self, a master of its environment), the ego also does multiple things that it in no way intends. In pulling out the chair, to follow Levinas's example, I scrape the floor or crease my jacket. These are actions that I might assent to, as it were, after the fact, but it certainly cannot be said that I also intend them along with intending to pull out the chair. Every concerted action is multiplied in a series of unintended co-actions and consequences that leave the ego as much mastered by as master of being. Thought also fails to break with being, but for a different and perhaps weightier reason—one that might be thought of as the tragic counterpart of action's comedy. Far from breaking with being, thought is precisely the measure of being on Levinas's reading of the philosophical tradition. Thinking and being are "the same," in the sense that anything of which we say that it *is* we thus conceive and render thinkable; and anything which we conceive or think to that extent at least *is*. An event that would break up being without passing beyond the limit of finitude must thus be sought elsewhere than in theory or praxis. Levinas first searches for such an event, as is well known, in death, erotic experience, and the having of children, or fecundity.

As the analyses of death, eros, and fecundity in *Existence and Existents* and *Time and the Other* are well known and have been discussed extensively elsewhere in the secondary literature, allow me to focus only on the way in which they fulfill this requirement to find an experience capable of breaking up the structures which bind the ego to being. Included in the troublesome section of *Totality and Infinity* entitled "Beyond the Face" is subsection E, "Transcendence and Fecundity."[16] Here Levinas presents the problem of transcendence much as he does in *Time and the Other* (1948), though more succinctly: the classical or traditional idea of transcendence, Levinas remarks, is "self-contradictory," since the subject that truly transcends must be "swept away in its transcendence," absorbed into the transcendent term toward which it moves. Such a transcending subject thus fails and "does not transcend itself," since it does not effectively survive the movement of transcendence; it does not remain itself throughout or after it (*TI* 274). In *Time and the Other*, this is precisely the situation we are said to face in confronting death. Death appears to us as an event we cannot master: in most cases we cannot predict its exact arrival and in no case can we master the event itself, since death is the end of our own existing. Levinas characterizes death as a "mystery" (a term closely associated with alterity in his early works) because it cannot be anticipated and grasped and thus enters into the present of consciousness only as "what does not enter it" (*TI* 77). But he asks, "How can the event that cannot be grasped still happen to me? . . . How can a being enter into relation with the other without allowing its very self to be crushed by the other?" (*TI* 77). In short, how can the ego transcend itself and still be preserved? How can being be "broken up" and "accomplished" at the same time? Death approximates transcendence as a movement toward absolute alterity, but ultimately fails to embody the transcendence relation since the ego does not survive its transcendence in this instance.

The problem of transcendence is answered in Levinas's early works by the now well-known, but at the time innovative move of claiming that the transcendence relation *par excellence* is the relation to the other person. The 1935 essay *On Escape* makes no mention whatsoever of the alterity of the other person and nowhere suggests that the erotic, social, or ethical relationship might serve as a path out of being or as a means of interrupting being's immanence. *Existence and Existents* and *Time and the Other* are the first of Levinas's texts to introduce the idea of the other as an *absolute* alterity and to connect alterity with transcendence. These texts argue that the other's alterity, or "exteriority," is "not simply an effect of space, which keeps separate what is conceptually identical"; nor is the other only an *alter ego*, since then the intersubjective relationship would be the "indifferent and reciprocal relationship of two interchangeable terms" (*EE* 95).[17] The relation to the other is an asymmetrical relationship that cannot be made reciprocal or symmetrical because the other's alterity is not a relative quality but rather the very content of her being: "The Other as Other is not only an alter ego: the Other is what I myself am not. The Other is this not because of the Other's character, or physiognomy, or psychology, but because of the Other's very alterity" (*TO* 83). The other "bears alterity as an essence" (*TO* 87–88). Levinas will adhere to this thesis about alterity throughout his major works, but in these early texts alterity remains subordinated to the problematic of escape. For example, Levinas writes in *Existence and Existents* that the relation to the other "is not something justified of itself," but is of interest only insofar as it constitutes "on the ontological level, the event of the most radical breakup of the very categories of the ego" (*EE* 85). It is this breakup, this path out of being, that concerns him, and the alterity of the other gains currency primarily because of the role it plays in opening this path.

Because Levinas identifies operations within being with power in these early texts, he seeks the break with being—transcendence—in a relation in which the ego is affected in its mode of being, but in which this being affected remains outside of models of domination or subordination. This is no doubt why love relationships, specifically the erotic relationship and the relation to one's child (Levinas almost always says "son"[18]), are initial exemplars of transcendence. Levinas remarks of the erotic relationship in particular that it is "a relationship that is impossible to translate into powers" (*EE* 88).[19] But even so, the erotic is not sufficient as a prototype of transcendence, because the ego does not *become other* in erotic love but only aims at alterity. The ego becomes other to itself, Levinas claims, "only in one way: through paternity" (*TO* 91). To have a child is to have a part of oneself *in* that child; it is to have become other than or other to oneself. "Paternity is the relationship with a stranger who, entirely while being Other, is myself, the relationship of the ego with a self who is nonetheless a stranger to me" (*TO* 91).[20] I am not the master of my child, as though she were my work or my property, Levinas says. Neither the concept of cause nor that of ownership are adequate to the relation, since I do not simply make or have my child. Rather, Levinas says, I *am* my child, but not with a relation of identity. Because she is also a self, a person, the child is not simply an event or ordeal that happens to one (though having a child can be this *in part*), nor is she merely an *alter ego*, another human being or creature of the same species as myself. The child is an event that accomplishes being at the same time as it makes being *plural*, breaks it up or shares it out between beings who cannot be united or identified or fused with one another, really or conceptually. Of course, by 1961 Levinas no longer saw the parental relationship or kinship as the prototype of a lived relation with alterity, but the structure identified here, as that which breaks up being without "leaving" being and in fact while "accomplishing" being, is the structure of transcendence throughout his mature philosophy.

The presentation of the problem thus far, like Levinas's own, foregrounds the existential or experiential dimension of transcendence, perhaps with the inadvertent result of intensifying our sense that Levinas's is a strange concern indeed. Why, after all, would one want to get out of being? What would it even mean to "get out" of being—especially when we are told that death is no more an exit than it is a solution to life's problems (*OE* 54)? Can we make sense of this desire to escape either existentially or conceptually? The problem is likely to appear to contemporary readers as a peculiar one, balanced uneasily between an existential psychology and an ontology of existence, neither of which are entirely compelling in today's intellectual landscape. "Escape" may well have been a "watchword" and a "*mal du siecle*" (*OE* 52) in Levinas's day, but it is no longer so in ours, and the sense of urgency that saturates Levinas's prose in these early texts may well leave today's reader only baffled or bemused. The problem of "escape" and of the possibility of "transcendence" or "excendence" in Levinas's sense may thus appear to us today as an odd and uncompelling problem—even if we are relatively inclined to accept the picture of philosophy that Levinas presents in connection with it.

All the same, it is not necessary to feel the desire to escape in order to appreciate the potential power of Levinas's notion of transcendence, which challenges what he terms the ontologism (*ontologisme*) of Western philosophy or its unacknowledged, positive valuation of being.[21] Levinas points out that, for the tradition, human finitude is conceived primarily as a lack or deficiency that would be removed in an ideal existence. Concomitantly, the plenitude of being, whether it is thought of as an infinite being or the totality of being, is conceived primarily or predominantly in terms of goodness and perfection. A challenge to both views is at the core of Levinas's mature thought. For Levinas, human finitude will not signify a lack or deficiency, but will be interpreted as the positive good of sociality—a kind of surplus in being that ultimately "breaks with" mere being. Similarly, the totality or plenitude of being (even when it is taken as an ideal rather than a given reality) is not identified with infinity as a positive term or ideal, but with an All or One that absorbs the concrete, here-and-now individual and reduces it to the meaning it has for the system. By contrast to this All or One, infinity on Levinas's view is not a static and completed state, a divine fullness or presence, but the infinitely repeated production within being of a break with being that nonetheless accomplishes being.[22] Levinas's conception of transcendence is thus ultimately deployed in the service of recuperating the significance (sense and importance) of each singular, embodied human being and its absolute resistance to a reductive move that makes it but a moment of being—though the difficulties of making this resistance visible will be all but insurmountable.

The Other Who "Counts as Such"

For Levinas, transcendence in the phenomenological tradition remains tied to the question of knowledge, not in the narrow sense of a subject's knowing an object, but in the broader sense in which what is at stake in Heidegger's inquiry into the mode of being of Dasein is an account of the intelligibility of the world or of our experience of the world as *making sense*. For Heidegger, transcendence is not a quality or property of Dasein, nor does it figure in his account in terms of an *explanation* for the intelligibility we experience. Just as Husserl sets out neither to solve nor dissolve the problem of cognition but attempts to give a careful, methodologically delimited description of how cognition achieves what it does, so Heidegger does not set out to prove that there is meaning in the world (as if this could sensibly be doubted) or even that there is something like "objective" meaning or "objective" truth. Rather, his intention is to illuminate the structures or modes of existing that combine to make up the meaningfulness of the world and by means of which we have the sort of experience we do.

In his essay "Is Ontology Fundamental?" (1951), Levinas argues that despite the groundbreaking character of Heidegger's work in *Being and Time*—a work that he later classes among the most important works of Western philosophy—this philosophy remains true to the structure of cognition or thought as it has always been conceived within the Western philosophical tradition (*BPW* 4). Insofar as Dasein's existence is identical with its transcendence or its understanding itself and entities from a world, Heidegger's thought rejoins the tradition in subordinating the singularity of the unique and irreplaceable "I" to the universality and generality of the concept. In other words, Heidegger subordinates existence to thought and beings to Being:

The understanding of a being will thus consist in going beyond that being (l'étant) into the *openness* and in perceiving it *upon the horizon of being.* That is to say, comprehension, in Heidegger, rejoins the great tradition of Western philosophy: to comprehend the particular being is already to place oneself beyond the particular. To comprehend is to be related to the particular that only exists through knowledge, which is always knowledge of the universal. (*BPW* 5)

Stated in the language of Heidegger's account of transcendence, Levinas's complaint is that Dasein "comes back" to particulars or encounters them meaningfully only on the basis of or out of a prior relationship to the world. The structure of transcendence, of what Heidegger in *Being and Time* calls the worldhood of the world, determines the meaning of each individual being.[23]

Levinas's resistance to Heidegger, which opposes the existence of singularities to the necessarily general and universal structures through which such singularities are known, recalls parallel critiques by Kierkegaard and Rosenzweig directed against Hegel's idealism. Judith Butler describes Kierkegaard's critique of Hegel as concerning "the failure of a philosophy of reflection to take account of what exceeds reflection" (Butler 1993, 363); and while her discussion is limited to Kierkegaard, the characterization is equally applicable to Rosenzweig's reading of Hegel and captures important aspects of Levinas's critique of phenomenology. For all three thinkers, though there are important differences in how they spell out this claim, what exceeds the totality that can be reflected in thought is the concrete, here-and-now existence of a singular human being. To the passion for system in Hegel's philosophy, Kierkegaard opposes a passionate individual asking where Hegel, the historically existing human being, stands in relation to the systematic totality he elaborates in his philosophy. Likewise, Rosenzweig's insistence upon the irreducibility of the "quite ordinary private subject" who has "a given and a family name" pits the reality of contingent, finite existence against the timeless, all-encompassing logic of Hegel's system (Rosenzweig 1937, 359).[24] So, too, Levinas takes the part of the singular against the universal, arguing for a relationship to the other person that is not mediated by knowledge or understanding and hence does not approach the other through the abstraction or generality of a horizon.[25]

Butler remarks on a "two-fold irony" in Kierkegaard's critique that in a very similar form becomes central to the structure of Levinas's position. In the first instance, "the very existence of Hegel, the existing philosopher, effectively . . . undermines what appears to be the most important claim in that philosophy, the claim to provide a comprehensive account of knowledge and reality." This is so because if Hegel, the actually existing philosopher, is "outside" the complete system, "then there is an 'outside' to that system, which is to say that the system is not as exhaustively descriptive and explanatory as it claims to be" (Butler 1993, 363). Kierkegaard, as Butler notes, is fully aware of this irony and exploits it thoroughly. But there is also a second irony which attends Kierkegaard's own claim to be writing in the name of what is "beyond" language, speculation, and reflection: by writing about what is purportedly beyond thought and language, Kierkegaard shows that precisely the opposite is true and that this "beyond" *can* be thought and expressed, at least in some form.

Both the question of exteriority (or transcendence in Wahl's sense) and the problem of writing or thinking about that which exceeds the structures of comprehension are central for Levinas, and are explicitly at issue in the essay on ontology.[26] Having concluded that in Heidegger's philosophy (as in the Western philosophical tradition generally) the particular is subordinated to the universal, Levinas remarks that in opposition to this tradition one cannot simply "*prefer* a relation with a being as the condition of ontology" (*BPW* 5). As soon as one engages in thought and discourse, one is seemingly committed to the same path as Heidegger and the tradition, since to reflect upon and say something about the singular necessarily involves grasping it through that in it which is general and universal. Levinas asks, "How, moreover, can the *relation* with a *being* be, from the outset, anything other than the *comprehension* of it as a being?" (*BPW* 5–6; translation modified). The problem is a central one for this early essay, since, with this recognition, the primacy of ontology that Levinas began by questioning—the primacy of understanding as the original mode of every relationship—appears to reassert itself.

Levinas claims that the relation to the other is unique in being irreducible to comprehension. His view is not that this relationship excludes or prohibits knowledge or a comprehension of the other, but that in every comprehension of the other there is always comprehension *plus* something more: "Our relation with the other certainly consists in wanting to comprehend him, but this relation overflows comprehension" (*BPW* 6). Levinas specifies that this something more in virtue of which the other affects us is not love or sympathy, modes of relation that have often been called non-cognitive and which, as thus outside of knowledge or understanding, might provide an alternative basis for ethical theory. Rather, the relation to the other exceeds the relation we have with objects or things in being a relation produced within discourse in which the other is never just my theme or the object of my speech but also its interlocutor: "The other (*autrui*) is not an object of comprehension first and an interlocutor second. The two relations are intertwined. In other words, the comprehension of the other is inseparable from his invocation" (*BPW* 6). From this point on in Levinas's writings, speech "designates an original relation" (*BPW* 6).

This vocative dimension of language, or what, following Jean Greisch, we might call its allocutionary dimension, is not subordinate to the constative function of language, nor even just something that runs alongside of the latter as a secondary possibility, something else one can do or mean by a given sentence.[27] In speaking about something, I speak about it *to* someone who is not herself thematized by the discourse. And even should she become my theme, this thematization or comprehension can never get beneath or ahead of the moment of invocation. As Levinas puts it in *Totality and Infinity*, "The word that bears on the Other as a theme seems to contain the Other. But already it is said to the Other who, as interlocutor, has quit the theme that encompassed him, and upsurges inevitably behind the said" (*TI* 195). The upshot is that *not everything can be said*: every statement, every instance of discourse enacts its own limit in enacting its relation to an exteriority that exceeds it. No matter how fast discourse runs, it can never catch up with this moment or recuperate it in a cognition that would contain the "One-All," nor can it ever make the moment of address be of a piece with the fabric of thought or consciousness. Levinas concludes, "Here the formula 'before being in relation with a being, I must first have comprehended it as a being' loses its strict application, for in comprehending a being I simultaneously tell this comprehension to this being. . . . Here perception is not projected toward a horizon . . . in order to grasp the individual upon a familiar foundation. It refers to the pure individual, to a being as such" (*BPW* 7). The force of Levinas's argument in this early essay on ontology is summed up when he writes that the other "does not affect us starting from a concept. He is a being (*étant*) and *counts as such*" (*BPW* 6; emphasis added).

The irreducibility of the singular other who faces me, expressed as the idea that the other is a being who "counts as such," is repeated throughout essays that Levinas published in the 1950s. "Ethics and Spirit" (1952) reprises the main line of argument from the ontology essay, linking discourse with the possibility of a face that presents itself in a way wholly different from the way in which things are given to us:

The Other is not only known, he is *greeted* [*salué*]. He is not only named, but also invoked. To put it in grammatical terms, the Other does not appear in the nominative, but in the vocative. I not only think of what he is for me, but also and simultaneously, and even before, I *am* for him. In applying a concept to him, in calling him this or that, I am already appealing to him. I do not only *know* something, I am also part of society. . . .What one says, the content communicated, is possible only thanks to this face-to-face relationship in which the Other counts as an interlocutor prior even to being known. (*DF* 7–8)

Here as elsewhere, Levinas identifies understanding or comprehension with an appropriating, possessive grasp that "seizes and disposes of the thing" (*DF* 8) and claims that the face opposes this kind of appropriation. Even though the face *can* be treated like a thing, and even though it is certainly known and named, it is never *only* known or named: "Knowledge seizes hold of its object. It possesses it. Possession denies the independence of being, without destroying that being—it denies and maintains. The face, for its part, is inviolable; those eyes, which are absolutely without protection, the most naked part of the human body, none the less offer an absolute resistance to possession, an absolute resistance in which the temptation to murder is inscribed: the temptation of absolute negation" (*DF* 8). In instrumental relationships (and it needs to be remembered that Heideg-ger's notion of equipmentality largely extends this status to all things and relationships to things), the alterity of what is other than me is suspended as I appropriate it for my own purposes. The tool resists me only in the sense that it may be too heavy for me to wield or it may be the wrong size or shape for the job. The ordinary suspension of alterity that characterizes use relationships is in no way possible, Levinas claims, in relationships with another person. No matter how great the extent of my domination or of the other's enslavement, possession of the sort I can have with tools simply is not possible with the other. To possess the other in the sense of having him wholly at my disposal would mean co-opting or controlling his will completely, which is possible only by making him no longer *him*, no longer a subject. To totally possess the other would be to kill him, and in this case I no longer possess him. This is why Levinas describes the temptation to possess the other as a temptation to absolute negation or murder and says that a human being is the only sort of being I can wish to murder.

"Freedom and Command," published just a year later, in 1953, again categorically distinguishes the subject-object or knower-known relationship from the social relationship with a face. Levinas notes that Hegel is undoubtedly correct in saying that "in the world of knowledge and action nothing is strictly individual" (*CPP* 20), since, from the perspective of knowledge, that which exists always exists in a system of pre-existing relations. The relationship with things is thus always, in a sense, indirect. The particular is grasped through or on the basis of a network of relationships or, in Heidegger's terms, within the horizon of a larger referential totality. The relation to a face, by contrast, is described as a "direct relationship . . . which puts us in contact with a being that is not simply uncovered, but divested of its form, of its categories, a being becoming naked, an unqualified substance breaking through its form and presenting a face" (*CPP* 20). While things take their meaning from the system of relationships in which they are embedded, the face "has a meaning not by virtue of the relationships in which it is found, but out of itself" (*CPP* 20). This manner of signifying independently of a context Levinas calls expression,[28] and he specifies that expression is to be altogether distinguished from the operation of a sign which exposes and conceals that which it signifies. The face, in Levinas's sense, neither exposes nor conceals, but simply *is* the presentation of the entity itself, "its personal presentation" (*CPP* 20). Things cannot present themselves in this personal way as individuals.

Again, in "The Ego and the Totality" (1954), we read that the other who is addressed or invoked in discourse "is not invoked as a concept, but as a person"; this other "is a being situated beyond every attribute which would have as its effect to qualify him, that is, to reduce him to what he has in common with other beings, to make of him a concept" (*CPP* 41). In this same passage, Levinas opposes any interpretation of the face which would take it as the signifier of a signified or as a mask dissimulating a real (*CPP* 42). The assemblage of brow, eyes, nose, and mouth is said instead to indicate a self-presence, a "hard and substantial interlocutor," a "you" outside of every system or totality (*CPP* 41).

Transcendence and Singularity

The problem of transcendence as Levinas raises it has both existential and ontological dimensions. It is existential because it is a problem about how we are situated in the world; it is ontological in both the ordinary and Heideggerian senses because it is a question about what there is and how meaning is produced. Jean-Luc Nancy describes Heidegger's fundamental ontology as concerned with the "givenness of being" and suggests that "*being itself is given to us as meaning*. Being does not *have* meaning, but being itself, the phenomenon of being, is meaning" (Nancy 2000, 2). Heidegger's account of meaning, as we saw above, suggests that all meaning is given through a referential totality—a web or network of practical assignments—that ultimately runs *from* a possibility of Dasein *to* a possibility of Dasein. This is not to be confused with an account of meaning as subjective or as laid over things in themselves in the way a tablecloth cloaks the table beneath. It suggests, rather, that meanings exist in virtue of the various possibilities in which Dasein finds itself, or which it has grown up with, or creates. Meaning is not exactly use on this account (at least, not in any narrow sense), but certainly Heidegger's understanding of meaning resonates with Wittgenstein's. Levinas is largely in agreement with this account of meaning, but departs radically from it where it concerns the other (*l'autrui*). It is not just that the other person is not to be conceived solely as a means for satisfying my own ends (something Kant already tells us), but that the relationship to the other is not meaningful solely in function of the sorts of things I *do* with others. It is not my own possibilities or the possibilities of Dasein as such that render the other meaningful, on Levinas's account. The other signifies outside of any horizon or context. She is a being who "counts as such."

Why should the other be the only exception to the rule, however? Why should all other relationships be adequately accounted for in terms of a system of practical comportments and possibilities of Dasein and, likewise, in terms of a relative notion of alterity *except for the other*? It is the exception that Levinas makes for the social relationship and the impossibility of giving a phenomenological justification for this exception that no doubt inspires Janicaud to describe Levinas's philosophy as a "swerve" and to condemn it as a return to theology. But is it? Though Janicaud misreads Levinas, he does so in a way that is ultimately instructive.

A double blindness structures Janicaud's reading of Levinas and parallels what he calls Levinas's double game or his two-timing relationship with phenomenology. On the side of transcendence, Janicaud refuses to credit that the term could have a meaning other than a dogmatically religious one, while on the side of phenomenological method he retains an unexplained faith in the power of "patient description" to render the world of immanent phenomena as they are in themselves. In this latter respect, indeed, Janicaud seems as zealously faithful to the power of phenomenology as Levinas is said to be committed to the God of the biblical tradition. A signal question for Janicaud concerns the coherence and admissibility of the notion of a "pure experience" that "does not pass into any concept" (*TI* 260). He quotes Levinas's statement that "the absolute experience is not disclosure but revelation," and remarks that "all of Levinas's discourse is suspended on this presupposition. Once he has made his reader assent to it, he may lawfully put all of its variants into circulation" (Janicaud 1991, 42). Once the reader has accepted the counterfeit bill as legal tender, an economy whose basic currency is theological can be deployed. For Janicaud, the decisive point is that assent to the proposition about revelation cannot come through phenomenological (or any other methodologically sound) channels. In effect, the problem he has is how an experience can be "pure," which here means conceptless, and also "present," which surely must mean present to the understanding and thus presentable in terms of general notions. "We will be told that the phenomenological reduction has been replaced by 'revelation'; in short, we will have to listen, again, to the refrain of the beyond. But this is always to put off the same question: Why keep playing along at phenomenology when the game is fixed?" (42). Janicaud formulates the stakes of this issue as a choice between "whether we can manipulate experience, or must, on the contrary patiently describe it in order to know it" (44). Husserl is said to have chosen the latter way, while for Levinas the "relation to experience is subordinated to the restoration of the metaphysical (and theological) dimension" (44).

The core of the issue raised here concerns what Levinas means when he talks about "experience," and more specifically, about the "absolute experience" of the face-to-face relation. The reading of alterity given to this point suggests that he is talking about experience in one quite ordinary sense at least: he is talking about our experience of sociality, of relationships with other human beings and how we are to understand them. But the last part of this is crucial: by what categories do we *understand* this relationship? Is it a relationship that can be grasped *understandingly*, which is to say through general concepts?

If we consider the "patient description" that Janicaud thinks is a hallmark of phenomenological research, we run into two problems that go unaddressed by Janicaud's report. First, and most immediately, there is a problem about the way in which cultural, political, and social institutions—in short, sociality and everything that ensues from it—shape perception and description alike (and we know them only as intertwined). The assumption that there is such a thing as neutral description can be maintained only by privileging certain cases of perception over others and abstracting perception as a whole from its social context. Famously, Descartes and Husserl both use examples in which the perception in question is perception of a simple object—this piece of wax or this piece of paper on the desk in front me. In each case, the object is viewed in a well-known context or in a context artificially constructed to aid the project of giving the sought after description. Husserl quite explicitly supposes himself to be talking about ordinary perception when he considers this example, and if he at all acknowledges the way in which the example neatly suits his theoretical purposes his discussion also suggests that any privilege granted to certain cases is the temporary and thus excusable privilege granted to a heuristic device that has no impact on the conclusions reached by means of it. In point of fact, Heidegger was quick to see that neither the so-called "natural" attitude nor the suspension of it by means of the *epoché* were natural or ordinary, but that both were heavily determined by philosophical assumptions and thus put the lie to any simple claims about phenomenology as pure, presuppositionless, descriptive science. For Heidegger, there is no "bare" perception that can be "patiently" described, only a hermeneutical circle that suggests one is already in the midst of various perceptual and descriptive processes at any given time. Levinas would certainly concur with this latter point of view.

A second and more crucial point about Janicaud's assumption concerns the link between description and generalization. When I describe a face, I have no choice but to describe it in general or universal terms that can be applied to other faces and that are already embedded in existing practices of description. The face, as Levinas often admits (and how could he do otherwise), is an assemblage of brow, eyes, nose, cheeks, mouth, chin. We describe the eyes as wide-set or close together, as blue or brown or green, the nose as snub or aqualine, the lips as full or thin; we focus on these aspects of the face and ignore those planes or negative spaces that, were the eye trained to see them, could be just as useful for identification, veneration, narration, and a host of other purposes. But even the most original description of the face will inevitably be general, portable from one face to another; *there is simply no way to do justice to the singularity of a face in a description.* Of course, in one sense this is as true for snowflakes or trees as it is for human faces and, particularity in this ordinary sense, does not seem to be especially mysterious or problematic. Moreover, it is a point of which Husserlian phenomenology was well aware and even helps us to understand: spatial objects, each of which is a particular, are intended as ideal unities, even though they are given to perception in constitutively incomplete series of *Abschattungen,* or perspectival "slices." We negotiate the move from the particular to the general in every case of intentionally relating to an object that appears spatially or temporally. Further, the problem of particularity can be solved for humans and objects alike by a convention of naming, that is, by assigning a proper name or number or some other symbol arbitrarily specified as uniquely designating *this* particular person or tree. However, it is not *particularity* which is at issue here, but *singularity,* and the difference is crucial. The idea that I can give a proper name to a tree as readily as to a human being—even if we ordinarily have little call to do so—indicates the troubling fact that at a certain level *language renders all others the same.* Animate and inanimate beings, humans, snowflakes, chairs, and trees are all alike "objects" that can be numbered and known. Levinas's point is that whatever this knowing amounts to, whether it is understood simply as "S knows that p . . . ," or in terms of the more richly, existentially textured structures of Heideggerian being-in-the-world, knowing cannot capture the singularity of the other who stands over against me. In effect, knowing is neither constitutive nor exhaustive of social relationships. Furthermore, the excess of sociality over knowing, the something "more" in virtue of which social relationships are irreducible to subject-object, knower-known relationships, cannot itself be described, because description inevitably renders every aspect in terms of a particular rather than a singular being. At the level of description, language seemingly cannot render the "fact" that in relation to a face I am in society with someone, whereas in relation to a tree—no matter how majestic, fragile, or precious—the relation is not one of sociality. In short, Levinas's plaint is that the categories available to us in describing and understanding our world are unable to capture the crucial dimension of the social relationship between human beings.

A presumption such as Janicaud's that permits only "patient description" in accordance with supposedly strict methodological constraints, and that fails—or, more accurately, definitionally refuses—to see the limitations imposed by this presumption, has no choice but to label the demand to recognize or acknowledge the distinct status of social relationships a theological importation and manipulation of "experience." Janicaud supposes that the only sort of evidence that can legitimately be brought to bear on the claim that the relation to a human other is different in kind than the relation to a thing must be phenomenological evidence—thus demanding that the categories appropriate to the description of physical objects and the evaluation of claims about physical objects be the ultimate categories of our thinking and evaluating. But, of course, as the forgoing discussion has shown, the problem of transcendence that is the spur to Levinas's philosophy is precisely the problem of whether these categories and modes of evaluation exhaust the whole of what is, or whether there is not in human experience a moment of transcendence when the sway of our relation to the world is pierced by another order, a sociality in which the other "appears" not only as a thing among things or a force ranged against us but as a singular being who "counts as such" and whose meaning, therefore, is not a function of a larger system or whole but signifies outside of every horizon or context.

Janicaud and Agamben share a view of Levinas as philosophizing in the service of a fixed point or guaranteed certainty that would provide the basis for a new ethics of respect and responsibility for the other human being. Now in one respect they are right: Levinas does have recourse to the idea of a "fixed point." In a passage in "The Ego and the Totality" concerned with the critique of knowledge (and with denying psychoanalysis this status), Levinas suggests that "one can inaugurate the work of criticism only if one can begin with a fixed point" (*CPP* 41). This point cannot be some purportedly incontestable truth or statement, since every statement is potentially subject to further analysis that would subvert or invert its truth status. The fixed point "can only be the absolute status of an interlocutor, a being, and not a truth about beings" (*CPP* 41). Stella Sanford reads passages such as this one and the one in which Levinas speaks of a "being who counts as such" as vestiges of an ontological language that Levinas later tries to do without (Sanford 2000, 12). She is no doubt right in this,[29] as in her claim that the term *autrui* is introduced "as that . . . which indicates something beyond ontology" (11). However, it is crucial that this *beyond* not be interpreted as a reference to something otherworldly. Transcendence, in the way Levinas uses it, does not designate an extraterrestrial phenomenon nor the interruption of the "here below" by a divine "beyond." Rather, transcendence functions as a trope to express the *inadequacy of every representation to the singularity of the other who faces me.* Sociality, as successive chapters will argue in detail, is excessive with respect to language or conceptualization, but this excess must be registered *in* language. The other *as a face*—as a "sociable" rather than an "intelligible" entity in the world, as *facing* rather than merely *being*—cannot be the object of an adequate representation. How, precisely, to conceive this inadequacy, and how to understand it as productive of an ethical relationship, is the focus of the following chapter.

2

Singularity:
The Unrepresentable Face

The immediate is the face to face.

—EMMANUEL LEVINAS

The first and immediate is always, as a concept, mediated and thus not the first.

—THEODOR ADORNO

The Dilemma of the Face

Few aspects of Levinas's thought have drawn more attention than his pivotal notion of the face of the other. In a 1982 interview, Philippe Nemo asks, "What does this phenomenology of the face, that is, this analysis of what happens when I look at the Other face to face, consist in and what is its purpose?" (*EI* 83). Levinas's reply is characteristic: "I do not know if one can speak of a 'phenomenology' of the face, since phenomenology describes what appears. So, too, I wonder if one can speak of a look turned toward the face, for the look is knowledge, perception. I think rather that access to the face is straightaway [*d'emblée*] ethical" (*EI* 85). The same point is made in almost the same words in an interview with François Poirié: "The face is not of the order of the *seen*, it is not an object, but it is he whose appearing . . . is also an appeal or an imperative given to your responsibility: to encounter a face is *straightaway* [*d'emblée*] to hear a demand and an order" (*IR*, 48; Poirié 1987, 94; emphasis in original).

The sheer number of pages devoted to the face in Levinas's thought and in commentaries on his work means that any discussion of this *mot-clef* is likely to have an air of the shopworn or obvious. But is it yet sufficiently obvious how we are to understand his claim that the encounter with a face is "straight off" or "right away" [*d'emblée*] ethical? In what sense is our encounter with a face an *immediately* ethical encounter? Surely, it is a banal fact of human existence that we do not always encounter one another in ways that manifest ethical respect or responsibility. Does the torturer fail to encounter a face? Does she encounter it, but somehow fail to recognize it? Do the faces of the homeless remain hidden, or is our walking by them a refusal to register what is patently there? That the ethical character of the encounter is not supposed to register either in the perceptual order or in the order of knowing is clear from what Levinas says. But how or where does it register? What does it demand and with what authority? And in what sense is our access to this demand immediate?

The face poses a dilemma that resists an easy solution. Consider first that if the face represents the singularity of the other (however problematically) and if singularity is understood in the ordinary sense of *uniqueness*, then it is unclear why the uniqueness of a face—its occurring in just this one instance—makes special ethical demands on me that the uniqueness of other things does not. After all, why should uniqueness command in a face and not when it is encountered in an animal, a tree, a stone, or a work of art? It is tempting to respond to this difficulty by saying that for Levinas notions such as alterity, singularity, and the face are ethical terms or categories from the start. On this view, alterity and the face are misunderstood if they are thought to be the ethically neutral catalysts to our entering into an ethical relation. Taking this line lands us on the other horn of the dilemma since, if uniqueness as it is encountered in a face is already ethical—that is, if singularity and the face have ethical force built into them—then the account seems circular and dogmatic. To be told that the ethical force of the face is there immediately or straight away and to be denied an account of it that is open to further scrutiny raises the suspicion that here one is dealing not with a philosophy but with something else. Thus, on the one hand, if we think of the face as an ethically neutral term, it is unclear how it generates anything like a responsibility or an ethical relationship.

But, on the other hand, if we grant that the face has ethical content built into it, it is unclear how Levinas's thought escapes the charge of circularity and dogmatism.

As we saw in the previous chapter, when Dominique Janicaud comes to this impasse, he concludes that Levinas's claims about the face are dogmatic importations from theology. As he sees it, the reader is confronted with the claim that she is infinitely responsible for the other, and when she asks for a justification, she is told that she must simply believe by the light of revelation that it is so. For Janicaud, "All of Levinas's discourse is suspended on this presupposition [of revelation]. Once he has made his reader assent to it, he may lawfully put all of its variants into circulation" (Janicaud 1991, 42). Janicaud writes of the urgent need to withhold that initial assent and thus to forestall the moment when phenomenology is abandoned for theology. Levinas was certainly cognizant of the possibility of this kind of criticism. In *Entre Nous*, he says of responsibility that it is not a matter of "receiving an order by perceiving it first and obeying it subsequently in a decision," but rather that "the subservience of obedience precedes the hearing of the order" (*EN* 151).[1] Having said this, however, he wryly observes that to ears conditioned by modern moral philosophy this idea will sound like a bit of "insanity," or an "absurd anachronism" (*EN* 151). For Janicaud, it is an anachronism indeed: the revelation of the face is no more than a leftover bit of religious tradition masquerading as philosophy.

Little relief is to be had from the idea that Levinas's thought rests on pre-philosophical experiences that cannot be made philosophically explicit or that cannot be fully justified by discursive means. Readers point to the texts of the Jewish tradition or to the events of the Shoah as providing underlying intuitions that guide the work without being available for critical assessment. In a related vein, Levinas's work is increasingly characterized in terms of ethical non-cognitivism. Simon Critchley appears to advance such a view when he writes: "The ethical relation takes place at the level of sensibility, not at the level of consciousness, and thus, in a way that recalls both Bentham's and Rousseau's criteria for ethical obligation . . . , it is in my *pre-reflective sentient disposition* towards the other's suffering that a basis for ethics and responsibility can be found" (Critchley 1999, 98; emphasis added). Is this to opt for insanity (in the form of a non-rational basis for ethics) rather than anachronism? Perhaps not, but whether one goes the route of assimilating Levinas's position to a theological ethics or to a species of non-cognitivism, the risk is that one abandons rational justification in favor of divine authority, the mechanisms of nature, intuition, or a moral sense. Moreover, though Critchley's remarks need not be read as positing a foundation for ethics in human nature, reading the face as a pre-discursive or pre-reflective basis for ethics risks reinstating the priority of ontology that Levinasian ethics is at pains to overturn. Todd May is right when he comments, "If ethics is either prediscursive or transcendent to cognition, then the content of our linguistic practices can never reach it; they can never make it a subject of discussion and debate. And if that is so, then ethics remains perpetually hostage to the ontological and totality" (May 1997, 147).

A third route beckons, but is just as problematic: perhaps these questions of justification are the wrong sort of questions. Perhaps they somehow miss the larger point of Levinas's account of the face. A defense of the notion of the face can seemingly be pursued only by means of the words and images that the view itself disavows as inadequate. And though the apologist is no worse off than Levinas himself in this respect, that may be little comfort indeed. When pressed in interviews to give concrete examples of the face-to-face relation, Levinas often cites small gestures of common decency, such as "After you, sir" or a simple "Hello." The commentator may well follow suit. Philippe Nemo, for one, invokes an example drawn from the extraordinary rather than the ordinary moments of human interaction: "War stories tell us in fact that it is difficult to kill someone who looks straight at you" (*EI* 86). Nemo means for the example to lend intuitive support to the account of the face as a directly ethical relation, but Levinas's response, quoted above, consists mainly in warning Nemo against attempting a phenomenology of what, strictly speaking, does not and cannot appear. Ironically, in an essay roughly contemporaneous with his conversation with Nemo, Levinas himself reports, "I have attempted a 'phenomenology' of sociality, taking as my point of departure the face of the other" (*EN* 169)! And in the essay "Signature," Levinas reports that freedom is "inhibited before the Other when I really stare, with a straightforwardness devoid of trickery or evasion, into his unguarded absolutely unprotected eyes" (*DF* 293). When Levinas can do no better, is it any wonder that commentators have either thrown up their hands in despair or pronounced themselves persuaded without the benefit of argument?

The reading of Levinas pursued here consciously forgoes the role of apologist for his notion of the face, but does not for all that abandon the problem of justification *as a problem*. Rather than smoothing the path that leads from Levinas's claims about the unrepresentability of the face to the demands of infinite responsibility, the aim here is to multiply the contradictions that structure Levinas's discussion of the face and to lay bare the detours, pitfalls, and uncertainties of the Levinasian route. The face is exposed as a figure of unreconstructed paradox: it represents that which it claims is unrepresentable; it presents immediacy through the mediation of an image; it makes an ethical claim that compels the hearer without ever becoming audible or legible. And if the last seems to approach thaumaturgic violence, it is worth knowing we have nothing more than Levinas's word that the face comes in perfect gentleness and goodness. The gamble here is that a commentary that reads *for* the tensions of Levinas's account may well succeed in a manner that those that want to reconcile or resolve the dilemmas of the face do not.[2]

To take this approach is to admit that the paradoxes generated by Levinas's discourse on the face are permanent and intractable: they cannot be resolved by patient exposition or by clever amendments to the account. But at the same time, admitting the difficulties need not condemn us to a view of Levinas's project as philosophically flawed, theologically motivated, non-cognitivist, or of interest only to those who share a penchant for the impossible. It will be suggested here that the tensions in Levinas's account of the face, and in particular the fraught nature of the question of authority or of how the face commands, are *constitutive* of the manner in which ethics is reconceived in his work. In particular, these tensions *perform* a desire for justification and a simultaneous frustration of that desire that are at the heart of the ethical relationship as Levinas reconceives it. This reading fully recognizes and credits a certain resistance to questions about how the face registers and with what authority it commands me, but it equally insists that such questions are not "out of order," nor external to the purview of Levinas's thought. These questions belong properly, if you will, to Levinas's account: they are internal to a Levinasian conception of ethical life. And that they cannot be satisfied either practically or theoretically does not impugn their claim to being constitutive.

The chapter begins by sketching Levinas's distinction between objects and faces or between objectifying intentionality and the ethical relation; next, it considers a constellation of tensions that arise in connection with this distinction and that render it deeply unstable; third, it examines the face as a figure or image; and, finally, it considers how these tensions produce a distinctive performance of the stakes of ethical life as Levinas conceives them.

Objects and Faces

Beginning in the 1950s, Levinas's essays distinguish between the face as an object of perception—the assemblage of nose, forehead, eyes, chin, cheeks, and so on—and the face as an ethical modality in which the other, present "somehow in a personal way" (*DF* 8), calls my naïve and egoistic freedom into question and founds it as responsibility. Whereas objects are given to consciousness in sensible experience through the mediation of images and concepts, the manifestation of a face is unmediated: "At each moment [the face] destroys and overflows the plastic image it leaves me" (*TI* 50–51). The face as ethical modality is not an object of cognition and is not accessed in an act of perception or knowing; it is, Levinas says, the "exceptional presentation of self by self, incommensurable with the presentation of realities simply given" (*TI* 202).

The fundamental thesis broached in the discussion of the face is the difference between the way in which objects are given to consciousness (the order of ontology) and the way in which human beings are encountered (the order of ethics). Levinas writes in *Totality and Infinity* that "*the difference between objectivity and transcendence will serve as a general guideline for all the analyses of this work*" (*TI* 49; emphasis in original). "Objectivity" as Levinas uses the term here makes it roughly synonymous with the Husserlian idea of the constitution of objects in intentional consciousness. "Transcendence," as we have already seen, is the name for the ethical relationship to the other. And though this relation, too, seems to be intentionally structured, inasmuch as it "aims" at another, Levinas insists that "the 'intentionality' of transcendence is unique in its kind" (*TI* 49) and that "one must end by seeing that it ruptures intentionality" (*EI* 32).

The picture of objectifying consciousness that Levinas sketches in *Totality and Infinity*, especially in the section on "Enjoyment and Representation," is drawn explicitly from Husserl's transcendental idealism, though Levinas consistently criticizes the intellectualist interpretation given to intentionality in Husserl's work (see *TIHP* 94–95, 155–58; *TI* 28; *DE* 120). For Husserl, the object constituted in consciousness is simultaneously distinct from consciousness and a product of consciousness through a meaning-giving act, or *Sinngebung* (*TI* 123). In contrast to some forms of idealism for which the mental representation or object—for example, "apple tree"—is really contained within the stream of conscious thought, Husserl maintains that the object taken as an ideal unity of thought is no more a part of the stream of conscious experience than the tree itself, which produces apples or can be burned for firewood. With a three-dimensional object like a tree, the perceiving ego cannot see or represent all sides of it at once; hence the act of perception consists in an infinite number of "adumbrations," or *Abschattungen,* of the object. These adumbrations are all that are "really" contained in the stream of conscious experience, but the object nonetheless falls "under the power of thought," in the sense that the ego posits these perspectival renderings as renderings of the same, single object (Husserl 1990).

Thought never fails to give itself the object as an ideal unity of meaning, which is why Levinas suggests that the movement proper to objectifying intentionality is one in which an exterior object is "given" or "delivered over" to a knowing subject "who encounters it as though it had been entirely determined by him" (*TI* 123). Representation may thus be viewed as a kind of creative mastering of the world through the production of intelligible or meaningful objects and events. Intelligibility implies the "total adequation of the thinker with what is thought, in the precise sense of a mastery exercised by the thinker upon what is thought, in which the object's resistance as an exterior being vanishes. This mastery . . . is accomplished as the giving of meaning" (*TI* 124).

The most important feature of representational intentionality is derived directly from this notion of a thought forever adequate to its object. In representation, the ego "determines" the other—that is, confers a meaning on it, assigns it to and recognizes its place in an intelligible or-der—*without being determined by it in return*. Representation involves a non-reciprocal determination of the other by the ego or "the same." Levi-nas describes the movement of objectifying consciousness as "the same," because what it brings out is "the identity of the I despite the multiplic-ity of its objects" (*TI* 126). Recalling the Kantian unity of transcendental apperception which "remains an empty form in the midst of its synthet-ic work" (*TI* 125–26), the "I" of representation retains all its freedom and spontaneity in relation to the world it knows: "The world which strikes against thought can do nothing against free thought—which is able to re-fuse inwardly, to take refuge in itself, to remain precisely a *free thought* be-fore the true, to return to itself, to reflect on itself and take itself to be the origin of what it receives, to master what precedes it through memory" (*CPP* 96). To be sure, it is not a question here of a creation or mastery that can project anything whatsoever onto the object. But even as representa-tion comes up against various limitations in its activity, *it constitutes these very limits as an object for consciousness*, thereby reestablishing its primacy and recovering its position at the origin of intelligibility. Levinas can thus describe the ego in representation as a "pure spontaneity" (*TI* 125) that re-duces every exteriority to a moment of its own thought (*TI* 127). As repre-sentational, thought remains free of its objects in the sense that it retains its power to withdraw from objects in reflection and is lived as a mastery of the world through constituting consciousness. Though Levinas agrees with Heidegger that representation is by no means the fundamental or pri-mordial form of our relationship to what is, it nonetheless has a privileged place "as the possibility of recalling the separation of the I" (*TI* 48).

The account of the face in *Totality and Infinity* and elsewhere sys-tematically inverts the fundamental features of objectifying consciousness. As Bernhard Waldenfels notes, this produces a "long and sometimes tire-some" list of negations (Critchley and Bernasconi 2002, 67): the relation to the face is not a matter of representation (*TI* 38); it cannot be under-stood in terms of comprehension or the grasping of an object in thought (*TI* 46); the face is not an image or form, but "destroys and overflows" its own "plastic image" (*TI* 51; *CPP* 55, 95–96); it is "neither seen nor touched" (*TI* 194); it refuses to be contained in a theme (*TI* 195) and is present only in its refusal of thematization (*TI* 199); it signifies outside of every context and without mediation (*CPP* 95; *EI* 86). In addition, the face puts the naïve freedom and spontaneity of the ego into question and calls the ego to goodness or responsibility (*TI* 200, 203). In short: (1) access to the face is not had in a meaning-granting act of representation directed at a sensuous object and grasping it as an ideal, formal unity—that is, the face is neither perceived nor known; (2) the encounter with a face is thus an experience of non-adequation rather than adequation; and (3) whereas the transcendental ego retains its freedom and spontaneity in relation to the objects or world that it thinks, the "I" who encounters a face loses its naïve being at home in the world and discovers itself bound by the other in ethical responsibility.

The Cartesian idea of infinity is the formal mechanism of the inversion from objectifying intentionality to ethical transcendence. Recalling Descartes' famous argument, Levinas is explicitly interested in the claim that while it is possible that I myself, as a finite substance, might be the cause of all of my ideas of other finite substances, I cannot by myself account for nor be the cause of the idea I have of infinity or God's perfection. For Descartes, I cannot arrive at the idea of the infinite through a negation of the concept of my own finitude, since it would not be possible to know that I am finite or imperfect, "that I doubt and desire, that is to say, that something is lacking to me . . . unless I had within me some idea of a Being more perfect than myself, in comparison with which I should recognize the deficiencies of my nature" (Descartes 1983, 166). Less interested in the question of God's existence than in the structure of the idea of infinity,[3] Levinas is struck by the suggestion that in the idea of infinity the distance between the idea and what it thinks is altogether different from that which normally separates the mental act from its object. In the latter case, the separation is overcome in the meaning-giving act, or *Sinngebung,* which delivers the object to thought as an ideal unity. By contrast, the gap between the idea of infinity and its ideatum can never be made up or filled in, since the ideatum can be exhibited in thought only as a surplus or excess over every idea the ego could have of it: "Infinity does not enter into the *idea* of infinity, is not grasped; this idea is not a concept" (*CPP* 54). "The idea of infinity is exceptional in that its ideatum surpasses its idea" (*TI* 49).

Like all intentional acts, the idea of infinity is an aiming at something or a "consciousness of something," but the "something" at which the idea aims—namely, God's perfection or infinity—is that which breaks with or outstrips the structures by which the meaningfulness of things or objects is produced. In the idea of the infinity, Levinas claims that thought cannot give itself its object by an act of pure thematizing intentionality: "Contrary to the ideas which always remain on the scale of the 'intentional object,' or on that of their *ideatum* . . . ; contrary to the ideas by which thinking progressively grasps the world, the idea of the Infinite would contain more than it was able to do. It would contain more than its capacity as a *cogito*. Thought would think in some manner beyond what it thinks" (*GCM* xiii). The idea of infinity thus represents the possibility of an idea whose object is not produced in a meaning-giving or objectifying act of consciousness. There is thus at least one "object" to which thought is inadequate, which it may neither grasp nor possess. The idea of infinity "is preeminently *non-adequation*" (*TI* 27).

In order to argue the third moment of the inversion, namely, that in relation to infinity the *cogito* does not retain its freedom, Levinas relies partly on the Cartesian idea that in having an idea of God's perfection we have an idea of our own imperfection, thus we have a check on the "naïve right" and "glorious spontaneity" of our own powers. But he also invokes in this regard the Platonic figure of desire as a form of delirium or a "winged thought" that breaks with rationality without necessarily taking on an "irrationalist significance" (*TI* 49). To think "what does not have the lineaments of an object is in reality to do more or better than think" (*TI* 49). It is to *desire*. "A thought that thinks more than it thinks is a desire. Desire 'measures' the infinity of the infinite" (*CPP* 56). In love, as the *Phaedrus* tells us, we are compelled to seek out the object of our desire, but this compulsion is not a form of violence but rather an extraordinary gift from the gods. Indeed, as Levinas reminds us, reason itself is the fourth type of delirium (*TI* 49), and philosophy is a love of wisdom. The idea of an orientation or commitment that we cannot account for because it conditions our very ability to produce an account or to engage in the activity of being accountable is crucial to Levinas's developing picture of ethical responsibility.

Totality and Infinity arrives explicitly at the notion of the face when Levinas says "we must now indicate the terms which will state the *deformalization* or *concretization* of the idea of infinity" (*TI* 50; emphasis added). Commentators have generally understood deformalization to involve the provision of a concrete experience in which the formal structure is realized (Peperzak 1993, 61).[4] We will return to this idea in the next chapter, but for the moment it can be noted that the move from formal to concrete is not entirely consonant with a move from a predominantly negative to a predominantly positive construal. Just as the idea of infinity includes both negative and positive characterizations (i.e., the idea of infinity is negatively an idea in which the idea is constitutively inadequate to its ideatum, and is positively an idea of God's perfection), so too the face is elaborated by means of a set of negative characterizations that are simultaneously given a positive import.

On the negative side, the account of the face once more inverts the standard features of intentionality. Within intentional consciousness, the object is produced in a meaning-giving act that grasps the object within a surrounding or environing horizon. In *Ideas I*, Husserl maintains that the act in which I attend to the piece of paper here in front of me has as its equally intentional complement an inattention to all those objects that form the horizon of this act. By turning my gaze, I can now pick out the other items on the desk, the desktop itself, the lamp, wall, or fireplace at my back, and so on beyond the confines of my study. My intentional act can thus ultimately encompass the entire world. Reinterpreting the notion of a horizon of unrealized acts that surrounds every intentional act, Heidegger posits a referential totality to which the paper belongs, a structure of "assignments" that are largely purposive in nature and that make possible my understanding of any given item I encounter within the world. Meaning for Heidegger and Husserl alike is meaning *within a context*. The face, by contrast, signifies *without a context* and outside of every referential totality: "The nakedness of the face is an extirpation from the context of the world, from the world signifying as context" (*EN* 57). Whereas Husserl and Heidegger both encourage us to think of the meaningful object in the manner of a "silhouette" acquiring a meaning by virtue of its appearance within a "luminous horizon," Levinas assures us that "the face *signifies* otherwise" (*EN* 10). It is "signification without context" (*EI* 86). Encountered in a face, the other is not encountered only through her social roles or in the context of human arrangements and purposes. Occupation, social status, economic class, heritage, race, gender, even the color of one's eyes are all beside the point where a face is concerned. "Ordinarily one is a 'character': a professor at the Sorbonne, a Supreme Court justice, son of so-and-so, everything that is in one's passport" (*EI* 86). In the extraordinary encounter with a face, however, the face does not derive its meaning from a context; it is "meaning all by itself" (*EI* 86).

Of course, even as Levinas insists that the face is a "thing" apart, he acknowledges that we *also* encounter faces as forms or images, vested with all the interests of social commerce: "The manifestation of the other is, to be sure, produced from the first conformably with the way every meaning is produced. Another is present in a cultural whole and is illuminated by this whole, as a text by its context" (*CPP* 95). But the "epiphany" or "revelation" of the face—both terms meant to suggest a means of manifestation totally distinct from perceptual appearance or cognition—also involves "a signifyingness of its own independent of this meaning received from the world. The other comes to us not only out of context, but also without mediation; he signifies by himself" (*CPP* 95).

In the relation to a face, the inadequacy of thought to its object takes on an overtly ethical significance. Whereas things are "integrated into the identity of the same," first as objects in meaning-giving acts of consciousness, and subsequently as that which the ego can appropriate to its own ends and purposes, the exteriority or absolute alterity of a face "is manifested in the absolute resistance which by its apparition, its epiphany, it opposes all my powers" (*CPP* 55). Once again, Levinas acknowledges the reality of ordinary power relations between human beings, even as he denies that these sorts of relations pertain to the face properly speaking:

To be sure, the other is exposed to all my powers, succumbs to all my ruses, all my crimes. Or he resists me with all his force and all the unpredictable resources of his own freedom. I measure myself against him. But he can also—and here is where he presents me his face—oppose himself to me beyond all measure, with the total uncoveredness and nakedness of his defenseless eyes, the straightforwardness, the absolute frankness of his gaze. The . . . true exteriority is in this gaze which forbids me my conquest. (*CPP* 55)

The face opposes me neither as a superior physical force nor with the technical force of strategy or art. In *Totality and Infinity*, Levinas notes that the other's resistance is not "like the hardness of a rock against which the effort of the hand comes to naught," nor is it like the "remoteness of a star in the immensity of space" (*TI* 197–98). It neither dwarfs nor overcomes my power, regardless of whether *power* is understood as physical capacity or as the capacity of consciousness to give itself an object. The face does not exceed my power by some measurable degree; it is a kind of *démesure*, an excess or infinity with respect to my power that can be indicated only through paradoxical phrases, as, for example, when Levinas writes that the face defies my "power for power" (*mon pouvoir de pouvoir*) (*TI* 198) or is "the resistance of what has no resistance" (*TI* 199). Or likewise when he suggests that the face "opposes" me by "inviting" me to responsibility; or that it is an "imposition" that nonetheless "does not limit" my freedom but promotes it (*TI* 200); or that it "commands" from utter "destitution" or is an "unshakeable" and "intransigent *no*" that, nonetheless, in the "contexture of the world . . . is a quasi-nothing" (*TI* 199).[5]

Contradictions in the Face

The distinction between objects and faces effectively underwrites the divisions between intentionality and transcendence and ontology and ethics that are canonical for Levinas's thought. And yet, the object/face distinction is everywhere in danger of collapse. The negations and inversions employed to differentiate the face from objects, the body, and spatiality seem to work in ways that bind the face all the more inextricably to the horizon of representation and objectification; that is, since the face can be delineated only in a negative fashion, it remains dependent both conceptually and practically on what it is not. That this is not a weakness in the account but produces the ethical interest of Levinas's text will be argued in the next chapter. For the moment, the aim is only to draw out these tensions and let them resound as fully as possible.

Let us begin again from objects and faces. Levinas's claim that thought is always adequate to its object is not, of course, an endorsement of a correspondence theory of truth, but indicates, as has already been shown, that representational thought never fails to give itself an object through a meaning-granting act of consciousness. The idea of infinity and, subsequently, the relation to the face are said by contrast to invert the structures of intentionality by presenting "objects" to which thought is constitutively inadequate. As Levinas often says, to "think" the infinite is "not to think an object" but "to do more or better than think" (*TI* 49). The "intentionality" of transcendence is thus said to be unique in kind, in that it is not the completion but the "ruin" of representational and objectifying thought. And yet, it must be said, representation is already significantly "in ruins" long before it comes face-to-face with an other.

Totality and Infinity writes of the body that it is "the permanent contestation of the prerogative attributed to consciousness of 'giving meaning' to each thing" (*TI* 129). The body intrudes on the relation between the act and object, asserts itself in the midst of the relation between representing and represented, because it is the place where representation "reverts" (see *TI* 127) into life and shows itself to be conditioned by the very things that it constitutes in consciousness. Eating, "for example" (*TI* 129)—and this is never a mere example for Levinas—cannot be reduced to consciousness of eating. Biting into one's food "measures the surplus of the reality of food [*l'aliment*] over every represented reality, a surplus that is not quantitative, but is the way the I, the absolute commencement, is suspended on the non-I" (*TI* 129). The I that represents bread, constituting it as an object for consciousness, is at the same time *conditioned* and sustained by the bread from which it lives: "The world I constitute nourishes me and bathes me" (*TI* 129). The body and its needs thus contest the possibility of a world fully mastered, shattering, even before the encounter with a face, the phantasmatic adequacy of the intentional aim to its object.

"The Ruin of Representation" was written in 1959 on the occasion of the hundredth anniversary of Husserl's birth and is widely recognized as marking a new chapter in Levinas's appraisal of Husserl. Here Levinas credits the Husserlian notion of *horizon* with making possible this idea of a constituting consciousness which is nonetheless conditioned by the world it constitutes. Moreover, he claims that this possibility in Husserl's work "compromises" or "puts into question" the "sovereignty of representation" more radically than the discovery of affective intentionalities (or the intentional structure of feeling) or of a pre-reflective engagement in the world (*DE* 116).[6] Insofar as "intentionality bears within itself the innumerable horizons of its implications and thinks of infinitely more 'things' than of the object upon which it is fixed" (*DE* 116), it opens the way to a philosophy of the lived body in which intentionality can be traced back to the "implicit" and "nonrepresented" dimensions of incarnate experience that serve as its sustaining but forgotten horizon (*DE* 117). That the constituting consciousness is conditioned by its own activity is a "paradoxical structure" that Levinas credits Heidegger with then making "evident" and putting to work "everywhere" (*DE* 118). In the "Ruin" essay, Levinas assimilates this movement, in which thought is conditioned by what it constitutes, to the figure of a thought that overflows itself or that thinks more than it thinks. The latter figure had already been employed in 1957 in "Philosophy and the Idea of Infinity" in connection with Descartes' idea of infinity and the ethical relation to alterity, but in the essay on Husserl it is sensuous experience and not the face that seems to bring about this rupture of representational adequacy and mastery.

Given these conflicting accounts, it is unclear whether it is the face that undoes and "ruins" representation or whether the conditions for this undoing are already there before the face-to-face encounter in the sensuous existing of the lived body. Can the face call me into question if the ground for such a call is not prepared in the body?[7] Are sensibility and embodiment pre-ethical conditions for ethics, or are they *themselves* ethical? Here the initial dilemma of the face reasserts itself, since if they are already ethical we can ask what makes them so. *Totality and Infinity* gives few if any unequivocal answers to such questions; it is as if the text cannot decide between body and face as sources that rupture totality and the mastery of representational thought.

There is an even deeper instability in the 1961 text in the relation between bodies and faces. Since Levinas says more than once that the "whole body" is a face, should we then conclude that the face is a body? In most respects, the answer is *no*. Whereas bodies can appear, the face does not and cannot; though the body can be made the object of science or knowledge, the face resists adequate representation and is not and cannot be an object of knowledge; whereas the body may be treated in many respects as a thing among things, this is precisely what the face, "properly" speaking, systematically and categorically refuses. And yet, as we have seen, Levinas admits again and again that the face is visible *in a sense*, does succumb to ordinary relations of power *in a sense*, and that human beings can be known *in the ordinary sense*. Interestingly, one of the very earliest occurrences of the word "face" in Levinas's work equates the face with form and with that which conceals alterity: "Form is that by which a being is turned toward the sun, that *by which it has a face*, through which it gives itself, by which it comes forward" (*EE* 40; emphasis added). Later uses of the term will preserve the aspect of self-presentation but will divest the face of every form, leaving us with a figure in which the self presents itself by itself but somehow without specific contours, without being illuminated against a horizon of meanings or projects.

If the relation of the face to the body is problematic, the tension grows when one considers the relation of the face and alterity to spatiality more generally. *Time and the Other*, for example, tells us that "exteriority is a property of space and leads the subject back to itself through light" (*TO* 76). Spatiality and light are quintessentially associated in this early text with knowledge and appropriation of the other. Light, for example, has the classic structure of Husserlian constituting consciousness: "Light is that through which something is other than myself, but already as if it came from me" (*TO* 64). Light illuminates the distance which the eye or the hand crosses in grasping an object; it separates the object from the ego, but in a way that prepares the object for appropriation and assimilation. "The light that permits encountering something other than the self, makes it encountered as if this thing came from the ego. The light, brightness, is intelligibility itself. . . . And in this sense knowledge never encounters anything truly other in the world" (*TO* 68). The exteriority of the other is thus better termed "alterity," Levinas tells us, in order that it not be understood in spatial terms (*TO* 76).

And yet, in *Time and the Other*, the word "exteriority" remains in use as a designation for the alterity of the other, each time with the caution that it is a non-spatial exteriority (see, e.g., *TO* 76, 84). *Totality and Infinity*, subtitled "*An Essay on Exteriority*," continues in this vein. But why use an obstinately spatial term to convey a supposedly non-spatial relationship? Indeed, why talk about a *relation* to alterity, which draws the I and the Other inevitably into spatial proximity to one another?[8] One need not go as far as Derrida's suggestion that metaphoric displacement is "the emergence of language itself" (though one might well go there in the end) to agree with him that it would be vain to try to purge language (and theoretical language in particular) of its dependence on a metaphorics of space: of concepts grasped, of lines of development, of levels of analysis, distances crossed, insides and outsides, interiority and exteriority. In part, Derrida's point is that conceptual language is inextricably bound to the deployment of spatial metaphors, hence any putting of alterity into words is bound to traduce this notion into a system of spatial relationships. Moreover, Derrida rightly asserts that alterity "would be lost more surely than ever" in some imagined non-spatial language (VM 113). Were it not for its exteriority, how could the alterity of the other be distinguished from our own dreams or hallucinations, which would surely range it all the more firmly within the same? How could the other be *other* without claiming exteriority? And at the same time, as we have seen, alterity in Levinas's sense requires that exteriority be "crossed out" as soon as it is invoked, since it implies a relative and not an absolute alterity—an exteriority that maintains itself by reference to and in relation to an interiority, and vice versa. This thought that writes and crosses out what it writes nonetheless allows spatiality to reassert itself, since the act of crossing out once more relies on a space traversed. The spatiality of language, Derrida concludes, is not like an image stamped on a coin that may be rubbed off or worn down to the point of being no longer recognizable, like a dead metaphor that no longer strikes us as a literary figure at all. Rather, metaphor is the very metal of language itself (VM 112).[9] "No philosophical language will ever be able to reduce the naturality of a spatial praxis in language" (VM 113). Thus, if alterity *must* be said, if its being said is an ethical imperative, it will necessarily fail to be said at the very moment when it is stated or its claims staked.

The simultaneous necessity and impossibility of stating or thinking alterity, infinity, and the face is the paradox that Derrida's essay, to borrow a phrase from Levinas, "puts to work everywhere":

That it is necessary to state infinity's *excess* over totality *in* the language of totality; that it is necessary to state the other in the language of the Same; that it is necessary to think *true* exteriority as non-*exteriority*, that is, still by means of the Inside-Outside structure and by spatial metaphor; and that it is necessary still to inhabit the metaphor in ruins, to dress oneself in tradition's shreds and the devil's patches—all this means, perhaps, that there is no philosophical logos which must not *first* let itself be expatriated into the structure Inside-Outside. (VM 112)

No *discourse* on alterity can do without exteriority and spatiality, not only because there can be no discourse at all without these, but also because alterity in Levinas's sense of infinity or absolute alterity can be said only by inverting, crossing out, negating, and exteriorizing. The face thus remains complicit with the terms whose inversion and negation are necessary to its being said, and what Derrida brings to our attention is the necessity of this and the compromise it involves. Hence, though it *may* be necessary— and Derrida habitually couches this necessity in a conditional form—to "[lodge] oneself within traditional conceptuality in order to destroy it" (VM 111), this *logement* is not without its consequences: "To say that the infinite exteriority of the other *is not* spatial, is *non*-exteriority and *non*-interiority, to be unable to designate it otherwise than negatively—is this not to acknowledge that the infinite (also designated negatively in its current positivity: in-finite) cannot be stated?" (VM 113).[10]

Derrida rings changes on this theme throughout "Violence and Metaphysics," and in reconsiderations of Levinas's thought in "At This Very Moment in This Work Here I Am" (1991a) and *Adieu to Emmanuel Levinas* (1999). Indeed, if "Violence and Metaphysics"—largely a reading of *Totality and Infinity*—emphasizes the impossibility of a complete rupture with traditional conceptuality and the ontological violence with which Levinas associates it, "At This Very Moment"—with a focus on *Otherwise Than Being*—observes that when the knot with ontology or conceptuality is retied, it "retains the trace of interruption despite itself" and thus that Levinas's text engages in a "retying without retying" of the strictures of logical discourse (Derrida 1991a, 27–28).

For the more immediate purposes of an analysis of the face, the most potent continuation of Derrida's point comes in his doubt that the face can be thought together with positive infinity or God: "The infinitely Other would not be what it is, other, if it was a positive infinity, and if it did not maintain within itself the negativity of the indefinite, of the *apeiron*" (VM 114). There are at least two difficulties here. First, in order to think the positive infinity of God, it is seemingly necessary to renounce language. This is the route classically taken by a negative theology that "was spoken in a speech that knew itself failed and finite, inferior to logos [or pure thought] as God's understanding" (VM 116). But Levinas, following Merleau-Ponty, refuses the separation of thought from language and most certainly refuses to privilege thought over language.[11] According to Levinas, speech is not the translation into words of a prior thought; it is not the failed linguistic means by which we approach a non-linguistic transcendence. Language on the Levinasian view *is* transcendence itself. Second, to the extent that language cannot be dissociated from spatiality, finitude, the play of interiority and exteriority, and the like, it cannot *say* positive infinity without rendering it finite, indefinite, and, to the extent that the face is a body, mortal. It may be, then, that "within *philosophical discourse* (supposing there are any others), one cannot simultaneously save the themes of positive infinity and of the face (the nonmetaphorical unity of body, glance, speech, and thought). . . . Infinite alterity as death cannot be reconciled with infinite alterity as positivity and presence (God)" (VM 114). Levinas, by rights then, must either renounce the connection between language and transcendence or renounce the link between transcendence and God.

It may be retorted that the face for Levinas is *both* finitude *and* transcendence. On one side, the face is body, mortality, hunger, destitution, and nudity, and on the other, infinity, height, and command. Indeed, this is the uniqueness of the position he advances, we may be told. The aim here is not to deny this, of course, but to recapture the strangeness with which these claims first struck us, before they became the weathered chestnuts of a Levinas industry. How can the face be at once body, mortality, finitude, *and* a positive infinity of which we cannot have even an idea? How does this unique, incomprehensible being, a face, present herself *in person* without becoming a thing or object, and why is this presentation or manifestation received as an *ethical command*? Before turning to these problems in the final section, there is one more tension to be examined: the face as a figure or representation of that which cannot be represented.

The Face as Figure

As Michèle Le Doeuff has noted, philosophers since Plato have habitually affirmed the non-philosophical character of images and rhetorical language (Le Doeuff 1989, 6). Levinas is no exception. In "Reality and Its Shadow," concepts are called the "muscles of the mind" while images are denounced (though not without ambivalence and sometimes appreciation) as "idols" (*CPP* 1–13). *Totality and Infinity* is likewise hard on speech that employs images, going to great lengths to exclude rhetoric from the sphere of ethical discourse (*TI* 70–72). Images in philosophical texts tend to be regarded by philosophers either as pedagogical aids (the need for which will be overcome as the student advances or as a more perfect philosophical language is developed) or as part of a stock of cultural forms that philosophers no less than others draw on unconsciously or unthinkingly but without significant theoretical consequence (Le Doeuff 1989, 6–7). In both cases, images are cast as expendable and extraneous parts of a philosophical enterprise. In a provocative reading of the philosophical imaginary, Le Doeuff suggests instead that we view images as unique coping mechanisms. She limits her analysis specifically to images in works of philosophy when she suggests that images in such texts occur either to resolve specific problems for which the given theoretical enterprise is otherwise unequipped or to evade an issue that presents an insuperable or intractable difficulty (4–5). Minimally, according to Le Doeuff, "imagery is inseparable from . . . the sensitive points of an intellectual venture" (3) and, maximally, it "occupies the place of theory's impossible" (5), sustaining something "which the system cannot itself justify, but which is nevertheless needed for its proper working" (3).

The figure of the face as it is found in Levinas's writings undoubtedly functions in accordance with both the minimalist and maximalist versions of Le Doeuff's thesis. Changing scarcely a word, we can say of the face what Le Doeuff says about the image of the northern isle in Kant's first *Critique*: in one way, it works toward the coherence of the philosophical enterprise—in it we are presented with the major theses of the critical project—but at the same time, and in a contradictory sense, the imagery reinstates everything that the project otherwise disavows or renounces (17). The figure of the face is emblematic of the thesis which posits an unbridgeable gulf between intentionality and transcendence, ontology and ethics; but even as we are told that the face of the other can be neither seen nor known, the face *as figure or image* reinstates the regimes of cognition and representation. The face of the other is the image of absolute alterity and unrepresentable singularity. It represents the inadequacy of every image to the task of representing the other and, as such, paradoxically, represents the impossibility of its own representational activity. Thus, in the figure of the face, Levinas's text does what must be done by conveying to the reader this notion of the face, and does what it explicitly maintains cannot be done, namely, it gives a form to that which "overflows" or "destroys" every form.

Two sets of conflicting imperatives cross in this figure of the face, and though they are deeply intertwined, we might assign one set of imperatives to the level of theory and the other to the dimension of ethical practice; equally, one could speak of imperatives that conflict at the level of their formal expression and in their concrete content. First, if the alterity or singularity of the other is to be the "object" of Levinas's discourse, it can be so only by appearing therein. That is, singularity—understood as that in the other which refuses the mastery of representation—must appear as a theoretic object, but, simultaneously, it is required to appear as that which cannot appear. Here, then, there are competing imperatives at the level of the formal demands of the theory: the face must be represented theoretically—it must be in some manner *conveyable*—but, equally, it must be conveyed as beyond or transcendent to representation in order to convey the ethical inadequacy (and even violence) attendant on practices of representation. The contradictions are reiterated at the level of the concrete, ethical content of the theory. To encounter a face, Levinas tells us again and again, is to encounter someone who *counts as such* rather than as a calculable quantity. But in order to count in any sense, the other must become *countable,* and here the betrayal of singularity inevitably begins as the other becomes just one more singular being among others. The paradox here is the one that Arendt identified when she remarked that "we are all the same, that is, human in such a way that nobody is ever the same as anyone else who ever lived, lives, or will live" (Arendt 1958, 8).

The reading of Levinas in "Violence and Metaphysics" presses us to accept not only that conceptuality is epistemologically unavoidable, but that representation is *ethically* necessary as well. Consider the line of thought that Derrida pursues in asking whether Levinas's notion of the other as an absolute alterity is preferable to the Husserlian view expressed in the fifth of the *Cartesian Meditations*—a text that Levinas translated (not entirely to Husserl's satisfaction). Derrida notes two systems of alterity in Husserl: the alterity of the transcendent thing and the alterity of the transcendent other. Both, he says, are irreducible alterities. In the first instance, the alterity of a thing is such "by means of the indefinite incompleteness of

my original perceptions" (VM 124). For example, because a perceiver cannot view all sides of an object at once, her perception of a thing is always
partial. With respect to the other person, Derrida notes, there are similar
dimensions of incompleteness (e.g., in my perception of the other's body
and in the history of our relationship). But there is also, for the Husserlian account, a further, "more profound dimension" of alterity, which is the
sort of ethical alterity presumably of interest to Levinas. Without the first
alterity, Derrida argues, "the second alterity could never emerge. The system of these two alterities, the one inscribed in the other, must be thought
together" (VM 124). Levinas and Husserl, he rightly suggests, are quite
close on this point (VM 125), but an important difference arises here. For
Derrida, when Husserl acknowledges that the first sort of alterity applies
to persons as well as things—that is, when he suggests that the other person's otherness is present in some form as an intentional modification of
the ego—he "gives himself the *right to speak* of the infinitely other as such,
accounting for the origin and legitimacy of his language" (VM 125). Husserl more than Levinas, according to Derrida, gives himself license to describe "the phenomenal system of nonphenomenality" (VM 125). Levinas,
by contrast, in refusing to acknowledge that the face in any way appears
in its alterity "deprives himself of the very foundation and possibility of his
own language" (VM 125).

Elaborating on this point, Derrida suggests that the other must be
recognized as a transcendental alter ego in order to be recognized as bearing the second sort of alterity. The other as other or as *alter ego* in Husserl
is not recognized as "another ego *like myself*" with the emphasis on the
other's life or being as a modification of my own life or being, but as "*another ego* like myself"; that is, the other is another origin of the world and
as such is exactly what I cannot absorb into my own being or possess in the
way that I possess and use food or tools.

If the other were not recognized as a transcendental alter *ego*, it would be entirely
in the world and not, as ego, the origin of the world. To refuse to see in it an ego in
this sense is, within the ethical order, the very gesture of all violence. . . . The other
as alter ego signifies the other as other, irreducible to *my* ego, precisely because it is
an ego, because it has the form of the ego. The egoity of the other permits him to
say "ego" as I do; and this is why he is Other, and not a stone, or a being without

speech *in my real economy.* This is why, if you will, he is a face, can speak to me, understand me, and eventually command me. (*VM* 125–26)

Alterity in the second sense, that is, ethical alterity, seems here to be dependent on or at least inextricable from alterity in the first, non-ethical sense: it is *because* the other is an ego who constitutes the world for herself in consciousness, just as I so constitute the world for myself, that she is a face with whom I can converse and who "eventually" commands me ethically. Stones, the passage suggests, do not make an ethical demand on me: they are part of the world; they have meaning within the world, as Heidegger would say; but they do not *have a world.* It is the having of a world that would seemingly be relevant for ethics. And Derrida suggests that to deny this would be tantamount to a form of ethical violence. (He also admits that Levinas would likely find intolerable the way in which the asymmetry of ethics is seen here as resting on a prior symmetry, and a systematic one at that.)

Once again there is a dilemma: either the face is treated as an object and suffers the violence of appropriation and reduction to the status of a thing, or the face is unrepresentable and suffers from going unrepresented, unseen, misrecognized. To represent the other, if it could be done, would be a form of violence; and yet, as Derrida maintains, failure to represent the other, understood as the failure to accord to the other ego the status of an *ego,* also involves an ethical failure and a form of violence against the other. On the one side, to resolve this tension in favor of the unrepresentability of the other—insisting, that is, on the other as outside all possible representation—is to court a mystical reading of the face that Levinas repeatedly says is not his aim and that Derrida too warns us against as a form of intolerable violence to the other. On the other side, to resolve the tension in favor of representation and a concept of the other is to give up on singularity in the name of some determinate characteristic by which we can then determine to whom we are responsible and to what extent.

Levinas rightly wants to avoid both poles of this alternative. The dangers of mysticism as he sees them are multiple. If mysticism involves the submersion of the ego in the mystical element, whether it be conceived as a divinity or something else, the loss of the individual entails the loss of the critical dimension of thought. If there is no one separate from me to demand a justification and to allow that the justification provided is sufficient, then any manner of violence becomes possible (*TI* 48). In effect, truth and ethics alike depend upon there being a plurality of discrete voices that do not all say the same thing or make the same judgments. When this multiplicity is submerged in a single voice, whether it be the voice of the *Volk*, or of a divine being, or of Reason itself, ethics is no longer possible. Likewise, ethical injunctions cannot be derived on the basis of *what* someone is: a rational animal, a pain-avoiding animal, one who looks like me and thus elicits my sympathy or activates my capacity for empathy. No one of these means for determining the proper object and scope of ethical responsibilities is sufficient to the singular face that stands before one. There will always be those who lack a full capacity for rational thought; there will always be questions about how to determine what sorts of thought patterns and practices are "rational," about who gets to decide and who is thereby included or excluded from the community of rational or reasonable beings; there are those who feel no pain but still cannot be ethically disregarded; and those who feel no sympathy or have diminished capacities for empathy who may or may not be exculpated on these grounds. Neither representation of the other nor the refusal of representation are unproblematic. Neither seems to render the other what is due to her.

In a discussion that is exceptionally evocative, though it is no more than a sketch, Le Doeuff suggests that images serve a twofold function whose sides can be separated only provisionally. In one respect, images are emblematic: they render the truth of the system in a kind of shorthand and come to symbolize the enterprise as a whole (Le Doeuff 1989, 11). The "face of the other" is most certainly emblematic in this sense; indeed, Levinas's ethics would be unrecognizable without this notion of the face. In a second respect, images serve a fantasy function: they are the means by which an otherwise critical, careful, and scrupulous enterprise can "engage in straightforward dogmatization," decreeing "'that's the way it is' without fear of counter-argument" (13). Images serve this purpose so cheerfully, not because they convey the gist of a complex idea in an immediate fashion (a claim which Le Doeuff challenges, since it is as hard to get students to understand an image as a concept), but because it is understood "that a good reader will by-pass such 'illustrations'—a convention which enables the image to do its work all the more effectively" (12). In its second function the image thus works a kind of seduction, producing and structuring a fantasy of naturalized truth: "That's just the way it is, as you can see for yourself." This dogmatism is most certainly recognizable in the figure of the face. Levinas never hesitates to remind his listener that access to the face is *straightaway* or *immediately* ethical. Though, again, whenever his listener succumbs to the seduction (as Nemo, e.g., does), Levinas is there to remind him that there can be no phenomenology of the face, no "seeing" for oneself after all!

The Face of Ethics

This chapter began by suggesting that questions of justification—of how and why the face makes me responsible to the other—have an internal connection to Levinas's thought. To say this, however, is not necessarily to maintain that the face serves as a justification for ethical responsibility, or as proof of our obligation to the other. It does not. And since it does not, it would be a mistake to class Levinas as either a cognitivist or noncognitivist about ethics. These labels assume that the question of justification can be answered in some fairly definitive manner and that the justification will either appeal to reason, in the case of cognitivism, or show why only an appeal to something non-cognitive, like emotion or sensibility, can serve as the final court of appeal. But the face is not that which justifies or stands behind particular moral claims, providing them with normative force or cast-iron motivational backing. It is not some sort of phenomenological evidence for our ethical responsibility to the other, nor that which moves us to act responsibly by engaging our moral sentiments or sympathy. More generally still, the face is not a criterion of moral standing; it is not that by which we know that the creature standing before us deserves or has a rightful claim to our moral consideration.[12]

It is of the first importance to resist a metaphysical or re-essentializing interpretation of the notion of the face. No doubt there are passages, especially in the essays from the 1950s and in *Totality and Infinity*, that lend support to such a reading, but the interpretation developed here has tried in every case to set such statements into a wider context, where they cannot be taken as simply descriptive of a phenomenon or event. For example, though Levinas writes, "That which escapes comprehension in the other is him, a being" (*BPW* 9), or "I, you—these are not individuals of a common concept" (*TI* 39), he is not suggesting that the other is possessed of some ineffable core of personality, some unique *je ne sais quoi* that eludes the understanding. Indeed, in *Totality and Infinity* Levinas reminds the reader that his aim is *not* to show that "the Other forever escapes knowing" (*TI*

89), and in *Outside the Subject* he is explicit: "It is not a question of putting knowledge in doubt. The human being clearly allows himself to be treated as an object, and delivers himself over to knowledge in the *truth* of perception and the light of the human sciences" (*OS* 3). The human being, who is the other par excellence for Levinas, can be known and represented as can a thing, but our relation to the other is not exhausted by the structure of comprehension or the constative dimension of language.[13] In every representation of the other as an object of thought, the invocation of the other in the very discourse that thematizes him means that something (or, more exactly, some*one*) escapes inclusion within the thematization. Singularity is this moment of invocation in which language exceeds its limits and enacts a relation to exteriority; this distinguishes Levinas's account altogether from a romantic conception of the other as an eternal mystery to the ego. The notion of a mystery implies the possibility of a solution: with infinite time, different circumstances, or more perfect insight, I might crack the code or enter the inner sanctum of the other's personality or being. But this is not the conception of alterity that comes to us from Levinas's work when we are attendant to the contradictions and tensions through which the notion of the face develops.

Everything Levinas says in *Totality and Infinity* concerning the face, alterity, and expression needs to be read in a manner that refuses to make of these new essences of the other. It is in this sense that Levinas can write toward the end of that work:

These differences between the Other and me do not depend on different "properties" that would be inherent in the "I," on the one hand, and on the other hand, in the Other, nor on different psychological dispositions which their minds would take on from the encounter. They are due to the I-Other conjuncture, to the inevitable orientation of being "starting from oneself" toward "the Other." *The priority of this orientation over the terms that are placed in it . . . summarizes the theses of the present work.* (*TI* 215; emphasis added)

The singularity signified in transcendence is not something we encounter or discover in the other—as we might discover, for example, that she is stubborn or a hopeless romantic. Singularity is not a property or quality of persons, but is produced or performed in an orientation toward the other. The face-to-face relationship and the face itself come about simultaneously. It is *in* this relationship and from this orientation that the other concerns me, claims me, or obliges me *as a face.* But this is also a misleading locution, because it suggests that there was a time before the relationship when the other did not so concern me, in which I would have been justified in treating her as a thing or an object. But this, of course, is something that Levinas's whole analysis rejects.

It needs to be said, and more than once: *the face does not exist before the encounter with it.* It is not a pre-existing "something" that the ego bumps up against or discovers—though Levinas will sometimes talk in ways that have this sort of feel to them. The face is not "there" by itself in a first moment and then encountered in another; rather, the encounter brings me face-to-face with the other. *It is in the encounter that the face is produced as such.*

If this is so, then why insist on the embodiment of the face? Why say that the whole body is a face? Why entangle the face with visibility, representation, knowledge, and the like, if the face is supposed to be invisible, unrepresentable, and unknowable? Why maintain that the transcendent par excellence is found in that which is most concrete, immanent, and down to earth, namely, a body? A first answer to such questions acknowledges that in order to talk about the face, Levinas must betray it by making it visible and representable. He must, as it were, thematize and theorize its unthematizability. But though the problem is one of language, it is not only that. The entanglement between face and body, invisible and visible, is not merely a matter of deploying language tactically or strategically in the name of saying what cannot be said (or cannot be *only* said).

The contradictions in the face give expression to competing requirements within our lived ethical situation, and it is these requirements that Levinas's thought captures so dynamically. On one side, the figure of the face expresses a desire for certainty—for an unimpeachable obligation, an unassailable and irrecusable responsibility, an ethical command that is undeniable or goes all the way down. This desire is amply present in Levinas's texts and gives rise to a host of canonical moments: those, for example, in which he speaks of the face as giving *immediate* access to the ethical, or those in which he writes of the impossibility of ignoring the other. A classic moment, and one to which we will return in the next chapter, occurs in the section of *Totality and Infinity* on the face, when he writes (purportedly quoting the treatise Sanhedrin) that leaving the other without food "is a fault that no circumstance attenuates" (*TI* 201). The language here implies that there can be no excuse for leaving the other without food: the demand for food institutes a kind of categorical duty that holds no matter the circumstances. It holds seemingly without exception—whether one has taken up a responsibility in this regard or not, whether one feels bound by the demand or not, whether one has food to give or not! But, of course, the moral skeptic is bound to ask why *must* I feed the other? What obligates me to give him not just bread, but the very bread that I was about to eat and the only bread I have? What justifies the other's claim on me? On the other side, there is not just the failure to answer the skeptic, but, as Levinas makes clear, the impossibility of anything that could meet the desire for a ground or ultimate justification of ethical obligation. The face is not a rational principle, but that which "opens" up or institutes rationality. The figure of the face conveys the desire for the possession of unshakable normative principles or an ethical *fundamentum*, but at the same times renders the basis for such principles null and void. But rather than leaving us with the certainty that we should abandon the search for reasons that would justify our lives and actions in ways that others would ratify,[14] the face represents the desire for a justification that would answer fully to an other—a desire that is lived as simultaneously compulsory and gratuitous. Suspended between the visible and the invisible, the immanent and the transcendent par excellence, the figure of the face is not a thesis about ethics but is the performance of ethical life. The tension between what this figure *does* (when it represents the other) and what it *says* (that the other is unrepresentable) is the enactment of our original ethical situation. To paraphrase what Levinas says about freedom, to be ethical in Levinas's sense is to know that ethics is in danger. Ethics is a matter not of having a secure principle, but of realizing that the principle is never secure enough. It is a matter of being overwhelmed by the infinity of the demand, the ever renewed demand of preserving ethical practices of reason-giving—and reason-giving that must meet not some abstract theoretical conditions, but that must respond to the hungry face, the embodied self, that here and now demands my aid. This conception of ethics will be developed in further detail in Chapter 3 in relation to Levinas's notion of responsibility, and in Chapter 4 in considering the relation of normativity to norms.

3

Responsibility: The Infinity of the Demand

In dreams begin responsibility.

—W. B. YEATS

. . . *as if* the other person were above all a face.

—EMMANUEL LEVINAS

Three Theses

"Everyone will readily agree that it is of the highest importance to know whether we are not duped by morality" (*TI* 21). So begins *Totality and Infinity*. The skeptic voices the suspicion that morality is for the weak and easily led, and Levinas's opening line hints there is a bit of the skeptic in all of us. We struggle with conflicts between the demands of morality and those of self-interest. We wonder why we should be moral at all. We suspect there is no such thing as a distinctly *moral* force and question how it moves us if not through self-interest or some other desire we already have. Such skeptical considerations may seem decidedly un-Levinasian and a strange beginning, unless one is convinced that *Totality and Infinity* has something to do, after all, with questions about the binding force of ethical claims. That it does is more than arguable. Structured as a classical phenomenology in successive strata (*OB,* xv), *Totality and Infin-*

ity equally exudes the air of a drama complete with protagonist, antagonist, conflict, and denouement. Especially in sections II, III, and IV there is an identifiable plot that might be summarized (a bit hastily, but still accurately) as follows: an ego absorbed in its needs and living in conditions of relative domestic security is confronted by a stranger who disrupts and calls into question its manner of being at home in the world. The result of this face-to-face encounter is that the ego finds itself in an ethical relationship in which it is divested of its egoism and invited to the serious work of goodness and responsibility. After recounting this history, the text ends by depicting the ego in a variety of intimate, familial, and fraternal relationships, some of which are shown to be only ambiguously ethical (e.g., erotic love), others of which are said to exhibit the concrete reality of ethical life (filiality and fraternity).

Of course, this tale of "I meets Other" was not meant by Levinas to be a tale at all, and its narrative structure is importantly at odds with the most original impulses of the work. I tell the tale here only to emphasize that the question of ethical force—of an encounter that issues in a summons to responsibility—is the pivot on which *Totality and Infinity* turns. The question of the ego's responsibility drives the work forward chronologically, logically, and dramatically, governing in almost every respect the relationships between its component parts. So the question becomes, what sort of story about ethical force or responsibility's hold on us does Levinas tell? And what reason does the skeptic have to be convinced?

The present chapter argues three theses in relation to the Levinasian notion of responsibility. First, Levinas uses the term "responsibility" in a way that systematically inverts core features of standard accounts of responsibility while nonetheless retaining the ordinary sense of responsibility as something which binds us without physical force. Contrary to a fairly common way of presenting Levinas's notion of responsibility, which distances it from more familiar philosophical and everyday senses of the term, this chapter argues that Levinas's conception of responsibility is directly dependent on those accounts, even as it inverts and subverts their standard tenets. In this respect, Levinas should be seen not as rejecting normative ethics wholesale, but as offering an original reconception of ethical or moral force. I call this the inversion thesis and develop it primarily in relation to the discussion of responsibility in *Totality and Infinity*.

Closely connected to the inversion thesis is a failure hypothesis. It remains a hypothesis because there is no way to decide (and perhaps little to be gained by deciding) between the claim that Levinas's account of responsibility in *Totality and Infinity* fails and the claim that its failure may be the only way it could succeed. Moreover, whether Levinas himself intended the book to work this way is beside the point. The hypothesis goes something like this: running beneath the surface of *Totality and Infinity* and feeding it much like an underground spring is an anxiety about whether the skeptical voice that opens the book can be answered with any certainty. To be sure, the sort of certainty that the book desires is not the certainty that would come from moral rules or precepts telling me definitively how to live or what to do. Levinas's text does not seek convictions of that kind, but neither does it completely abandon the desire for ethical certainty. It oscillates, rather desperately at times, between the impossibility of a foundation or ground for ethical life and the certainty that the face of the other produces an ethical demand to which I cannot be indifferent and from which there is no escape. The ethical relation to the face and the infinity of one's responsibility to this other are written about in most of the text's moments with a hyperbolic certainty (which some have taken for religious dogmatism and others for prophetism); and yet that same face-to-face relation, as the previous chapter has shown, is shot through with uncertainty, with a refusal to function as the ground or condition for an ethics. One could, without straining credibility too far, describe the principal task of *Totality and Infinity* as finding a way to secure the force of the encounter with the face without grounding it either in a mute and ambiguous nature or in the false transcendence of a world behind the world. But on the reading developed below, this is precisely what it cannot do. A good portion of this chapter will be devoted to tracing the devolution of responsibility in Levinas's 1961 text.

The final thesis concerns the fate of this failure in the works leading up to *Otherwise Than Being, or Beyond Essence*. If the quest for certainty is an implicit or explicit motivating force in the earlier text, and if it gives Levinas's discussion of responsibility a decidedly normative or at least normativity-seeking cast, the later texts are explicit in acknowledging that the skeptic's demand will never be met. Whereas the predominant mood of the earlier discussion of the face is a certainty that covers over its insecurities with bravado, the tone of the later work—going so deep as to shape the very syntax of the sentences—is one of hesitation, of an ethical life glimpsed but never possessed. This is not to say that *Otherwise Than Being* embraces ethical uncertainty or a constitutive, deconstructive undecidability. Ethics is lived, as will be argued in Chapter 4, not in the mode of either certainty or uncertainty, but as the always vulnerable desire and demand for ethical justification. The failure of *Totality and Infinity* is taken up and turned to good account in the later works, as the demand for ethics becomes the only positive content of ethics. To be ethical is not to achieve moral certainty, but never to let go of the demand for it. This is why Levinas ultimately compares the "movement" of responsibility to the phases of a skepticism that is refuted, only to return as the legitimate heir of the very philosophy that would have done with it. Ethical demands are likewise refuted, ignored, or dismissed as *resentment* or a fool's game, only to return with an obsessive urgency that is the mark of the ethical itself. Whereas *Totality and Infinity* seemed to want to make of the epiphany of the face a beacon or guiding star, *Otherwise Than Being* speaks of traces, lapses, invisible traumas, anarchic beginnings, a blinking and enigmatic transcendence whose ambiguities cannot be resolved or fixed into constancy and light. In the present chapter, the three subsections elaborate these three theses respectively, though the final thesis will get its full elaboration only in a subsequent chapter.

Inverting the Standard Account

The common assumption that alterity and the face are themes of Levinas's earlier work and responsibility predominates only in later text overlooks the fact that responsibility is there in Levinas's *oeuvre* in a significant form as early as 1954.[1] Moreover, the core elements of the later account—which presents responsibility as infinite, irrecusable, and asymmetrical—are already present in *Totality and Infinity*. Indeed, these core features come about as *Totality and Infinity* effects a calculated inversion of what we ordinarily understand by "responsibility." This inversion is the starting point for the interpretation developed in this chapter.

In our everyday ways of talking, responsibility is more or less synonymous with accountability. One is held responsible for actions one has done oneself, for what is one's own doing or one's own affair. Accounts of responsibility in contemporary moral philosophy mirror our everyday understanding to a great extent, and despite important differences, most philosophical treatments share a commitment to the idea that responsibility is limited in scope, restricted to voluntary action, and applies to everyone in more or less similar ways. This contrasts directly with Levinas's notion of a responsibility that is quite literally infinite, irrecusable (in being beyond the distinction between voluntary and involuntary action), and asymmetrical or mine alone.

For standard accounts, responsibility is limited at its broadest reach by possibility: an agent can be held responsible to perform an action only if it is in fact possible for her to do it. This is expressed in the well-known dictum "Ought implies can." If I *ought* to do something, this presupposes that it is possible for me to do it, that I *can* do it. More narrowly, the standard account thinks of responsibility as limited to one's own actions and the fairly immediate and expected consequences of those actions. It is obvious on such an account that I cannot be held responsible for something that I have not done, or for a state of affairs that I have had no part in bringing about. In an age of global economies the impact of individual actions and the agent's consequent responsibility may be more difficult to determine, but most views nonetheless maintain that there is indeed a limit to that for which I can be held responsible and this limit is generally determined through a consideration of the proximity of the agent's action to the matter or affair in question. To take but one example, utilitarianism urges us to produce the greatest good for the greatest number. All the same, it does not think one's duty in this regard is, strictly speaking, unlimited: it permits the agent to favor his own interests some of the time, even if such actions contribute to his failure to produce the greatest amount of good overall. Shelley Kagan calls such permissions "agent-centered options," or just "options," and gives the example of ordinary morality requiring me to sacrifice some of my interests to save a drowning child but stopping short of demanding that I sacrifice all of my interests or my very life (Kagan 1989, 3–4). The more distant the other who ostensibly would benefit from my aid, the more ordinary morality understands and condones the exercise of my "options."

Another restriction central to both philosophical and everyday understandings of moral responsibility says that an agent can be held responsible only for actions that are done voluntarily. Harry Frankfurt famously avoids thorny questions about whether any action can be said to be freely performed by formulating this intuition in terms of a "principle of alternative possibilities": "A person is responsible for what he has done only if he could have done otherwise" (quoted in Fischer 1986, 143). Frankfurt notes that though the meaning of "could have done otherwise" can be debated, "practically no one . . . seems inclined to deny or even question that the principle of alternative possibilities (construed in some way or other) is true" (ibid.). If I truly had no other options, then I can hardly be faulted for acting as I did. Of course, as Frankfurt recognizes, the quandary lies in determining just whether an agent had alternative possibilities, and of what sort.

Finally, responsibility on the standard account is universal and reciprocal: it applies to everyone in more or less the same way. This does not mean, of course, that everyone has the same responsibilities, but rather that the reasons that justify my responsibility for some action in some particular set of circumstances will hold for all relevantly similar agents, actions, and circumstances. If I am responsible for making some effort to save the child in danger, so are others who find themselves in this or a similar situation. This is so because of the close tie on the standard account between responsibility and reasons. Reasons clarify the basis for an agent's action; they say why she acted as she did and are capable of exculpating her in the right circumstances. Responsibility on the standard account is attributable when the agent has the right relationship to (and thus the right reasons and motive for) the action in question. The specification of this right relationship in a general theory of responsibility provides rules or guidelines that hold equally for all agents. The possibility of such a general theory is thus also a central tenet of standard accounts.

In stark contrast to these features of ordinary morality, Levinas speaks of a responsibility that goes beyond what it is possible to do, beyond my actions and their consequences, beyond the distinction between the voluntary and the involuntary, to an infinite and irrecusable responsibility for the other. As a kind shorthand for his own view, Levinas is fond of quoting Alyosha's statement in *The Brother's Karamazov*: "We are all guilty of all and for all men before all, and I more than the others" (Dostoyevsky 1957, 264). I find myself responsible, Levinas maintains, "not owing to such and such a guilt which is really mine, or to offenses that I would have committed; but because I am responsible for a total responsibility, which answers for all the others and for all in the others, even for their responsibility. The I always has one responsibility *more* than all the others" (*EI* 99). By such lights, I am responsible even for what I have not done, for what is not my doing or my affair, indeed for what does not "matter" to me at all. Or rather, I am responsible for precisely what does matter to me (i.e., what ought to matter to me, or what matters to me whether I acknowledge it or not), the "face" of the other (*EI* 95–96). Far from being understood as limited, responsibility in Levinas's sense is an *unlimited* obligation; it seemingly annihilates those agent-centered options that Kagan talks about. To be infinitely responsible is to be ever on call, always at one's post, impaled upon one's obligation, never quits with it, never with an option to take a day or an hour or even a minute for one's own cares.

No matter how appealing such a severe notion of responsibility may be to some, readers have rightly wondered whether the concept of responsibility remains meaningful if its scope is infinitely extended in this way. In what sense can I really be responsible for everything? Might it not be argued that if I am responsible for everything, I am *in fact* responsible for nothing? Against the idea of a limitless responsibility for others, we hear that the idea is pathological, counter to human psychology, even destructive of morality itself, since by denying that we can ever succeed it may destroy our motivation to try to live up to our ethical responsibilities. Moreover, what are we to make of Levinas's suggestion, advanced to be sure with the greatest hesitation, that I am responsible to the point of being responsible for my own persecution and for the evil that the other does to me (*EI* 99)? Some of Levinas's readers, notably Paul Ricoeur, have exclaimed that this last thesis borders on the morally scandalous.[2] In part, the question raised by critics is whether Levinas's conception of responsibility denies the requirement that the scope of responsibility not exceed the power of an individual to meet the demand (that *ought* not exceed *can*). That it does will become more explicit in the later writings, as for example when Levinas refers to infinite responsibility quite pointedly as a "demand" that is "without regard for what is possible," adding, "For the order of contemplation, [this is] simply demented [*insensée*]" (*OB* 113).

Just as it subverts "ought implies can," so too does the Levinasian account challenge the usual understanding of the relationship of responsibility to voluntary action. In *Totality and Infinity* Levinas quotes a remarkable passage that he attributes to the treatise Sanhedrin (at page 104b). "'To leave men without food is a fault that no circumstance attenuates; the distinction between the voluntary and the involuntary does not apply here,' says Rabbi Yochanan."[3] Commenting on the passage, Levinas adds, "Before the hunger of men responsibility is measured only 'objectively'; it is irrecusable" (*TI* 201). The passage suggests that if I leave someone without food, I am guilty of a fault for which there can be no excuse. Extenuating circumstances—that I have only enough food for myself, or indeed that I have none at all—are ruled irrelevant to the determination of responsibility. Does this mean that Levinas takes our reasons for acting to be a fact of little or no moral consequence? Is there really, for Levinas, no morally relevant difference between leaving the other without food because I have no food to give and having food but withholding it? This is certainly a view that few modern readers would be willing to accept!

This difficulty might be mitigated if the view were that everyone is equally called to the task of feeding the hungry, but Levinas again thwarts our usual expectations. Asked whether the other is not as responsible for me as I am for him, Levinas says, "One of the themes of *Totality and Infinity* . . . is that the intersubjective relationship is a non-symmetrical relationship. In this sense, I am responsible for the other without waiting for reciprocity, were I to die for it" (*EI* 98). The asymmetry of responsibility doubly affects the ego. The ego does not demand justice for herself but for the other: "I seek . . . peace not for *me* but for the other" (Levinas and Kearney 1986, 31). And concomitantly, the prescriptions of morality do not apply to the others, but only to the self: "If I say that 'virtue is its own reward,' I can only say so *for myself*" (ibid.). To hold the other to this standard is already "to exploit him, for what I am then saying is: be virtuous toward me—work for me, love me, serve me, and so on" (ibid.). To students of moral philosophy today this line of reasoning must sound strange indeed. Can I make no moral claims on my own behalf? And why should

I be moral if no one else must be? Moreover, what of duties to oneself, or simply of justified self-concern?

For *Totality and Infinity*, the ego is both less and more than the other, but never a mere *semblable*, a fellow human being, or fellow citizen (*TI* 215). To see oneself as just "someone" and the other as just another "someone" is to take up a point of view which, though it may be inevitable or even a sign of rational maturity,[4] is also for Levinas the condition for moral indifference. When I compare our two positions in order to decide whether to share my stores with you, for instance, I am not engaged in an exercise of moral conscience on the Levinasian view, but am taking the first steps toward your exploitation. By contrast, "the accomplishing of the I qua I and morality constitute one sole and same process in being: morality comes to birth not in equality, but in the fact that infinite demands, those of serving the poor, the stranger, the widow, and the orphan, converge at one point of the universe"—namely, me (*TI* 245; translation modified).

Equality, reciprocity, accountability: these are the stuff of the standard view of responsibility. By comparison, Levinas appears to show us a responsibility seen through the looking glass. It is a responsibility out of the ordinary walk of life, an extraordinary and hyperbolic exigency. The worries about the coherence of the concept, about its feasibility and livability, about the role of reason-giving, and the asymmetrical nature of the demand—these are real worries that should not be swept under the rug. Likewise demanding a response are the questions posed by the skeptic: Why think this extraordinary responsibility is anything but *resentiment* taken to its most sublime height? Why think responsibility on the Levinasian account is anything but the ultimate dupe? In other words, how is this seemingly unworldly responsibility grounded or justified to worldly beings?

Before developing a Levinasian response to such questions, it is worth setting aside one way in which their force is wrongly blunted. Faced with a disbelieving reader who can make little sense of a responsibility that deepens with every step I take to fulfill it, that cannot be assumed or cast off, and that seemingly holds only for me and not also for others, it has been tempting for Levinas's readers to say that Levinas is not talking about responsibility in the ordinary sense at all and therefore should not be expected to be intelligible in those terms. Like the word "ethics" as it is used in connection with Levinas's thought, it will be said that "responsibility" means something different here, something that has been overlooked by moral philosophy, either because it lies in its deepest recesses or because it is that from which our thought flees allergically or in anguish. Those who pursue this sort of reply habitually make much of the link between response and responsibility: responsibility is not accountability, they say, but an *ability* to *respond*; it is a response-ability.

The puzzled critic is likely to find this answer question-begging, and rightly so. Certainly Levinas is using the term in a way that challenges ordinary, overly legalistic senses of responsibility, but his articulation of a new conception is deeply parasitic on the ordinary sense. His account draws its rhetorical force precisely from its inversion of our ordinary expectations and perceptions about responsibility. And, more importantly, in at least one crucial respect, Levinas is talking about responsibility as we ordinarily mean it: he is talking about a *moral* rather than a causal force, or the force of prudential or self-interested considerations. This is explicit at *TI* 225—"The force of the Other is already and henceforth moral"—but it is equally evident when Levinas speaks of the relation to the face as different in kind from empirical experience (*TI* 101), as an "ethical resistance" (*TI* 199), as arousing the ego's goodness (*TI* 200), as instituting a discourse "whose first word is obligation" as convincing even those who "'do not wish to listen'" (*TI* 201). Responsibility is a "summons" (*TI* 215) and an "election" (*TI* 245); it is an infinite demand addressed to one's freedom (*TI* 304). All of these passages invoke responsibility as a non-causal, nonphysical but still binding force: it arouses, resists, commands, demands, convinces, summons, elects. All of these terms have been used in the history of Western philosophy as thinkers have tried to give voice and shape to the unique mode in which ethical considerations make themselves felt. It is the contention here that *Totality and Infinity* is not only concerned with the question of moral or ethical force, it is in a certain sense obsessed by the idea. How does the face of the other command me or concern me? What is subjectivity such that it is open to this command? These are explicit concerns within the text of Levinas's first major work—even though, as the next section argues, they do not receive a wholly satisfying answer within those pages.

The "Failure" of the Totality and Infinity Account

Responsibility as Moral Conscience

When Levinas uses the term "responsibility" in the period of *Totality and Infinity*, it is more akin to the idea of a moral conscience than to the discharge of a specific duty, though the latter notion plays a secondary role. This is perhaps most evident in the essay "Philosophy and the Idea of Infinity," where Levinas speaks of the "life of freedom discovering itself to be unjust" as the "converse" of the self-sufficient, spontaneous freedom of modern accounts of the ego. The "life of freedom in heteronomy," as he also calls it,

consists in an infinite movement of freedom putting itself ever more into question. This is how the very depth of inwardness is hollowed out. The augmentation of exigency I have in regard to myself aggravates the judgment that is borne on me, that is, my responsibility. And the aggravation of my responsibility increases these exigencies. In this movement my freedom does not have the last word; I never find my solitude again—or, one might say, moral conscience is essentially unsatisfied, or again, is always a desire. (*CPP* 58)

Totality and Infinity uses the same language to introduce the idea of an infinite responsibility:

The calling in question of oneself is all the more severe the more rigorously the self is in control of itself. This receding of the goal in the very measure one approaches it is the life of conscience [*conscience morale*]. The increase of my demands with regard to myself aggravates the judgment that is borne upon me, increases my responsibility. It is in this very concrete sense that the judgment that is borne upon me is never assumed by me. (*TI* 100)

Phenomenologically this makes good sense: the more I understand the connection of my own life to the lives of those whose circumstances are altogether foreign to my own and whose way of living may be almost unimaginable to me, the more I feel the weight of living responsibly in relation to these others. Thus does the ego develop a moral conscience, and this way of orienting one's actions and choices discloses further situations in which care or concern is required. To have a moral conscience is to be, in a sense, tuned in to the situation of others. It does not mean that I can stand in their shoes or that I know what is best for them, but it means that I am aware of their demand for aid, for apology, for an end to suffering, or for the freedom to pursue their own form of life. This phenomenology of conscience accords well with Levinas's statement that the "infinity of responsibility denotes not its actual immensity, but a responsibility increasing in the measure that it is assumed" (*TI* 244). The more I fulfill my responsibility, on this view, the more responsible I become. The better I accomplish my obligations, the more demands I find addressed to me. It is not a matter of the actual number of demands increasing, but a matter of my sensitivity increasing so that demands and injustices of which I was formerly unaware now come to press on my attention and weigh on my conscience.

Construing infinite responsibility as moral conscience rather than as an innumerable collection of duties also makes better sense of Levinas's approval of the Sanhedrin passage. Rather than thinking that Levinas's ethics makes reason-giving irrelevant, a more plausible way to interpret his stance sees it as rejecting the default assumption of the standard view that one is not responsible unless one's own actions, performed voluntarily and with sufficient knowledge and reflection, render one accountable. This may be true of legal responsibility, especially in political systems where those charged are "innocent until proven guilty," but it does not hold for moral responsibility on Levinas's account. "If I do not know that my neighbor has gone without dinner, and perhaps without breakfast and lunch as well, and if ordinary morality does not expect me to know this, then how can I be held responsible for failing to feed him?" asks someone who subscribes to the standard account of responsibility. On Levinas's view, this person makes a kind of category mistake. They look to give reasons, when it is food that the other requires; to do so is to be on the lookout for the possibility of a morally sanctioned indifference to the other. By contrast with a responsibility within "reasonable limits," Levinas suggests that, at its most fundamental level, "responsibility"—the having of a conscience—means the impossibility of being indifferent to the other. Responsibility is the impossibility of saying "This is not my affair" or "This is none of my own doing" when another human being goes hungry or is persecuted.

It is worth noting that this interpretation does not make reasons morally irrelevant, though it alters their moral significance. Formerly my reasons played a role in determining whether or not I *was* responsible, where that meant justifiably open to censure or reward. The reasons I give for my actions, on the standard account, serve not only as an explanation of my actions but as an exoneration or condemnation. They show why I cannot reasonably be held responsible for what has happened, or why I can. If I am already responsible, by contrast, exoneration or condemnation is no longer quite the issue. On Levinas's view, my reasons still serve as an explanation, but it is my prior responsibility which makes an explanation necessary. Reasons then serve as an apology. They are an admission and acknowledgment of my connection to others, and of an orientation that does not permit me to disregard the other as if he were no more or no different than a stone. To have a moral conscience means owing an account of myself to the other. It is to be oriented toward others in a way that leaves one unable to turn one's back.

In Levinas's own words: "To hear [the Other's] destitution which cries out for justice is not to represent an image to oneself, but is to posit oneself as responsible, both as more and as less than the being that presents itself in the face. Less, for the face summons me to my obligations and judges me. . . . More, for my position as *I* consists in being able to respond to this essential destitution of the Other, finding resources in myself" (*TI* 215). One can hear the other's cry as a cry for aid only within an already ethical orientation—that is, from the perspective afforded by moral conscience. Suppose that the other, dying of hunger, asks me for food and my first reaction is to calculate whether, given my own stores and needs, I can really be held responsible for giving aid. Everything in the standard account of responsibility is set up to suppose that this is, in fact, the default position of the moral agent, even if most of us would think this a callous and cold-hearted response. On Levinas's view, to hear the other's cry *as a cry* means hearing it as something from which I cannot coldly turn away. I may turn away, to be sure, but not in complete indifference or with the certainty that it is none of my affair or, more exactly, without it having even crossed my mind that I should do something to help. To find one's freedom called into question means, for Levinas, to find oneself under a judgment, and this in turn "lies in a new orientation of the inner life" (*TI* 246).

The Investiture of Freedom

If we understand responsibility in this way, we can read much of *Totality and Infinity* as telling the story of how the "separated" or "atheist" ego acquires a moral conscience. The key moment for this story concerns the "investiture of freedom," that is, the moment in which my freedom is put into question by the other and "invested" as goodness. This moment is recounted at two distinct points in the itinerary of Levinas's 1961 text. It is first introduced in the section on "Truth and Justice," where the presentation is as systematic as anything Levinas ever writes and moves primarily over epistemological terrain. The second account comes in those well-known sections on "Ethics and the Face" that make up the third quarter of Levinas's book.

In "Truth and Justice," beginning from the claim that critique "is the essence of knowing," Levinas argues that the movement of critique is misunderstood if it is thought to be accomplished by knowledge freely taking itself as its own object. The account of a spontaneously generated critique might go something like this: I see a round tower in the distance but realize upon reaching it that it is in fact square; I thus come to realize that my senses sometimes deceive me. In this picture, the impetus to critical reflection arises naturally and accidentally as the ego spontaneously corrects its earlier error in judgment. For Levinas, by contrast, reflection is an "unnatural" position (*TI* 81, quotation marks in the original) that involves "a calling into question of oneself, a critical attitude which is itself produced [only] in face of the other and under his authority" (*TI* 81). Reflection is not "an accident in the life of consciousness" (*TI* 81), but is brought about in an intersubjective relationship. It is the other and not nature or reason or experience that halts the ego's spontaneous action and calls on it to undertake reflection and justification. If this seems to conflict with the story of a natural correction in error, consider that for a solitary ego it would be no more "logical" to deduce that one's earlier perception was in error than to deduce that the structure had magically changed from round to square, and did so every time someone approached. In order to determine that this is not the case will require at least two subjects in an intersubjective relation. Unlike Kant, then, who identifies critique with reason's coming of its own free accord to know its limitations, Levinas suggests that critique comes about only when one concrete reasoning being stands before another who calls the first to account and demands a justification.

Levinas's idea that even theoretical knowledge has a social basis resonates with similar theses found in thinkers from the Frankfurt school, perhaps especially with the idea that all knowledge is interested or motivated.[5] However, for Levinas, the motivation at bottom is always the same: it is the other's scrutiny that puts the spontaneous flow of understanding in check and calls for a critique that raises it to the level of theory or knowledge. What is proper to knowing is that it be able to "put itself in question" by penetrating "beneath its own condition" (*TI* 81). Levinas argues that the meaning of this putting in question cannot be reduced to an objective cognition of cognition. My interest in truth-telling or in knowing something objectively is not a function of practical goals I just happen to have, but of a moral or ethical orientation awakened in me by the other who faces me. It is the other who both demands the truth from me and makes truth-telling and reason-giving possible.

For Levinas, the ethical relationship is "prior to"[6] or conditions the subject's theoretical relation to objects, since theory comes about only because the other demands that I justify myself: "We think that existence *for itself* is not the ultimate meaning of knowing, but rather the putting back into question of the self, the turning back to what is prior to oneself, in the presence of the Other. . . . The essence of reason consists not in securing for man a foundation and powers, but in calling him in question and inviting him to justice" (*TI* 88). The ego's spontaneous action within and appropriation of the world is suspended and turns into critical reflection only in virtue of being face-to-face with another and called to defend my actions and claims.

When the theme of a freedom called into question is introduced for a second time, in the sections on "Ethics and the Face," the relation to truth and knowledge is still there, but the emphasis and order of presentation is inverted. Rather than beginning with knowledge and seeking beneath it for its ethical conditions, the investiture of freedom is now considered beginning from the infinity of the face. Levinas once more rehearses the formal features of the idea of infinity as they are deformalized or concretized in the expression of the face: the face refuses to be contained in a form or image (*TI* 194); it is the transcendence of an interlocutor who is invoked prior to being the theme of a discourse (*TI* 195); it is an expression that functions as a moral summons and as that which puts the I in question (*TI* 196). How does it summon the ego? In a key passage, Levinas writes:

This infinity, stronger than murder, already resists us in [the Other's] face, is his face, is the primordial *expression*, is the first word: "you shall not commit murder." The infinite paralyses power by its infinite resistance to murder. . . . There is here a relation not with a very great resistance, but with something absolutely *other*: the resistance of what has no resistance—the ethical resistance. (*TI* 199)

The other's command is not backed up by some sovereign power, but by the lack of all defenses. He is absolutely denuded and exposed and yet there issues from this nudity and defenselessness the supreme resistance of the ethical as the other's first word—the first word of all words, according to Levinas, and a prohibition on murder.

The reader is told that this prohibition is not merely negative, however. It does not merely forbid certain actions: "The impossibility of killing does not have a simply negative and formal signification" (*TI* 199). The proscription must be understood as an invitation: "The face opens the primordial discourse whose first word is obligation, which no 'interiority' permits avoiding. It is that discourse that obliges the entering into discourse, the commencement of discourse rationalism prays for, a 'force' that convinces even 'the people who do not wish to listen' and thus founds the true universality of reason" (*TI* 201). The face does not dogmatically prohibit murder, nor does it make a plea coming from its own interest in self-preservation; rather, the face here issues an invitation (albeit one that cannot be refused) to enter into rational discourse, which is to say, into a discourse in which *reasons* are required on all sides.

Here the two presentations of the investiture of freedom coalesce into a single view. The ethical relationship is not simply prior to and a condition for rationality; it is, in fact, the demand for a life of reason and for rational critique. The face invites the ego or commands it—and the difference is difficult to determine on Levinas's account—to enter into a rational discourse, meaning a discourse that puts the world in common between us and demands of me an account recognizable by you.

In light of this way of reading Levinas's concern, the skeptic's question might be reformulated this way: Why must I enter into a life of reason-giving? What force could compel me or oblige me to be rational, to give an account of myself, to care whether the other accepts this account or not? Given all that Levinas says about the face—its unrepresentability, its lack of physical resistance, and so on—one ought to conclude that there can be no such obliging per se. There is no *force* in the physical sense that can compel me to be ethical or rational, just as there is no physical resistance that magically protects the face from the cold steel of a gun or knife wielded against it. Likewise, there is no psychological compulsion to ethics: the force of the ethical is not the force of prudence, self-interest, sympathy, or any other inherent desire or need that would provide the subject with a naturally occurring motive. How then does this *ethical* resistance— this resistance of what has no resistance—work? How, specifically, does the face introduce into the ego a moral conscience where none existed before?[7] *Totality and Infinity* gives two not entirely compatible responses to this question.

The Face as Interruption

The first response is perhaps the more familiar one, not because it is more prevalent in Levinas's writings, but because it predominates in the secondary literature. According to this reading, the face of the other interrupts, disrupts, de-centers, or otherwise breaks in on the naïve and spontaneous egoism of the ego, putting the latter into question and calling it to responsibility. Evidence for such a view comes early in *Totality and Infinity* as we read that the "imperialism of the same is the whole essence of [egoistic] freedom" and that "the Other imposes himself as an exigency that dominates this freedom" (*TI* 87). Of course, Levinas consistently maintains that this imposition is not experienced as a violation by the ego, though at one point he paradoxically writes of the relation that "it is imposed upon the I beyond all violence by a violence that calls it entirely into question" (*TI* 47). The other is not experienced as a force to be subdued, overcome, or dominated—in the first place because he eludes or outstrips every such relation and in the second because the relation with him takes place as discourse, whose essential nature, Levinas says, is teaching (*TI* 89). The other's imposition, as it were, is welcomed and does not overwhelm us: "The face in which the other—the absolutely other—presents himself does not negate the same, does not do violence to it as do opinion or authority or the thaumaturgic supernatural. It remains commensurate with him who welcomes; it remains terrestrial" (*TI* 203). Preeminently nonviolent, "instead of offending my freedom [the other] calls it to responsibility and founds it" (*TI* 203).

Phenomenologically as well as formally, discourse provides Levinas with the exemplar of a situation in which the one who imposes himself does so without violence. Take, for example, the case where another calls my name and I stop. He has imposed himself on my attention, he has "made" me stop, but without violence. Language, for Levinas, "is a relation between separated terms" neither of which absorbs or engulfs the other (*TI* 195). In language, and Levinas especially has the spoken word in mind, the other may become the theme of my discourse, but cannot be reduced to being no more than the theme, since the "word that bears on the Other as a theme" and seems to "contain" him is also "said to the Other who, as interlocutor, has quit the theme that encompassed him, and upsurges inevitably behind the said" (*TI* 195). Language, as was already evident in Levinas's work in the 1950s, thus becomes the formal figure of transcendence, since in it the other is invoked in a manner irreducible to a *consciousness of.* Even when the other is represented, he is always *more* than represented, since the representation is *addressed to* this very same being. And Levinas sees in this divergence between the other as object of knowledge and the other as noumenal interlocutor "the ethical inviolability of the Other" (*TI* 195).

Supposing that the account can get around questions about whether all language is aptly characterized as a discourse between interlocutors, the question remains as to whether Levinas moves with any justification from the other as interlocutor to the other as author of an ethical command. Why must this interlocutor whom my discourse cannot fix affect me in an ethical manner? The position face-to-face "can be *only* as a moral summons," Levinas intones (*TI* 196, emphasis added). The ego's selfish appropriation of the world is said to be put in question as it faces the other, and though we are repeatedly assured that this putting in question "does not limit the freedom of the same" but calls it to responsibility, indeed, though we are told that the face of the other "founds" and "justifies" the ego's freedom, we are not told *how.* "The 'resistance' of the other does not do violence to me, does not act negatively; it has a positive structure: ethical"

(*TI* 197). But the move from an interlocutor who cannot be thematized to one who puts me in question and introduces into me a moral conscience is seemingly accomplished in a manner no less mysterious than the process by which alchemists turn iron ore into gold.

Subsection 2 of "Ethics and the Face" purportedly expounds this movement from the formal structure of language to its positive ethical content. There Levinas begins from the recognition that the face is a "thing among things," and repeats his claim that in rising up as an interlocutor behind the theme of discourse, the face "breaks through" the form that meant to contain it or make it an object ready-to-hand. "This means concretely: the face speaks to me and invites me to a relation incommensurate with a power exercised, be it enjoyment or knowledge" (*TI* 198). This incommensurate relationship which exceeds the ego's power or the *I can* of its egoistic life occurs, according to Levinas, in a decisively ethical dimension. "The epiphany of the face is ethical" (*TI* 199). It engages me with a moral rather than a physical or causal necessity: "Infinity presents itself as a face in the ethical resistance that paralyses my powers and from the depths of defenseless eyes rises firm and absolute in its nudity and destitution" (*TI* 200). This rising up, this epiphany, this "expression" of the other as a being with meaning comes not from its place in a totality, but from itself, and is both imposition and appeal: "The being that expresses itself imposes itself, but does so precisely by appealing to me with its destitution and nudity— its hunger—without my being able to be deaf to that appeal" (*TI* 200). The other's nonviolent imposition is "the first rational teaching" and "the condition for all teaching," as the other "introduces into me what was not in me" (*TI* 203). This moment, where deafness eludes me, is the moment of responsibility. It binds expression to responsibility in Levinas's account and constitutes both as the essence of language (*TI* 200).

For the skeptical reader, this will no doubt seem like more of the same alchemy. It is only mobsters, after all, who issue "invitations" that cannot be refused! How can such an invitation be ethical, and why, in any case, must I accept it? Can't I simply turn my back on the other's expression? Indeed, why assume I even hear his demands as intelligible? After all, some teaching never takes, regardless of the skills of the instructor. Socrates speculates in the *Apology* that the world is divided between those who think it is always wrong to return a harm for a harm and those who sanction revenge or permit harm in the name of self-defense. The suggestion is that rational argument and every other sort of persuasion may simply fail to convince those on one side to adopt the stance of the other. Why might it not be like this with the other's teaching? Why is the other's expression one that will convince even those—and here Levinas most explicitly has the opening of Plato's *Republic* in mind—"who do not wish to listen"?

There appears to be a contradiction between the idea of the face as *imposed* on the ego and the claim that the face is necessarily *welcomed.* Levinas never quite says so explicitly, but in moving without hesitation from the language of interruption, disruption, and imposition to that of welcome and teaching, he implies that these two ways of understanding the relation to the face are one and the same. But if I welcome the face, don't I remain master of the encounter, and aren't the other's alterity and his judgment thereby suspended and appropriated as my own? And if I do not welcome him, but am put in question by him despite my wishes, then isn't this, despite everything Levinas has said, a violent imposition indicating that ethics begins in my submission to an exterior being? John Caputo, following Lyotard's analysis in *The Differend*, speaks similarly of the "scandal" and "dilemma" of obligation in Levinas: "If I understand an obligation, if it is a universal and intelligible principle, then I have made it mine, one of my projects, something I have appropriated and made my own, and so not an obligation at all, but another bit of my freedom, another good idea I have and want to pursue. If I do not understand an obligation, then it is arbitrary; and then I am unable to distinguish among obligations, to distinguish, say, the command that Yahweh gave to Abraham ('that Isaac die') from the command issued to the Nazi guards ('that the Jews die')" (Caputo 1993, 8–9). Lyotard raises this possibility that God's command may be no more intelligible than a Nazi order as part of an argument to the effect that the content of a law has nothing to do with its power to put the addressee under an obligation. The content of the law is not indifferent, to be sure, "but it does not allow one to distinguish the rightful authority from its imposture" (Lyotard 1988, 108).

In a most thought-provoking analysis of obligation in Lyotard and Levinas, Hent de Vries makes clear that the two philosophers agree in maintaining that there is no way to know *objectively* that one is under an obligation. There can be no certainty that could be transmitted from one subject to another, no guarantee of my obligation through a process of intersubjective verification. Speaking of Lyotard's analysis, de Vries notes: "Abraham obeys . . . because he is somehow, mysteriously, paradoxically, 'affected.' He—and *he alone*—is being addressed by the voice of God. Lyotard cites Wittgenstein's *Zettel* to underscore the loneliness of this singular address: 'You can't hear God speak to someone else, you can hear him only if you are being addressed'" (de Vries 1998, 84).[8] In parallel fashion for Levinas, it is only *me*, singularized in the accusative, who experiences the advent of a face as the advent of responsibility. Responsibility literally cannot be made plain from a perspective outside the relation. I can hear the other's cry only if or when I am in the position of the one addressed, and from there the cry is undeniable. A less prosaic way to put the point is to say that it is only if I have a moral conscience already that its demands strike me as intelligible and as addressed to me. But then, paradoxically, I must have a moral conscience already in order to be in a position to be affected by the other who demands that I have just such a conscience!

This paradox will become central to the account of responsibility in Levinas's later work. In *Totality and Infinity*, however, it is as if Levinas is still under a compulsion to make responsibility visible, to show not just that it occurs, but how it is produced—in effect, providing a narrative justification for obligation or for the obligation to have obligations. To this end, much of the analysis of subjectivity or the interiority of the ego that occupies the middle sections of the work is devoted to showing that though the ego is a separated being totally absorbed in and with the world, within the conditions of its egoist existence there is a certain openness to the other. This view of the ego as both open and closed constitutes the second line of response to be considered here and reflects again the tension already seen in relation to the interruptive reading of the face.

The Face as Welcomed and Welcoming

The ego is described as both "open and closed" in connection with Levinas's analysis of enjoyment in the sections on the ego and interiority. The life of the ego in enjoyment is conveyed in the figure of Rabelais' Messer Gaster (literally, Mr. Stomach[9]). Gaster is not a self-interested creature pitting his interests against those of others, but neither is he altruistic nor naturally other-regarding. Gaster is simply *unaware* of the others; he is, as Levinas characterizes him, a hungry stomach "without ears," without a way for the others and their concerns to make themselves known. Here is the "innocently egoist" I (*TI* 134), sincerely and single-mindedly pursuing the satisfaction of its needs, eating much in the way that very young children eat, with focus and a deafness to the world around them. Gaster, for Levinas, is the figure of a finite being conceived as wholly without a relation to the infinite or transcendent other, such a situation being conceivable "only as contentment" and "sensibility" (*TI* 135).

In point of fact, Levinas thinks that an ego like Gaster's cannot be a fully developed reality (*TI* 139). Not only is there no subject who is not already in relation to others, but the things of the world are given to experience having already "undergone labor" (*TI* 137), having been worked up into objects, both practically and theoretically. The apple I eat has been cultivated, picked, packaged, and sold; to have a relation to it that does not pass through others is nearly impossible. But even though sensible objects—even naturally occurring ones—are mostly given in contexts replete with the presence of others, Levinas nonetheless sees the sincerity of Gaster's enjoyment, his contentment, lurking "behind the relation with things" (*TI* 137). I am content with my own corner of the world, with the aspect presented to me by the things of my daily life, by "this city or this neighborhood or this street in which I move, this horizon within which I live"—*this* is the everyday remnant or continuation of Gaster's contentment. I do not ground these things in a larger system of meanings or purposes; rather, *they ground me* (*TI* 137).

In furnishing the ground of my being, like the corporeality of which it is part and parcel, enjoyment is an absorption *in* the world and an absorption *of* the world. The ego appropriates that on which it depends for its sustenance and enjoyment. Here again we meet the Levinasian ego who is conditioned by the very things it constitutes for itself in consciousness and practical comportments. This situation, in which "living from . . . " indicates a simultaneous mastery and dependence, is the heart of the egoism that Levinas describes as both "open and closed." The extraordinary passage in which Levinas introduces this terminology is worth quoting at length, though it does not quite speak for itself:

The interiority that ensures separation [of the ego from the Other] . . . must produce a being absolutely closed over upon itself [*fermé sur lui*], not deriving its isolation dialectically from its opposition to the Other. And this closedness must not prevent egress [*la sortie*] from interiority, so that exteriority could speak to it, reveal itself to it, in an unforeseeable movement which the isolation of the separated being could not provoke by simple contrast. In the separated being the door to the outside must hence be *at the same time open and closed* [emphasis added]. The closedness of the separated being must be ambiguous enough for, on the one hand, the interiority necessary to the idea of infinity to remain *real* and not apparent only, for the destiny of the interior being to be pursued in an egoist atheism refuted by nothing exterior, for it to be pursued without the being who is descending into itself, in each of the movements of [its] descent into interiority, referring to exteriority by a pure play of the dialectic and in the form of an abstract correlation. But on the other hand *within the very interiority* hollowed out by enjoyment a heteronomy must be produced, a heteronomy that incites to a destiny other than this animal complacency in oneself. If the dimension of interiority cannot belie its interiority by the apparition of a heterogeneous element in the course of this descent into itself along the path of pleasure (a descent which in fact first hollows out this dimension), still in this descent a shock [*heurt*] must be produced which, without inverting the movement of interiorization, without breaking the thread of the interior substance, would furnish the *occasion* for a resumption of relations with exteriority. Interiority must be at the same time closed or open [*fermée ou ouverte*]. The possibility of rising from the animal condition is assuredly thus described. (*TI* 148–49; translation modified; emphasis in original except as noted)

While there is more here than can adequately be commented upon, it should be noted that the first aim of this passage is to establish that the separation, or "atheism," of the ego is not produced through a formal, logical, or dialectical opposition to the other, which in Levinas's view would be no opposition at all. The separation of the ego is *concrete*. On this account, it is the ego's enjoyments that give it the weight or "substance" (though Levinas uses the latter term advisedly) that make of it a genuinely independent being and that provide it with an interior life. But at the same time, this interiority must not be so closed in upon itself as to make a relation with exteriority impossible. Somehow, in the midst of interior life, without destroying its reality and without stopping its movement, it must be possible for a "shock" to register and for the ego thus to find itself exposed to an absolute exteriority.

It is not always clear from the passages that follow whether the shock to interiority is delivered by the advent of the face or by the insecure conditions of enjoyment. Levinas writes that "in interiority a dimension opens through which it [the ego] will be able to await and welcome the revelation of transcendence" (*TI* 150). He labels this dimension "concern for the morrow" or the "uncertain future of sensibility" (*TI* 150). The possible vanishing of the things or the elements that support my enjoyment introduces an instability and insecurity into contented being (*TI* 141). Our enjoyment of the air, the sun, the water we drink, and the food we eat is everywhere surrounded by the possibility that these same elements will turn on us through storm or drought and bring about our devastation and misery rather than our contented sustenance. In this possibility, the ego strikes up against something other, but here it is not the alterity of transcendence but the otherness of an indeterminate element: "To be affected by a side of being while its whole depth remains undetermined and comes upon me from nowhere is to be bent toward the insecurity of the morrow" (*TI* 142). The independence of enjoyment is thus as precarious as a ship at sea. When it floats on calm waters it seems master of the elements through which it moves, but this mastery is backed up against the indeterminateness of the elements, which threaten at every moment to envelop its independence in dependence. This insecurity does not suppress the fundamental agreeableness of life—indeed, enjoyment agrees to be troubled and takes delight in its needs, not just in their satisfaction (*TI* 144). But at the same time, the insecurity at the heart of enjoyment is said to open a dimension through which or in which a relation to transcendence becomes possible.

Levinas writes that this "insecurity brings into the interiority of enjoyment a frontier that comes neither from the revelation of the Other nor from any heterogeneous content, but somehow from nothingness" (*TI* 150)! For the question of how the ego comes to be bound by an infinite responsibility, everything rides on this moment. It is at this frontier, seemingly generated neither by interiority itself nor by something exterior to it, that the encounter with the other becomes possible. Insecurity "delineates a margin of nothingness about the interior life" (*TI* 150). The French is more evocative and more exact: "Cette insécurité . . . dessine ainsi un liséré de néant autour de la vie interieur." *Liséré* is a term used primarily in relation to the weaving of fabric, where it indicates a decorative stripe, often at the edge of the material, as for example in the single or double stripe of a different color which edges the collar of a polo shirt. This decorative element is not an external addition, but of a piece with the fabric into which it is woven. The method involves bringing to the surface supplementary warp threads that otherwise go unused and unnoticed in the weaving of the fabric. Thus, the nothingness that edges interior life is not foreign to it but something that in the ordinary weave of enjoyment goes unobserved within it. It is raised to the surface only at the extreme edges of the life of the ego. How then does this fundamental insecurity furnish the opening for transcendence? How does it open that "dimension" through which the ego "will be able to await and welcome the revelation of transcendence" (*TI* 150)?

Insecurity, the Feminine Face, and Failure

Insecurity is lived, Levinas tells us, as "concern for the morrow." Habitation in a home, labor, possession—indeed, all of economic life, in which Levinas includes recollection and representation—are aimed at postponing or delaying the hour of the ego's undoing. An ego with the foresight to store up provisions against a season of drought or cold is one capable of gathering together its thoughts (*se recueillir*) in recollection and representation. Critical to the account developed from this point forward is Levinas's claim that these economic activities "imply a first revelation of the Other" (*TI* 151). The "feminine face" (*TI* 150) is this first revelation: "In founding the intimacy of the home the idea of infinity provokes separation not by some force of opposition and dialectical evocation, but by the feminine grace of its radiance" (*TI* 151).

Levinas's conception of the feminine other has been written about extensively in the secondary literature, and the problems of the account are well known. Most often criticism has focused on his seemingly derogatory account of the erotic relationship, though feminist-minded readers have also remarked on those sections of "The Dwelling" that, on the one hand, portray a domestic feminine presence in the home as the condition for the ethical relation to a transcendent other but, on the other, deny that such a presence is the presence of a full-fledged "face," in the sense that counts for Levinasian ethics. "The Other who welcomes in intimacy is not the *you* [*vous*] of the face that reveals itself in a dimension of height, but precisely the *thou* [*tu*] of familiarity: a language without teaching, a silent language, an understanding without words, an expression in secret" (*TI* 155). Levinas says point-blank in a passage just preceding this one that this familiar and feminine other "is the Woman. The woman is the condition for recollection, the interiority of the Home, and inhabitation" (*TI* 155). A few passages later he adds that there is no question here of presupposing that every home in fact has a woman that keeps it; rather, the feminine is "one of the cardinal points of the horizon in which the inner life takes place" (*TI* 158). Whether or not there is a flesh-and-blood being of the "feminine sex" (a term which Levinas, too, puts in scare quotes), the "dimension of femininity" and the welcome it creates are indispensable moments of the analysis (*TI* 158).

Our interest in this account is not, for the moment, feminist in nature. That is, it is not a question of whether Levinas accords women full subjectivity or whether he adequately concedes that they too enter into ethical life and are more than the silent means for accomplishing a homosocial bond between men—a bond that, were it in fact accomplished across and through the silenced bodies of women, would make of Levinasian ethics the same old fraternity and equality that have too rarely included or protected women's freedom. Legitimate as such concerns are, they are secondary here to the question of why and whether the account needs this proto-ethical encounter as the condition of possibility for a fully ethical face-to-face relationship.

Characterizing the ego prior to its encounter with the feminine other as a *conatus* whose only concern is its own persistence in being. Catherine Chalier writes that the "feminine compels the conquering and virile attitude to stop and to start thinking. It stops the project of being, a project that is deaf and blind to all that does not belong to the strength that persists. She who welcomes in her dwelling helps to find the way of interiority that stops this blind strength" (Bernasconi and Critchley 1991, 122). As a cardinal point of Levinas's analysis, the feminine has the "ontological function" of turning the ego from being for itself to being for the other (123). According to Chalier, the masculine spirit by itself would be sterile; it produces works but lives in a world where they cannot be defended and are thus there for the taking. The masculine economy would be one where might makes right and there is no "care of the Other" (ibid.). "The feminine has to help it [the masculine ego] go beyond this alienation. Since the feminine function is not to create, it cannot be wrapped into its works. It has to give birth to 'a place' in space that will allow man to learn how to turn his natural way of living into ethics" (ibid.).

Chalier notes that if her reading is correct, then the feminine welcome is "but a condition of ethics"; the intimacy and gentleness radiated by a feminine face do not come from "*height* which is, according to Levinas, the only authentic ethical dimension. It means that the feminine (and he often says 'the woman') would be excluded from the highest destiny of human being" (ibid.). This is a strong indictment indeed, and one that should trouble the reader. But just as fundamentally, and still unanswered within Chalier's own very fine reading of Levinas, is how the feminine accomplishes the move to ethics. On Chalier's interpretation, it is a feminine spirit, or perhaps Woman—not necessarily *a woman*—that turns, or "converts," the masculine ego to a life of ethics. *But who converts her?* Is she "naturally" more ethical than he is? Is she inherently possessed of a conscience? Is her natural moral capacity, her moral sense, as it were, then taken up by man and reworked in a way that makes of it a fully ethical position, since in man moral conscience makes the final break with nature? It is worth recalling in this context Levinas's claim that it is in a being both open and closed that one "assuredly" escapes the animal condition.

The feminine face is problematic not just because it is gendered according to a set of stereotypes widely questioned by feminists at least since Beauvoir's *Second Sex*, but because it is a narrative device, a figure employed to do work required by the argument but likewise prohibited within its own terms. Like the role of the pineal gland in Descartes' "resolution" of the mind-body relation, the feminine face is a mechanism meant to serve as the interface between incommensurable orders. That Levinas employs the figure of *the feminine* to bridge the gap between ontology and ethics—a gap he elsewhere implies is unbridgeable—is not incidental. No doubt, conceptions of the feminine prevalent in both Western philosophy and literature and in the texts of the Jewish tradition prefigure and aid Levinas's deployment of this trope. Turning to these sources and understanding Levinas's account in light of them does not, however, change the fundamental fact that the work this figure is meant to do is undoable. The feminine other purportedly solves the problem of how the other imposes itself without violence and turns the ego to goodness and responsibility. And there is much in traditional conceptions of the feminine that lends itself to this work: the connection of the feminine with materiality and nurturing; the perception of femininity as unable to impose itself through force and as thus developing other modes of persuasion; the idea of women as naturally more moral than men (a notion that in the nineteenth century put women on a pedestal that very effectively kept them out of the "dirty" and "corrupt" spheres of public life)—all of these images are potentially deployed by Levinas's account.

For Levinas, the nurturing nature of the feminine permits the narrative to ignore the question of how she rises out of *her* animal complacency, how *she* develops the ears with which to hear another's cry. Perhaps we are to assume that answering the cries of a newborn babe is a natural tutelage and that it is a short step from maternal instinct to a generally other-regarding demeanor. And a natural progression too, perhaps, from nurturing and educating her young to doing the same for her assumedly masculine and immature mate. Whether Levinas might have presumed any such picture, consciously or unconsciously, is certainly subject to debate. Whether his narrative frames women—those empirically existing creatures—and their social contributions in a positive or negative light is also debatable and subject to whether one thinks the story he tells is meant to be the whole story about women or only its first chapter. What is the case in any event—and what especially matters here—is that Levinas's account trades on unacknowledged links between femininity, nature, and nurturing behavior to effect the move from the egoist life in enjoyment to the face-to-face encounter with an other who invites me to an infinite responsibility.

That Levinas gives a fundamental place to the body and that, as early as the essay on Hitlerism, he rejects a vulgar materialist interpretation of embodiment speaks against a criticism of his account as simply reducing femininity to materiality or woman to the body (*RPH*). That is not the complaint here. However, materiality still figures significantly in the way the feminine face "works"—if it works. If Gaster's contentment "lurks" behind all of our relationship to things, which is to say that if a certain deafness to others is characteristic of the ego in enjoyment, then the conversion of the ego has to have a material component. There must be a way for the other, literally and materially, to get me in his grasp, to pull me out of my complacency in order to turn me, or convert me, to good works. But it is a requirement of Levinas's account that this grasp be nonviolent, and thus it is to the account's advantage to be able to portray the moment in which the other first gets hold of me as one in which I am drawn gently into a "space" or "place"—the home—where the "shock" of transcendence can register without annihilating the subject who receives it.

The feminine is positioned in *Totality and Infinity* between ontology and ethics, between bodily needs and spiritual ones, between animal being and ethical transcendence. She is, in Irigaray's terms, an angelic figure, a figure of the passage from one region to another.[10] But she can perform this function only so long as her own status remains unexamined. Returning again to Le Doeuff's insight that images mark the place of a theory's impossible, the claim advanced here is that the figure of the feminine locates the place where the narrative of *Totality and Infinity* falls into ruins and cannot be put back together again. Without the feminine face, it is unclear how Gaster would ever develop the ears to hear the other's cry. Without the feminine, it is unclear why a subject with ears couldn't nonetheless turn a deaf ear to the other and contentedly eat his way through the world.

The ambiguity that attaches to egoist being attaches itself tenaciously to everything in separated being. Without belaboring the point, Levinas's entire discussion of interiority in section II could be read as a paean to ambiguity: the ambiguity of the body and corporeality, of enjoyment, of representation, labor, the feminine other, the dwelling, and works—in short, everything that touches and is touched by materiality. Levinas is explicit that this ambiguity also touches the ethical:

> The separated being can close itself up in its egoism, that is, in the very accomplishment of its isolation. And this possibility of forgetting the transcendence of the Other—of banishing with impunity all hospitality (that is, all language) from one's home, banishing the transcendental relation that alone permits the I to shut itself up in itself—evinces the absolute truth, the radicalism, of separation. (*TI* 173)

Though "the possibility for the home to open to the Other is as essential to the essence of the home as closed doors and windows," it is not clear whether the doors and windows are opened from within or without, by

the ego or the other's initiative, in welcome or as an imposition and disturbance. Moreover, even if one admits that a certain openness or opening in
egoistic life paves the way for the relation to the other, it is unclear how the
ethical relation can be insulated against the other side of openness, namely,
the ego's ability to turn a deaf ear and retreat into the complacent pleasures
of life at its own hearth. And *Totality and Infinity*, such is the reading proposed here, may have no definitive answer to give.

In sum, there are two requirements in the *Totality and Infinity* account of responsibility that are difficult and perhaps impossible to reconcile. On one side is the demand for an "atheist" ego whose egoism is accomplished in enjoyment; on the other side, the insistence that the advent
of ethics be nonviolent. The idea of the ego in enjoyment requires that
the encounter with the face be figured as a disturbance and interruption
of the ego's complacent persistence in being. If the ego were preordained
to an ethical life, either by the possession of inherent social instincts or by
a naturally occurring moral sensibility, its goodness would also be prede-
termined. Like the acorn that can become an oak or nothing at all, an ego
preordained to ethical responsibility would flower or wither without its essence ever being put into question; the only question would be whether
environmental conditions were in favor of it or against it. If ethics is conceived, as it most assuredly is in Levinas, as that which breaks with nature
and is the advent of the human (Rolland 2000, 22), it cannot come about
in the natural course of the ego's life in enjoyment. As the long passage cited above makes plain, ethics is a "shock" to the egoist system. Nonetheless,
and here the second requirement makes itself felt, this shock must come
as the supreme gentleness of an invitation and a teaching. Were the conversion—this turn from being-for-itself to being-for-the-other—achieved
through physical force or compulsion, it would not be ethical. It would be,
as Derrida argues it must be, a violence deployed in the name of reducing
violence, of having the least violence possible.[11] Levinas's account, to the
degree that it demands an ethical relation that is quintessentially nonviolent and to the extent that it insists on an ego who begins in the deafness
of enjoyment, seemingly has little choice but to employ some figure to me-
diate these conflicting demands of the system. The figure of the feminine
bridges the gap between materiality and ethics, body and face, the deafness of a "hungry stomach without ears" and a moral conscience who is

all ears, ever open to the other's command, a pure *response-ability.* Like the face, the feminine does work that Levinas's account needs to do in order to succeed but that is prohibited in the strict terms set by the account itself. For what remains forever unclear on Levinas's account is how the feminine other raises *herself* above the conditions of enjoyment and moral turpitude. Where Levinas asks the reader to see in the domestic figure of the feminine a figure of man's ethical redemption, the reading developed here sees instead a troubled marriage and the breakdown of the text's major narrative. Indeed, as we have argued above, though it is not incidental that it is the feminine that Levinas relies on to do this work, the problem is not with the feminine *per se,* but with the task for which it is so neatly suited but which neither it nor any figure could rightfully or legitimately accomplish. If one admits that the dual requirements of the text cannot be met, then we are left with a text (and an ego) oscillating between the demands of ethics and those of enjoyment, between moral conscience and moral deafness, between responsibility and *conatus essendi,* with no way to decide between them or come down decisively on one side or the other. Does *Otherwise Than Being* share this fate, or is the question in some measure resolved? That is the question to which the analysis now turns.

Emphatic Responsibility

Readers have differed over how to see the relationship between *Totality and Infinity* and *Otherwise Than Being, or Beyond Essence.* Jacques Rolland has argued the case for a "radical difference" between the two books, crediting Derrida's critique in "Violence and Metaphysics" with effecting a "global reorientation" of Levinas's thought (Rolland 2000, 12, 15). Rolland credits Derrida with seeing that as soon as *Totality and Infinity* posits *le Moi* as an *ego,* "it becomes unclear how it can envision the other otherwise than as a phenomena" (88). And a phenomenal other is one who is not *Tout-Autre,* but is in essential respects an *alter ego* ranged within the same. In seeing this, Derrida effected what Rolland describes as a "demolition by delegitimation" of all that Levinas's 1961 text had risked: its analyses of alterity, separation, and ethical responsibility. According to Rolland, a decisive paradigm shift occurs in *Otherwise Than Being,* as *moi* no longer designates a generalized subject or ego, but an identity singularized and produced in the accusative. "It is no longer a question," Levinas writes, "of the Ego [*du Moi*], but of me [*de moi*]" (*OB* 13). In passing from the nominalized and often capitalized *Moi* to *moi* in the accusative, identity is no longer conceived as the act of a self-positing re-identification, but as a unicity that comes "from the impossibility of slipping away from responsibility" (*OB* 14; translation modified). In effect, the subjectivity of the subject is now constituted not by egoism but by responsibility. Looking to contemporary physics, Rolland compares the difference between *Totality and Infinity* and *Otherwise Than Being* to the difference between the realm of human perception and that of subatomic particles: statements that are plainly valid in one order lose their sense in the shift to the other. So, too, with Levinas's thought, which undergoes a veritable "*changement d'ordre de grandeur*" from the first work to the second (Rolland 2000, 16).

One might see Derrida's approach in *Adieu* (1999) as moving in a direction opposed to Rolland's reading. As Rolland himself admits, Derrida tends to stress the continuities of problematic and theme rather than major differences between Levinas's two main works, reading them together as a complex meditation on *hospitality*—not, of course, without attending to differences between the definition of the subject as a "host" in the earlier work (*TI* 299) and as a "hostage" thereafter (*OB* 112).[12] Levinas himself stresses a shift in language from his first major book to his second, but rarely speaks of more thematic differences. The language of *Totality and Infinity*, on his view, remained too ontological (Wright, Hughes, and Ainley 1988, 171). This is not the confession of a covert commitment to being or to the ontological difference, but reflects the manner in which the analyses of Levinas's early and middle period tend toward the description of *existentiales,* or fundamental structures, of our mode of being.[13] Levinas mentions that the ontological flaws of the earlier work are due to its trying to avoid psychological descriptions (ibid.), but as the preceding section suggests, the narrative commitments of this ontological approach work directly against the ethical orientation or responsibility that the text otherwise seeks to disengage from being.

Content and form, what is said and how it is said, are inseparably intertwined in *Otherwise Than Being,* whereas in the earlier works it is the conflict between these orders or levels that produces an extraordinarily rich thought, but also one which cannot fully proceed to its term. In this,

Rolland is right. *Otherwise Than Being* works differently than the way in which the earlier texts work: its statements operate in a different way as they consciously, explicitly compromise themselves with being in order to "say" an otherwise than being. That they cannot say directly what they "want" to say is explicitly recognized, being raised indeed to the level of method. But this difference can be recognized without denying that the problematic that guides the later work is inherited directly from *Totality and Infinity*. Although I read Levinas's two works together through a different prism than the one which animates Derrida's "Word of Welcome," it is a presumption of the interpretation here that there are deep thematic connections between the two works. Indeed, were it not beyond the scope of the present work, I would argue that *Otherwise Than Being* is likely to be misunderstood should it be divorced from the questions raised (without resolution) in *Totality and Infinity*. Without the earlier work—and especially without its failure—responsibility in the later account is all too likely to be read either in falsely theologizing terms or falsely naturalizing ones, both of which miss by a significant distance the place of the ethical in Levinas's thought.[14]

Levinas's response to and appropriation of the failure of the *Totality and Infinity* account is noticeable first in three essays published close on the heels of the 1961 work. "The Trace of the Other" appeared in French in 1963 in *Tijdschrift voor Philosophie*. "Meaning and Sense" was published in 1964 in the *Revue de Métaphysique et de Morale* and later as the first chapter of *Humanisme de l'autre homme* (1972). A third text, "Phenomena and Enigma," was published in 1965 in the Catholic journal *Esprit* and included in the 1967 edition of *En découvrant l'existence avec Husserl et Heidegger*.[15] These three essays pose anew the question of the possibility of an experience of the absolutely other. That Levinas feels the need to return to this theme repeatedly in the years immediately following the defense of his *doctorat d'état* is telling on several counts. The question is clearly unfinished business, despite the considerable resources devoted to it in *Totality and Infinity*, and no doubt Rolland is right to read Levinas's return to this topic as at least partially motivated by Derrida's deflationary reading in "Violence and Metaphysics." Equally telling is that in each essay the question of the experience of transcendence is framed in terms of the question of whether talk of transcendence can be philosophical talk. The issue is not only whether the subject can in some sense "have" an experience that does not pass through the mediation of concepts or the intentional aim of consciousness; it is whether such an experience has to be described in non-philosophical terms, such as that of faith. That Levinas is not interested in a faith-based discourse on transcendence is clear. His texts, early and late, are quite rightly described as "anti-theological," in the sense both that they abjure the consolations of religion and reject a theological foundation or justification for the positions they advance (Ricoeur 1997, 25). That an *experience* of transcendence would be one that confounds reason or "maddens the subject," as Levinas puts it (*CPP* 62), is also plain. Levinas suggests that what he seeks in these essays is a "third way" of describing the experience of alterity that portrays it neither as theological revelation nor as the disclosure of being (*CPP* 103). Moreover, Levinas legitimates his search by recalling that this third way is one that philosophers themselves have pointed to—for example, in Plato's Good beyond being, in Plotinus's One, and in Descartes' idea of infinity, to mention but three sources that Levinas often appeals to in this period. Whereas elsewhere Levinas tends to oppose transcendence to being and ethics to ontology by invoking the complex relation of Jewish to Greek sources, in these essays immediately antecedent to *Totality and Infinity* the dispute is not between philosophy and its other but concerns a possibility within philosophy itself. Claiming this possibility *for* philosophy means mitigating the earlier tendency to identify Western philosophy too exclusively with ontology, and paves the way for the idea that philosophy is, after all, required by the ethical *saying* as that which potentially prevents saying from congealing too solidly in a said. Effectively, it is philosophy's skepticism and its knack for ambiguity that makes it possible to "retain an echo" of the ethical interruption of being within being itself (*OB* 44).

This ethical interruption is now figured as a "trace," which Levinas describes as a signification that "consists in signifying without making appear" (*CPP* 104). Traces in the ordinary sense are, as Jill Robbins terms them, "residual phenomena" (Peperzak 1995, 177). They are like the fingerprints of a criminal or the tracks of animals (*CPP* 104). "This kind of trace is a mark *in* the world, the *effect* of a cause *in* the same world . . . [and] accessible to an interpreter who would decode them" (Peperzak 1995, 177). Like a sign, such traces reflect the activity of someone no longer present, and they permit the detective to reconstruct the original scene. For Levinas, a trace is not a sign in this way, but the comparison with such signs is instructive. If the fingerprint of the criminal is a sign of his having been where he says he was not, the trace would be like a mark unintentionally left by the wiping away of these traces. "He who left traces in wiping out his traces did not mean to say or do anything by the traces he left" (*CPP* 104). The trace is an "overprinting" that disturbs the order of appearance without appearing *within* that order, that is, without being assimilated to an order in which each thing bears a reference to another both contributing to and deriving its meaning from the whole (*CPP* 104). The trace is not the mark of an absence, Robbins points out, but "the mark of the effacement of a mark that was already the mark of an absence" (Peperzak 1995, 177). In this sense, Levinas maintains, every sign is a trace, since in addition to what it signifies, it signifies the past of the one who emitted the sound or wrote the word or made the gesture. A sign "stands in this trace" (*CPP* 105).

The salient point about traces is not that they are unintentional whereas signs are intentionally produced, nor that signs belong to concerted patterns of action whereas traces do not. The idea, rather, is the same one that Levinas has always had in attempting to isolate or make meaningful the possibility of a signifyingness (*significance*) that does not pass through the ontological structures that make of the world an intelligible totality constituted by an ego in consciousness. Just as the invocation of the other that accompanies every discourse escapes thematization within the time of the discourse itself, the trace signals a "lapse" in the temporal order, a moment that escapes the play of retention and prolepsis that sustains the present moment and makes it of a piece with everything else that occurs. That there should be signifyingness that is not a making-present again of what is absent is the gamble of Levinas's thought, and the trace but its newest expression. The other, transcendence, alterity, saying—all of these imprint their trace on the thematization in which they are brought to concepts and by which they are rendered no longer other, transcendent, or absolute (see *OB* 46).

In Levinas's analysis of the relation to alterity in the essays just after *Totality and Infinity*, the trace does away with the need for a mediating figure between the face as an *imposition* and the face as *welcomed*. "In what sense, then, does the *absolutely other* concern me?" Levinas asks ("Trace," 347). He concerns me as a *trace*, which is to say that he does not directly grasp me or turn me toward the good. Rather, the face is now said to disturb the phenomenal order "without settling into the horizon of the world" (*CPP* 102). In responding to a trace, Levinas says we respond to an order that is "utterly bygone," a "deep yore" or "irreversible past" that cannot be made present and which "no memory could follow" (*CPP* 103). These claims are effectively retained from the *Totality and Infinity* account, but without the narrative of the feminine figure that mediated them there. There is no longer a need to explain how the imposition of a face both shatters the egoism of the ego and comes in the greatest gentleness, since the disturbance is no longer in the same temporal order as its effect. The effect belongs to phenomenality, whereas the disturbance does not appear, is not present even in its absence, but signifies only as a trace, that mark of the erasure of marks.

The notion of the trace developed in these essays, and its extension in the notion of *illeity*, are not so much at variance with *Totality and Infinity*'s narrative as they are its exact claims stripped of the narrative form that previously worked against their content. To be sure, a small vestige of the earlier reliance on narrative can be found in "Phenomenology and Enigma," though the different end to which it is fated is instructive. Levinas writes: "Someone unknown to me rang my doorbell and interrupted my work. I dissipated a few of his illusions. But he brought me into his affairs and his difficulties, troubling my good conscience" (*CPP* 64). Is this an irreducible disturbance, Levinas asks. It disturbs my home life, my being *chez moi*, but does it do so in a manner that eludes capture within this immanence? Until this essay—indeed, until this moment—the predominant answer in Levinas's *oeuvre* would have affirmed the radical and irreducible character of the disturbance. Here, however, Levinas admits that the ringing of my doorbell, the appearance of this other and his affairs, the break in my calm and security, can all be reabsorbed into the everyday workings and meanings of the world. The disturbance can be rewoven into the narrative of my day, my week, my life. It might institute a new phase of that life, as when I become so embroiled in the other's affairs that it changes the shape of my own. Then I might say that this ringing doorbell was the beginning of the end, the moment when everything changed; but to tell the story of this change is to make of it a moment of a larger order wherein it makes sense and becomes of a piece with all that preceded and followed it. "The disturbance was a precursor of a more concrete totality, a world, a history. That strident ringing of the bell is reabsorbed into significations; the break in my universe was a new signification that came to it" (*CPP* 64). And the face? The shock of it will be denied, Levinas says!

"Phenomena and Enigma" affirms that the disturbance brought by a face is of an altogether equivocal kind. Even the language in which this equivocation is stated equivocates. When the essay asks how an irreducible disturbance could occur, the answer never comes in a declarative sentence, but always in the conditional: "What would be needed for such a disturbance . . . " or "Everything depends on the possibility . . . ," Levinas says. The reader is never told with certainty that this need has been met or such a possibility realized. Wondering how we can refer to "a past which this very reference would not bring back, contrary to memory which retrieves the past, contrary to signs which recapture the signified," Levinas writes, "what would be needed would be an indication acknowledging the withdrawal of the indicated, instead of a reference that rejoins it. Such is a trace in its emptiness and desolation" (*CPP* 65). The words that state the conditions for the reference themselves enact the withdrawal of certainty. They do not tell us that there *is* a trace. Perhaps not quite as awkward in French as in the English, the last sentence of the passage just quoted begins, "Telle la trace . . . " (*CPP* 65). The missing copula indicates the withdrawal through its refusal to indicate the being or existence of the trace structure.

The disturbance created by a trace is described in "Phenomena and Enigma" as that which "disturbs order without troubling it seriously" (*CPP* 66). The trace is like diplomatic language or sexual innuendo, Levinas says, in that its proposals are made in terms such that "if one likes, nothing has been said" (*CPP* 66). It is an insinuation that "remains only for him who would like to take it up" (*CPP* 66). "This way the other has of seeking my recognition while preserving his incognito, . . . this way of manifesting himself without manifesting himself, we call enigma . . . and [contrast] it with the indiscreet and victorious appearing of the phenomena" (*CPP* 66). The stranger who knocks at my door no longer interrupts absolutely, and his singularity is seemingly no longer a pure self-presentation that commands even those who do not want to listen. The ethical disturbance, if indeed there "is" one, passes in a trace that is altogether inapparent. The face no longer *imposes* itself, but passes in a modality that is eminently discreet, liable to be missed, ignored, or denied. Levinas describes the enigma as the "intervention of a meaning [*sens*] which disturbs phenomena but is quite ready to withdraw like an undesirable stranger, unless one harkens to those footsteps that depart" (*CPP* 70).

If *Totality and Infinity* explained the possibility of the ego's deafness to the other's ethical summons as a result of the lurking complacency of enjoyment, "Phenomena and Enigma" suggests that this deafness is a permanent possibility, inseparable from the modality in which the face signifies. Indeed, Levinas goes so far in this essay as to suggest that it is "vain to posit an absolute you [*un Toi absolu*]" (*CPP* 73). To be sure, earlier he had already suggested that a Thou (*Tu*) would be too familiar, and *Totality and Infinity* especially associates this term with the feminine face which lacks the unbreachable uprightness of the ethical other (*Vous*) (*TI* 155). But now the claim is that the face, strictly speaking, is never a *Vous*, but always an ambiguous *Tu* animated by or standing in the trace of an immemorial *Il*. Levinas now acknowledges that if the other is to *concern me* without being enmeshed in being and finitude, the infinite cannot be "incarnated" in a face, which would then function as the end or term of my desire (*CPP* 73). The infinite "solicits across a face," and the face is no longer identical to this infinite since it is the always material and ambiguous "term" of my good works. "A Thou [*Tu*] is inserted between the I [*Je*] and the absolute He [*Il*]" (*CPP* 73; translation modified). The *Tu* is never absolute, never absolves himself completely from the compromise with being and consciousness; and the *Il* is likewise never manifest, never present, but comes only "enigmatically . . . from the infinite and its immemorial past" (*CPP* 73).

To respond then to the question that pervades these three essays following the publication of *Totality and Infinity*, to respond, that is, to the question of whether there can be an experience of the absolute other, the Levinasian answer is "yes," "no," "perhaps." The face has become thoroughly enigmatic; it interrupts the phenomenal order and thus in a certain way "appears" there, but in the manner of a trace or a "saying which has already withdrawn from the said" (*CPP* 69) or withdrawn from the scene of phenomenality. The face bears a trace of illeity—an illeity that "has never been presence" (*CPP* 73) and that belongs to a past beyond the past that one could remember and represent in the present—but the very significations which bear this trace "forthwith contest and efface" it (*CPP* 69).

One might say that in its more sober moments *Totality and Infinity* was already forced to acknowledge the equivocation of the face, and that the book's best readers have long hazarded that the face could not be altogether freed of its phenomenality even as it contested the limits of ontology and phenomenology. But a retrospective reading of this sort has to be balanced against everything in the 1961 work that rejected and eschewed equivocation, whether it be the equivocation of the beloved and the erotic relationship or the duplicities and circumlocutions of rhetoric. Both were explicitly ruled out as exemplifications of the ethical relationship and ethical language, paradoxically despite Levinas's own necessary turn to figurative language and the contradictions in his notion of the face. When in "Phenomena and Enigma" equivocation and enigma become central to Levinas's account of the face and the ethical relation, it marks not so much a break with or radical reorientation of the earlier view, but a capitulation to an ineradicable ambiguity within it. Unable to overcome the equivocations which may well spell the failure of the *Totality and Infinity* account, Levinas's subsequent work takes up this equivocation and makes it the very modality in which the infinite gains a foothold in being and disturbs phenomenality without settling into its horizons.

Reprising the analysis of the caress in *Time and the Other*, and with a nod toward Merleau-Ponty's last writings, *Otherwise Than Being* finds in skin an exemplary site of the ambiguity of the face. Skin is not just an envelope for the organs or the surface of the body (*OB* 89), but neither is it the presentation of a self "somehow" in person (the quintessential definition of the face in Levinas's earlier works, where he also says that the whole body is a face). Skin is not the paradoxical manifestation of that which cannot appear, but is rather "the divergence [*écart*] between the visible and the invisible" (*OB* 89). This gap is reminiscent of the reversibility that Merleau-Ponty notes in all perception, where the one who touches is at the same time touched, or the eye that palpates the world is simultaneously palpated or moved by it. There is no unassailable distinction here between subject and object, since toucher and touched reverse places or, if one likes, one is never just one or the other. Likewise, Levinas's references to the skin's tender surface confound the distinctions between phenomenal and non-phenomenal. The tenderness of skin is something we *perceive,* and yet we do not read it off the surface of the body like the coarseness of burlap or the smoothness of silk. Tenderness here doesn't refer to the texture of the skin, but to its simultaneous invitation and susceptibility, to its reversibility as toucher and touched. Skin reflects an oscillation between visibility and invisibility not because it is a tissue-thin pellicle—even a skin so thin as to be almost nothing is still of a measurable thickness. Rather, skin indicates the equivocation of the face because its tenderness—which invites caresses but also blows—betokens the very "gap [*décalage*] between approach and approached" (*OB* 90).

Otherwise Than Being affirms that the trace of the infinite signifies "through these ambiguities," not in spite of them (*OB* 91). Already in *Totality and Infinity*, Levinas insisted that the face was both more and less than the ego: it commanded from a position of extreme height, but this height was due to its equally extreme poverty and destitution. This destitution, understood materially in the earlier work, is now shown to be not just the vulnerability of the body to "real" ailments, hunger, or the force of blows; it is also the metaphysical poverty of the face or of the trace. The face, if it still commands absolutely, does so in a trace that can always be ignored. The face of the other "obsesses me" without ever appearing, without becoming more than a trace which is already "less than nothing" (*OB* 93). And what evidence is there that an infinite has passed by in a trace? Only my obsession, only my responsibility. Thus, despite the urgency with which Levinas still writes of my responsibility to the other, it is crucial to remember that this responsibility depends on a trace that is "less than nothing."

Totality and Infinity engaged in an extended narrative that purported to show how a separated and atheist ego could nonetheless come to be commanded by and responsible for an other. If the ego had not been separate, if it were but a dependent moment of the ethical relation, its becoming ethical would be an unremarkable achievement. And if it were brought to ethics by compulsion, if there were a violence at the beginning of the ethical relationship, this too would compromise the extraordinary event of sociality. In *Totality and Infinity*, the narrative form (in conflict, at times, with its content) leads one to expect an answer to the skeptic. You are responsible whether you know it or not, says this text; but the narrative form implies that one could in fact be *brought* to know, that a narrative could be produced that would show the ego to itself in the right light, despite its own attempt to position responsibility outside cognition and intentionality. *Otherwise Than Being* explicitly abandons the narrative commitments of the earlier work and is explicit about the problematic status of its own discourse. Levinas rejects the narrative aspects of the earlier presentation, now saying of responsibility that it is not an event that happens to "an ego already posited and fully identified," not a "trial that would lead [the ego] to being more conscious of itself, and make it more apt to put itself in the place of others" (*OB* 115–16).[16] There is no ego who pre-exists its responsibility and who might thus serve as the protagonist of the story that *Totality and Infinity* tells. Similarly, Levinas now remarks that the first moment of responsibility cannot be one of welcoming the other's command (since this would still be an activity of the subject) and says that it has to be something like obeying an order that has yet to be formulated. Though even this way of putting the point, Levinas says, is "still perhaps a quite narrative, epic, way of speaking" (*OB* 13). Moreover, whereas *Totality and Infinity* moves from interiority to exteriority, and from formal structures to concrete situations, giving the appearance of developments that move the argument forward, Paul Ricoeur rightly remarks that "one notes no visible progression in the argument" of *Otherwise Than Being* (Ricoeur 1997, 3). Everything has already been said in the introductory chapter, entitled "Argument," and the successive chapters do not advance beyond this initial statement, but "unfold" and "deploy" what is already contained therein (ibid.).

As the narrative of the ego coming to moral conscience is abandoned, the conception of responsibility undergoes a correspondingly important shift. The core features of responsibility remain stable between Levinas's two works, but they are rendered in *Otherwise Than Being* in increasingly hyperbolic terms. Thus, Levinas speaks of an *infinite responsibility* increasing in the measure it is fulfilled (*OB* 93), without regard for what is possible or impossible (*OB* 113), always with one responsibility more (*OB* 10, 84), to the point where the persecuted "is liable to answer for the persecutor" (*OB* 111). Similarly, it is an *irrecusable responsibility* that cannot be declined, because it is prior to every free commitment (*OB* 10), "preceding every free consent, every pact, every contract" (*OB* 88), justified by no action of a subject because it is an absolute passion (*OB* 102–3), an "irremissible guilt" that makes of my own skin a Nessus tunic, rendering me totally susceptible to the other (*OB* 109). Again, it is a one-way or unique orientation, an *asymmetrical responsibility*, like a persecution undergone (*OB* 102, 111), or an obsession (*OB* 101 and passim); I am "irreplaceable" in responsibility (*OB* 103), a "hostage" to the other (*OB* 112, 114), since the other "is abandoned to me without anyone being able to take my place as the one responsible for him" (*OB* 153).

Ricoeur speaks with frustration of the "verbal terrorism" of such passages (Ricoeur 1997, 26), though Levinas anticipates such complaints, readily acknowledging that his approach is exasperating, and suggesting even that it raises exasperation to the level of method. His use of emphasis—understood here as a formal figure of rhetoric as well as in its ordinary sense—is strategic: in passing "from one idea to its superlative, to the point of its emphasis," one sees that "a new idea—in no way implicated in the first—flows, or emanates, from the overstatement. The new idea finds itself justified not on the *basis* of the first, but by its sublimation. . . . Emphasis signifies at the same time a figure of rhetoric, an excess of expression, a manner of overstating oneself, and a manner of showing oneself. . . . Exasperation as a method of philosophy!" (*GCM* 89). The usual connotations of responsibility are "exasperated," worn out and overwhelmed, though not at all lost or given up in being pushed to their extreme limit in Levinas's text. The older and more familiar notions of responsibility are not the *basis* on which a new account is built or justified; rather, hyperbole renders the older notions vulnerable or susceptible to showing responsibility differently and permitting a new sense (meaning and orientation) to emerge. It is possible to see now how Levinas's understanding of responsibility can be dependent on the ordinary notion of responsibility—indeed, to the point of being parasitic on it—and at the same time can liberate a sense of responsibility that was previously unheard in the term.

Initially, Levinas proceeds by inversion: if ought implies can, we are told of a responsibility where ought outstrips can; if usually one can be held responsible only for actions done voluntarily or for events connected to the agent's agency through the right channels, we are told of a responsibility that goes beyond anything I have done or freely committed to and of a responsibility for which the voluntary/involuntary distinction does not matter; if we ordinarily think of responsibility as something of which a general account can be given that shows how it applies to every or any ego, we are now told of a responsibility that is "mine" alone, which cannot even be generalized to each one who says "mine." From these inversions Levinas pushes still further: responsibility is so far from being an active commitment of a free ego that it is a passivity more passive than the passivity of receptivity—receptivity, after all, being still a *capacity* to receive. Responsibility is a passion undergone without there yet being anyone who submits to it or undergoes it. Responsibility in this extravagant version is not just other-regarding behavior, but is a being-*for*-the-other, the one-for-the-other of a substitution constitutive of the subjectivity of the subject.

And though we are infinitely far here from any *Sollen* (which Levinas writes in German), from a Kantian *ought* or a moralist *should*, Levinas can nonetheless with perfect right pull the account up short by insisting that responsibility in this new sense involves good works. It is not just an ethereal orientation toward the Good, a well-meaning but vague or empty intention to give due regard to the other. To be responsible means going toward the other with one's hands full, that is, in concrete actions that end the other's suffering (*OB* 12).

In doubling up the ego's responsibilities to the point of seeing in them an infinite demand, outstripping the subject's capacity to assume or take on such obligations, Levinas ultimately passes "beyond" the notion of the subject itself. The infinity of responsibility is not only the idea of an ego who always has "one responsibility more," but of a being whose very subjectivity consists in its expiation for the other. This is not the expiation of religious, or at any rate Christian, theology. It is not an atonement for the other's sins, since the very notion of sin presupposes a sinner, a subject who acts. Expiation here indicates only that "the relationship with the non-ego precedes any relationship of the ego with itself" (*OB* 119). Before being for myself—indeed, before being a self or as the condition of self-becoming—I am for the other. "Why does the other concern me? What is Hecuba to me? Am I my brother's keeper?" Levinas asks, invoking Hamlet and the story of Cain and Abel. Such questions are meaningful "only if one has already supposed that the ego is concerned only with itself" (*OB* 117). From such a perspective, it "indeed remains incomprehensible" that the other could come to matter to me and matter to me more than my own life. But Levinas has pushed responsibility to the point where this notion of a pre-existing ego collapses in on itself, imploded under the weight of responsibility. And at this extreme limit of its undergoing, responsibility affords a glimpse of subjectivity as an original *for*-the-other.

In a well-known passage at the very center of the analysis of substitution, Levinas writes, "The word *I* [*Je*] means *here I am* [*me voici*], answering for everything and everyone. Responsibility for the others has not been a return to oneself, but an exasperated contracting, which the limits of identity cannot retain. Recurrence becomes identity in breaking up the limits of identity, breaking up the *principle* of being in me, the intolerable rest in itself characteristic of definition" (*OB* 114). The passage continues, exaggerating the notion of restlessness until it becomes the idea of the self as a "gnawing away" at itself, which would be the only modality of its having a hold on itself (*OB* 114). The gnawing that hollows out the minimal distance of the self from itself that is necessary for self-consciousness is nonetheless an auto-ingestion that precedes my being a self; moreover, Levinas says, it is not alienation of the self from itself, but inspiration by an other. In a further elaboration or emphasis of the notion of inspiration: "This inspiration is the psyche. The psyche can signify this alterity in the other without alienation in the form of incarnation, as being-in-one-skin, having-the-other-in-one's skin" (*OB* 114–15). The other is in the same, like air in the bottom of the lung, where the structures that are elsewhere differentiable into inside and outside can no long be fully distinguished. The "atomic unity" of the self, as of the organism, is exposed to the other as that from which it lives, as its own very substance or core (*OB* 107).

In passages such as these one experiences the method of emphasis. The text does not make an argument in the sense of leading the reader from one justified claim to the next; rather, it passes from one term to another along a chain of rhetorically linked figures that through hyperbole, emphasis, and exasperation of their limits breathlessly forms and unfolds the itinerary outlined in the introduction to the text.

In what sense are we any longer in the realm of an ethical responsibility recognizable as such? Of an ethics recognizable as such? Nothing Levinas says about responsibility is empirically verifiable or justified in any of the usual ways relied on by philosophers, nor is it meant to be. Nor is it the case, as was at least a possibility in *Totality and Infinity*, that one could come to recognize oneself in the descriptions offered. Levinas's text is literary in a deep sense, to be sure, but it is not akin to recent attempts to see in literature an exemplar of ethical life that could instruct us about our passions, fragilities, and vulnerabilities. Indeed, we should be suspicious of anyone who is at home with or who recognizes his or her own life in Levinas's words. Ricoeur at least has what must be the only decent reaction one can have to *Otherwise Than Being*. He is horrified and disturbed (interrupted and made uneasy) by its hyperbolic responsibility. This disturbance moves him to take up the terms of the text anew, to turn them over in his own mouth, to pose questions about them—indeed, to treat them with an abiding skepticism.

Levinas not only anticipates this response but finds in it the enactment of the ethical: "The responsibility for another is precisely a saying prior to anything said. . . . [This] miracle of ethics before the light, this astonishing saying, comes to light through the very gravity of the questions that assail it" (*OB* 43–44). Not only "must" saying be assembled in a said, posited, hypostatized, sedimented in the knowledge of a particular time and place, it also "calls for philosophy in order that the light that occurs not congeal into essence what is beyond essence" (*OB* 44). Philosophy has the task of unsaying the said, though this is not a matter of bringing forth the saying as a revelation that would be of a different order but equal in status to the concepts of Western logic. Rather, as "endless critique, or skepticism," philosophy destroys the conjunction of saying and said (*OB* 44). When asked whether philosophy's skeptical attitude is consistent with "the attitude of faith" (and the questioner implies without saying so that Levinas's philosophy might prize the latter over the former), Levinas's reply is itself skeptical. As discrete as his questioner, and as unwilling to be straightforward, his response implies that skepticism might be the only way to be faithful, if one is willing to credit the distinction to begin with. *Skeptical,* he says, "only means . . . the fact of posing questions" (*GCM* 86). And questioning, as an "original attitude," is already a relation to that which "no response can contain" (*GCM* 86). To question is already to direct one's question *to someone*; it is invocation, in the sense given to the term in "Is Ontology Fundamental?" But it likewise means that one has already been called into question, that a response has been demanded, that one has been taken hold of in a manner that goes beyond anything in the question itself. To question, one has already to be susceptible, which within the emphatic method Levinas deploys is just a step or two away from being vulnerable and exposed to the other in an infinite responsibility. The skeptic is not a figure without the ears to hear—he is not Messer Gaster, deaf to the call of reason or the plaints of the others. As a skeptical attitude, philosophy "arouses a drama between philosophers and an intersubjective movement which does not resemble the dialogue of teamworkers in science, nor even the Platonic dialogue which is the reminiscence of a drama rather than the drama itself" (*OB* 20). Philosophy as the work of two concrete philosophers, rather than as the dialogue of the soul with itself or the unfolding of a world spirit or reason, thus enacts that which prevents the saying from being frozen or hardened in a said. In the history of philosophy, new interlocutors come on the scene and resay what has come before, answering to past and present objections. Levinas writes, "Despite this lack of 'certainty in one's movements' or because of it, no one is allowed a relaxation of attention or a lack of strictness" (*OB* 20).

The next chapter returns to Levinas's engagement with skepticism as a figure for ethical life. For the moment, suffice it to say that skepticism is a wholly warranted response to Levinas's thought. It is perhaps the only one that preserves the ambiguity on which ethical transcendence depends. To be ethical means to have a part in the skepticism that opens *Totality and Infinity*; and to be skeptical means already to have a part in the ethical. Just what part is what remains to be said, though never, of course, unequivocably or finally.

Ethics: Normativity and Norms

And so, when the question of what justice consists in is raised, the answer is: "It remains to be seen in each case."

—JEAN-FRANÇOIS LYOTARD

Normativity without Norms

There is a widespread view according to which Levinas is not engaged in *ethics* in any of the usual senses in which philosophers, legal scholars, political theorists, or others generally employ the term. Commentaries routinely distance Levinas's from traditional schemas that divide ethics into normative, descriptive, and meta-ethical spheres of inquiry, and that further divide normative ethics by whether an author is chiefly concerned with duty, consequences, or human character and virtue.[1] We read: "Levinas does not treat 'ethics' as one branch of philosophy amongst others. And neither does he attempt to construct a normative moral philosophy. Rather his work is a search for the significance of ethics and the ethical" (Ciaramelli 1991, 85). Likewise: "Levinas's work cannot be said to provide us with what we normally think of as an ethics, namely a theory of justice or an account of general rules, principles and procedures that would allow us to assess the acceptability of specific maxims or judgments relating to social action, civic duty, or whatever" (Critchley and Bernasconi 2002, 27). Just as *Being and Time* is not an ontology in the usual sense, but rather a fundamental inquiry into the question of the meaning of being, so too we hear that Levinas's work is not an ethics per se, but rather a radical re-thinking of the question of the meaning of the ethical. Whereas Heidegger retrieves the question of the ontological difference from the oblivion into which it had fallen, Levinas likewise rescues the question of ethical transcendence from a neglect he attributes not just to a certain forgetting but to an actively allergic reaction (Robbins 1991, 101). Levinas himself largely underwrites this view, which puts his work at a substantial remove from traditional ethical concerns. In his well-known interview with Philippe Nemo, Levinas states, "My task does not consist in constructing an ethics; I only try to find its meaning" (*EI* 90). He adds, however, and this line is rarely quoted: "One can without doubt construct an ethics in function of what I have just said, but this is not my own theme" (*EI* 90).

It is not the aim of this chapter to construct a Levinasian moral system; indeed, I am less convinced than Levinas himself that such a thing is possible. But at the same time, this chapter *is* a defense of the idea that Levinas's thought offers us an account of normativity or the force of ethical claims. Despite the fact that Levinas's commentators regularly want to divorce his work from so-called normative ethics, almost no one actually adheres to the terms of such a divorce. When Levinas's work is employed to identify and redress social, political, and economic injustices, when it is invoked as calling us to a new respect for alterity, difference, diversity, or simply "the other," when it is cited as a way to rethink the ethical dimension of the relationship between teachers and students, caregivers and patients, judges and defendants, when it is appealed to by a host of disciplines from psychology and sociology to literary theory and communication studies as they make the "turn to ethics," it is well-nigh impossible to read these invocations as having nothing to do with normative ethical concerns. Indeed, to the extent that Levinas's thought has had an impact outside of narrowly phenomenological and theological discourses, it is his *ethical stance* that has captured readers' attention. Robert Bernasconi makes it plain that this is as it should be: the "reorientation of thinking that is Levinas's goal . . . matters not at all unless it impacts on our approach to concrete situations so that we come to see them as ethical" (Bernasconi 2002, 250). Bernasconi's remark suggests that if Levinas's notion of responsibility has no practical impact, that is, if it does not change the way we see ourselves or the situations we confront, then there is little point in invoking his work as a fundamental investigation into the meaning of something vaguely called "the ethical." But what sort of impact is Levinas's thought supposed to have? What sort *can* it have if it forgoes all connection to normativity and norms? Is it enough merely to be inspired by Levinas's writings to see ourselves as in an ethical relation to the other? To think this is surely to concede too much to those already tempted to view Levinas as no more than a pious moralizer whose writings are accepted by "disciples" without argument and without the possibility of philosophical justification. I have argued in the previous chapter that responsibility in the Levinasian sense requires giving a defense of oneself, justifying oneself before the other. This is the sense in which he speaks of responsibility as *apology*. To be called to an ethical life, then, is not to be called to a life of pious thoughts or inspired sentiments—no matter how other-regarding or generous they may be; it is to be called to justify one's life and one's construal of the world to others. It is to respond to the other's demand for justification. The aim here is to show as directly as possible why that justification is not optional, but required; that is, why the demand for it is normatively binding.

To implicate Levinas's thought in a certain understanding or articulation of normativity is not, however, to suggest that his philosophy provides direct *norms of action*. His philosophy is not and cannot be in the business of telling us what we ought to do or what it is right or good or saintly to do. This does not mean that his work ends in relativism or the dismissal of constructive ethical projects; nor does it mean that his work has nothing to do with normativity or normative questions. In what follows, it is argued that Levinas's thought *does* provide us with an account of why and how it is that we are bound to justify ourselves to other people. He gives us a compelling account of why others' needs, concerns, and very lives are something which makes a claim on us and toward which we cannot be wholly indifferent. As such, I argue that he gives us an account of normative force, that is, of how we come to be bound to respond to others' claims. But it is a *normativity without norms*. What his philosophy cannot provide is a rule or algorithm by which to test and evaluate specific claims. From a Levinasian perspective, specific norms of action arise in determinate historical contexts. They are the claims of individuals within concrete communities. The Levinasian account of responsibility tells us why they must be taken seriously—which means that they must be subject to critical evaluation and response—but this interpretation rejects the idea that any such norms can be developed *universally* and *ahistorically* from a mere consideration of the basic or formal structure of the face-to-face relationship.

This chapter begins from two fundamental features of Levinas's account of responsibility—its ambiguity with respect to grounds and its simultaneous status as constitutive of subjectivity. I then construct an argument to show how responsibility in this sense responds to the moral skeptic who professes indifference to the other's moral demands. In effect, seeing how Levinas responds to the skeptic allows us to see how normativity is at work in his thought. Finally, the essay addresses the question of why normativity in Levinas's sense nonetheless does not produce or underwrite specific norms or moral principles.

Responsibility and the Condition of Ethics

Two features of Levinas's notion of responsibility are important for the question at issue here. In the opening sections of *Otherwise Than Being*, responsibility is described as "a response answering to a non-thematizable provocation" (*OB* 12). The provocation or call cannot be thematized because that which evokes it is not an object for consciousness or something that appears: "This response answers, before any understanding, for a debt contracted before any freedom and before any consciousness and any present, but it does answer, as though the invisible that bypasses the present left a trace by the very fact of bypassing the present. That trace lights up as the face of a neighbor" (*OB* 12). The "trace," in the Levinasian sense, is not a mark within the world; it is not like the tracks of an animal or the prints left by a thief, both of which represent absence through the presence of a sign. A sign "is a mark *in* the world, the *effect* of a cause *in* the same world . . . [and] accessible to an interpreter who would decode them" (Peperzak 1995, 177). The trace, in Levinas's sense, is like the mark that occurs when a thief wipes away his prints. It is an "overprinting" that is not perceptible as such (*CPP* 104).

Since responsibility, for Levinas, has the structure of a trace—that is, since it is a response to a face that never appears as such—then the face may be said to be something like the site of normativity but not its origin or source. Indeed, there will be nothing that functions so foundationally in the Levinasian account. In a sentence whose hesitations and evasions might be read as themselves enacting the effacement that structures the trace, Levinas writes of the face of the neighbor as a "trace lost in a trace, less than nothing in the trace of an excessive, but always ambiguously (trace of itself, possibly a mask, in a void, possibly nothingness)" (*OB* 93). Later he says more clearly that the face "does not function . . . as a sign of a hidden God who would impose the neighbor on me. It is a trace of itself, a trace in the trace of an abandonment, where the equivocation is never dissipated" (*OB* 94). The face is thus misunderstood if it is thought to operate like a cause or origin of our responsibility, and Levinas is clear that it cannot serve as the point of departure for a demonstration of the truth or reality of responsibility. One can neither deduce ethical obligation from the trace nor find unambiguous evidence of the passing of a face in ethical responsibility. The "infinite that calls for or commands my response is thoroughly "ambiguous, "enigmatic," and "equivocal" (*OB* 12). In an evocative description, Levinas compares the trace to diplomatic language and sexual innuendo in which "if one likes, nothing has been said" (*CPP* 66). Thus, the face that "commands" or "ordains" one to an infinite responsibility is nothing certain or unambiguous.[2] If one likes, one has never been called! This intractable ambiguity is the first point to be noted for the reading developed here.

To be obliged by a face that passes only in a trace means that "I am obliged without this obligation having begun in me, as though an order slipped into my consciousness like a thief" (*OB* 13).[3] Levinas notes that this will appear paradoxical to views, like those he credits to phenomenology, according to which nothing can be totally alien to the consciousness that thinks it. Responsibility confounds the structure of constituting consciousness since it is prior to my freedom to assume or decline it. It is "as though" responsibility consisted in a movement of obeying before an order had been formulated, or as though the order was "formulated in the very obedience of the one who obeys" (*OB* 13; translation modified). The response to the other becomes the site or moment in which the order to respond is given. In later sections of *Otherwise Than Being*, Levinas speaks of a command that commands me "by my own mouth" (*OB* 147) and of an order that is heard only in the response that obeys: "The order has not been the cause of my response, nor even a question that would have preceded it in a dialogue. I find the order in my response itself" (*OB* 150). I am subjected to this order "before hearing it," or "I hear [it] in my own saying" (*OB* 150).[4] This strange structure of an order that forms in the syllables and on the lips of the one who responds corresponds "concretely," Levinas says, to the ordinary event of responsibility for the neighbor (*OB* 100). This proximity to the neighbor "is already an assignation, an extremely urgent assignation—an obligation" (*OB* 100). Prior to any commitment on my part, before I can invest this assignation with meaning or make of it a theme for consciousness, I am affected by the other. Indeed, Levinas goes so far as to say that before being for myself, I am *for another*. It is as if the other were the condition of my own subjectivity. And this is the second feature of the account that matters for us here.

Being *for* the other is not to be conceived as an activity of the subject or an accomplishment of its will; rather, it must be conceived, Levinas says, as a radical or hyperbolic passivity, pure exposure to the other without even the initiative found in the capacity to receive. In a development that gives bite to Levinas's claim that responsibility is not a modality of cognition, the one-for-the-other of substitution is figured as the vulnerability of the body: it is a susceptibility to the other that "cannot be reduced to an experience that a subject would have of it" (*OB* 54). Here the subject is affected without being able to attach an "I think" or "I perceive" to this affection. It is an emphatic, hyperbolic affectivity undergone in the way one undergoes ageing—that is, without consenting to it but in the recognition that it is uniquely one's own senescence, not imposed on one from without.

In the middle chapters of *Otherwise Than Being* maternity becomes the principal figure of this affective relationship in which extreme susceptibility to the other becomes a being *for* the other or "the possibility of giving" (*OB* 69). Levinas portrays sensibility as a kind of irritation, the "restlessness" of someone persecuted or uncomfortable in their own skin, someone "torn up from themselves," unable to close themselves off, unable to be at rest or complacent in their own being (*OB* 75). And in a passage whose imagery is as unsentimental as any ever written about pregnancy, Levinas writes, "Is not the restlessness of someone persecuted but a modification of maternity, the groaning of the wounded entrails by those it will bear or has borne?" (*OB* 75). Maternity signifies as a responsibility, "to the point of substitution for others and suffering both from the effect of persecution and from the persecuting itself in which the persecutor sinks. Maternity . . . bears even responsibility for the persecuting by the persecutor" (*OB* 75). Maternity betokens a manner of conceiving materiality that sees in it not the dumb and formless matter of Aristotelian metaphysics but a materiality that *already signifies*, that is already the "very locus of the for-the-other" (*OB* 77). To be sure, there is an "insurmountable ambiguity" in embodiment. Pregnancy, like any other bodily experience, can be affirmed as nothing more than an animal function (*OB* 79). But this ambiguity, Levinas says, employing a tactic that will mark the most significant advances of *Otherwise Than Being*, "is the condition of vulnerability itself, that is, of sensibility as signification" (*OB* 80). The ego's enjoyment and self-complacency, which were the starting point for the account in *Totality and Infinity* and which had to be overcome in responsibility, are here seen as secondary possibilities attributable to a more original or pre-original vulnerability and susceptibility, but one whose signification is never unambiguous. It is only because I am *for* the other, Levinas says, that enjoyment or suffering *by* another become possible (*OB* 90). Being for-the-other is the pre-condition for all other subjective experiences. Substitution as the pre-original *for-the-other* of responsibility thus appears to be positioned as a condition for the possibility of all subjective experience.

The Skeptic's Question

Asked, "What would you respond to someone who said that he did not . . . feel this call of the other, or more simply that the other left him indifferent?" Levinas replied, "I do not believe that is truly possible. It is a matter here of our first experience, *the very one that constitutes us*, and which is as if the ground of our existence" (*IR* 184; emphasis added). Suppose that Levinas's account of responsibility were meant to respond to the moral skeptic who claims indifference to the face of the other and who expresses doubt that there is any such ethical relation to the other or any such moral demand being made. The skeptic asks, "What is the other to me?" or "Why ought I value the other's demands?" Such questions imply that only a fool is duped into thinking that the other's claims to moral consideration have any kind of binding force apart from that already provided by utility or other prudential considerations.[5] In effect, the skeptic doubts that there are uniquely moral reasons and doubts that such reasons have a normative force that cannot be reduced to self-interest. The skeptic thus asks what reasons there are to value something or someone she has been told she has an obligation to value. She asks why she should think that the other has *moral* value or deserves moral consideration.[6]

Faced with this ordinary sort of moral skepticism, a Levinasian response might begin like this[7]: the idea of valuing something presupposes a world in which this something is meaningful or intelligible. If I value something—regardless of the value I assign to it—this implies I have taken its measure, weighed it against other objects or possibilities, and in some manner understood its connection to my own life and to others. To be sure, I can be wrong in the judgments I make in any of these spheres. I can underestimate the value of what I have and realize my error only too late. Equally, I can overestimate something's value and later come to see that, after all, it was something I was able to live without. Further, my valuing something need not mean that I have gone through an explicit or conscious process of evaluative reflection on the thing or relationship in question. Much of our valuing in fact comes about without direct reflection, but *a relationship is not one of valuing unless it is possible for it to have been accompanied by some such process.*

Someone may raise an early objection that the picture painted here doesn't seem quite right as an account of the way in which I value myself or my own life, and it might also be questioned as an account of the way in which we value our children or those we love. In both cases, the valuing seems more immediate, more like an impulse or an emotion than like a reflective act. With characteristic freshness of insight, Virginia Held argues just the opposite point of view, taking the example of children and giving birth as her focus. We are often told about the reasons human beings have for dying, she notes, but just as we can die for a reason, we can also give birth for a reason. This is true, Held argues, even for women who have little reproductive freedom or control (Held 1989, 365–66). People "can die for noble causes and die heroically. They can die out of loyalty, out of duty, out of commitment. They can die for a better future, for themselves, for their children, for human kind. They can die to give birth to a nation, or democracy, to put an end to tyranny, or war. They can die for God, for civilization, for justice, for freedom" (364). That human beings can make such choices is "part of what it is to be distinctively human" (ibid.). Most deaths, to be sure, are not the result of such dramatic choices, and many people live without sustained reflection on what things are worth dying for or on what makes a life worth living. "Nevertheless, that a human being can choose what to die for, and what to live for, characterizes our concepts of being human, and our concept of dying a human death and living a human life" (367). If reflection and choice are appropriate when we are talking about what to die for, we should consider, Held suggests, that they are equally appropriate when we ask what we give birth for. The upshot of Held's argument is that valuing and evaluating cannot be gotten around by trying to claim that they happen naturally. We are beset with the problem of evaluating our choices and justifying what we choose to value. Valuing is a reflective activity. Neither self-love nor love of a child, neither the choice to bring the latter into the world nor the choice to maintain oneself there are simply natural, biological processes that are closed to reflection. Held's example effectively points out that we would not be human, or would not be human in the way we take ourselves to be, if they were.

To return to our Levinasian argument then: valuing requires and expresses the fact that I am *already reflectively in a world.* To be in-the-world can be understood here with the full richness Heidegger gives to the term. I am immersed in an open-ended system of relationships, many of which I understand and control, some of which I do not, all of which refer to possibilities of the kind of being that I am myself. What are we to say about how I came to be there? While Heidegger takes the question of the world-hood of the world to be one of the fundamental questions of ontology, he would no doubt read the question of *how* we come to find ourselves in a world as an ontic question of little direct interest. On the Levinasian account, however, how we answer the question is crucial. Being-in-the-world, for Levinas, is neither the achievement of a self-sufficient subject nor the ontological birthright of *Dasein.* Being in a world presupposes an other who has *opened that world to me and with me.* I do not meet the other *in* the world; rather, to have a world (which means being capable of reflection) is already to be in a relationship to the other. Without the other, there is no world; without the world, there is no ego who could be the subject or bearer of experiences within the world.[8] The relation to the other is thus constitutive of my having a world at all.

Though Levinas shies away from developmental models almost as much as Heidegger, we might consider the case of a newborn to illustrate this point: at just a few months old, the newborn uses another's hand to grasp what he wants to grasp. He holds his father's hand, for example, as that hand grasps a toy or a spoonful of fruit. The other's limbs become an extension of the infant's body as he reaches for something out of his grasp or beyond his ability to manage. Likewise, the toddler's early words, her first demands and observations, are intelligible only to those who have been keenly watching for them and who can interpret the rough sylla-bles as meaningful words and phrases. Context in such cases is everything. Knowing which objects are the child's favorites, and which things she is likely to be "talking" about, a parent mediates the child's early attempts at conversation to others, helping her be a part of the world long before she can hold her own there. Such observations are as much in an Irigarayan vein as in a Levinasian one perhaps, but then, Irigaray's notion of the touch and the caress is deeply indebted to Levinas's own elaboration of these themes in *Totality and Infinity* and later texts. What is clear, in any case, for Levinas and Irigaray is that others are not just "there" *with* me in a world; they are the condition for my having a world *at all*. Others are not co-orig-inary with the world, for Levinas, they are the pre-original condition for any subjectivity and any relation to the world whatsoever.

In *Otherwise Than Being*, Levinas writes somewhat enigmatically that responsibility arises in an "overemphasis of openness" (*OB* 119). The suggestion developed here is that we can read this openness as the open-ing of and to a world. If subjectivity signifies for Levinas as "being affected by the other whom I do not know" (*OB* 119), this needn't mean that the other is literally a stranger or a remote and absent other. She may well be unknown, because there is as yet no "I" to do the knowing. By the time *I* am *me*—by the time, in other words, that I achieve subjectivity—I am not just susceptible to an other, but deeply vulnerable to a host of others, be-cause my subjectivity has been constituted within a series of intimate and dependent relationships that make my meaningful relations to the world possible. Responsibility—exposure and non-indifference to the other—is thus the condition of subjectivity and mediates its formation. The relation to the other mediates the subject's entrance into the world, though, strictly speaking, the subject does not pre-exist the relation itself.

Levinas's thought, both early and late, insists that the ethical relation precedes the possibility of reason in us, and by reason he means the possibility of critical reflection. He rarely concerns himself with the question of what sort of thing reason is, except to insist that it is not an abstract, universal Reason with a capital "R," but something embodied and creaturely.[9] Rationality, like subjectivity itself for Levinas, is a distinctly social product. To be in a world, to be reflective, to be rational, all have the same condition: the relation to an other who even as he or she is constituted by my reflective, conscious activity is equally the condition of its possibility.[10] This realization prepares the final step in the argument, which now reads in full as follows: (1) The idea of holding anything as a value presupposes a world in which the thing valued is already meaningful or intelligible. To value thus means that I am already reflectively situated in a world. (2) Being reflectively in the world is the product of a social relationship, which is to say that the relation to the other is constitutive of my being able to value anything whatsoever. (3) Thus, the other person is not merely something or someone that I can value or fail to value. Without an other, there is no world and no meaningful valuing. Hence, the skeptic's question of whether I am obliged to value the other and on what grounds always comes *too late*. It mistakes the other for an object within the world, rather than seeing the relationship to the other as the condition of my having a world at all and being able to find value in it. If I value *anything* at all, then, I am already in a relationship to the other. He or she *already* concerns me. What could my continuing to ask for proof of this mean except that I have failed to understand what sort of relationship we have? The other can never be only an object of value within the world concerning which I might rightfully ask why she or her needs should matter to me. By the time I ask these questions, I have already shown myself to be immersed in a complex evaluative practice. In effect, to ask for reasons, to ask why I should concern myself with the other, is itself already indicative of such concern. The skeptic's question thus indicates that the other has already passed that way, already introduced her into a world in which critical reflection is possible.

The reading advanced here, though it often departs from Levinas's own idiom, nonetheless conforms closely to the structure of his thought.

If Cain (and sometimes Hamlet) is Levinas's exemplar of the moral skeptic, the skeptical question is this: "Why does the other concern me? What is Hecuba to me? Am I my brother's keeper?" (*OB* 117). Levinas emphasizes that such questions are meaningful only for a subject who pre-exists its encounter with an other: "These questions have meaning only if one has already supposed that the ego is concerned only with itself, is only a concern for itself. In this hypothesis it indeed remains incomprehensible that the absolute outside-of-me, the other, would concern me" (*OB* 117). By contrast, for a subject whose very subjectivity is formed as a response to the other, such questions always come on the scene, as it were, *too late,* and it is always too late to be concerned *only* with oneself. Responsibility is not the concern of the subject who already has a history, who already exists; rather, Levinas says, responsibility "speaks" in the "pre-history" of the ego (*OB* 117). It is to capture this idea that Levinas employs the figure of the "hostage." I am already bound to the other, already his or her hostage, when "I" take up my position in being: "The self is through and through a hostage, older than the ego, prior to principles" (*OB* 117). It is also for this reason that Levinas is doing more than playing on words when he says that to posit oneself in being, to be posited there or to pose oneself there (*se poser*), is to be exposed (*s'exposer*) to the other, to be already outside oneself, not oneself, or unable to close oneself up in oneself. From the very first moment that one takes up a position as a subject, one is already exposed to and in relation to an other (*GCM* 89). "It is through the condition of being hostage that there can be in the world pity, compassion, pardon and proximity—even the little there is, even the simple 'After you, sir'" (*OB* 117). The events we recognize as ethical, from the polite gestures of social commerce to the selfless lives of saints, and everything in between, are predicated upon or find their condition in the "unconditionality of being hostage" (*OB* 117). This unconditionality "is not the limit case of solidarity, but the condition for all solidarity" (*OB* 117).

The Freedom of Others and Founding Possibilities

One aspect of the argument I have constructed for Levinas is found explicitly in Simone de Beauvoir's *Ethics of Ambiguity.* For Beauvoir, the world is opened to the subject *by means of the other.* Describing a "young man" who wills himself free and who sees others primarily as enemies to the free realization of his projects, Beauvoir admits the kernel of truth in Hegel's comment that each consciousness "seeks the death of the other" (quoted in Beauvoir 1994, 74). But this perception is naïve insofar as it fails to see that if the ego's freedom were everything or the only reality—if it were the All—the "world would be empty. There would be nothing to possess, and I myself would be nothing" (75). To be free, Beauvoir explains, "is not to have the power to do anything you like; it is to be able to surpass the given toward an open future" (91). Others are the means by which this future remains open or is closed down. This happens in a variety of ways. Others are the basis of my own willing, in the sense that projects have a social and cultural context that provides the horizon within which or against which they can be seen as meaningful (even if only to a single individual). Likewise, others are the means by which my projects are extended or frustrated; as Sartre pointed out, if I develop a political party, it is others who make that party a reality or let it fall into oblivion. Insofar as all willing has this social basis and prosthesis, "the existence of others as a freedom defines my situation and is even the condition of my own freedom" (91). In a more technical sense, to the extent that freedom in the existentialist account requires a situation as the site of its exercise, others are necessary to freedom in an almost metaphysical sense.

For Beauvoir, perhaps the most salient interconnection between my freedom and that of others is the more ordinary one in which "it is other men who open the future to me, it is they who, setting up the world of tomorrow, define my future" (82). Others can promote the scope of our freedom, just as they can diminish our opportunities to act and to be purveyors and creators of social meaning. If I have any project at all, I am thus already entangled with others, not just as potential obstacles to the realization of my project but as those who provide the basis on which my project is meaningful and as those who make my willing possible. My own willing depends on others and can be effective only where others also will freely; hence, for Beauvoir, to will one's own freedom is to will freedom universally: "To will oneself free is also to will others free" (73).

There is a similar idea in Kelly Oliver's notion of "witnessing," as she likewise emphasizes the interdependence of human possibilities and takes this as the basis for a universal responsibility to others.[11] Witnessing indicates in the first instance a kind of testimony to what one has seen or experienced firsthand. But this rather juridical sense shares space in Oliver's account with an admittedly religious sense of the term as testifying to that which must be taken on "blind faith" (86). Moreover, she sees the two senses as connected. First-person testimony differs from third-person accounts, Oliver argues, not in giving a more accurate or objectively true description of an event, but in being performative in a way historical narrative is not: first-person testimony re-presents an historical event at the same time as it dramatizes the impossibility of making that event fully present for another. Testimony thus gives something to be known and marks the impossibility of full knowledge: you to whom I testify and before whom I testify cannot have a first-person perspective on these events. "What makes testimony powerful is its dramatization of the impossibility of testifying to the event" (ibid.).

While Oliver often uses the term "witnessing" in a way that suggests it is the activity of a pre-existing or already recognizable subject, she also means for the term to refer to the process by which subjects come into being. Witnessing in this sense plays a role similar to that played by interpellation in a theory like Althusser's. But whereas the latter accords exclusive authority to the other in constituting the "I," Oliver privileges the relational process over either of its terms. Subjectivity, she says, "requires a witness" (88), and it is impossible to bear witness without an addressee (91). Rather than seeing subjectivity as being called into existence by the address of another who recognizes me or confers upon me a certain social intelligibility, Oliver sees witnessing as involving structures of address-ability and response-ability that can only be understood as emerging from within the I-Other relation.

Combining this sense of witnessing to subjectivity (our own and the other's) with the idea that first-person testimony performs its own impossibility, Oliver concludes that we are obligated "to recognize the impossibility of recognizing others" (88). Witnessing both performs this impossibility and makes this performance *obligatory*. Why obligatory? Oliver effectively suggests that witnessing to the simultaneous reality and incomprehensibility of the lives or experiences of others is necessary because witnessing, as address-ability and response-ability, is the condition of being a self or subject. Thus, insofar as we can be said to have an obligation to our own most fundamental possibility, we have an obligation to preserve and maintain the conditions for witnessing generally. "Subjectivity requires the possibility of a witness, and the witnessing at the heart of subjectivity brings with it responsibility, response-ability, and ethical responsibility. . . . Responsibility, then, has the double sense of opening up the ability to respond—response-ability—and ethically obligating subjects to respond by virtue of their very subjectivity itself" (91). Oliver cites Eva Kittay, who maintains that "a subject who 'refuses to support this bond [between the conditions of its own subjectivity and that of others] absolves itself from its most fundamental obligation—its obligation to its founding possibility'" (Kittay 1998, 131, quoted in Oliver 2001, 91). We witness to the subjectivity of others, in effect, because of their role in witnessing to our subjectivity, or, to put it in terms other than those of self-interest (which admittedly distort the intent of Oliver's work), we are obligated to keep the pathways of witnessing as open and unobstructed as possible because our own subjectivity directly depends on it. Witnessing, in effect, is something I cannot but engage in if I am to be a self, but it is also something that I *ought* to engage in as extensively as possible so as to keep my own subjectivity viable.

The argument here is similar to Beauvoir's, and the structure of both arguments problematically parallels Kant's argument about the imperfect duty to beneficence. For Kant, roughly, we have a duty to help others because we are the sorts of beings who at some point will require help ourselves, and to the extent that we create a society in which help is rarely or never forthcoming or is given only grudgingly, we participate in instituting a culture that contradicts the conditions of our own willing. That benevolence is an imperfect duty means there can be no strict rule about how much help to give or when it is allowable to refuse. The question of what constitutes tolerable limits of indifference to others would then be an empirical one: how much indifference destroys the culture of aid that we all need to flourish or to exist as subjects with a will? To put this in terms of Beauvoir's argument, willing my own freedom certainly involves willing the freedom of *some* others, enough to keep my future reasonably open, but it is not clear that either practically or theoretically it justifies the claim that freedom *must* be willed universally. In particular, it is not obvious that the freedom of an oppressed minority is a real liability to the dominant group's freedom, especially if there is otherwise a diversity of viewpoints, projects, passions, and the like within the dominant group. That oppression is deplorable we may agree, but Beauvoir's argument appears to want to show that it is somehow illogical as well, or contrary to the structures of freedom itself; it is not clear she achieves this. Likewise in Oliver's argument we are said to have a categorical reason to witness to some events or subjects (enough, presumably, to keep the general process viable), but we do not have a strict obligation to witnessing *as such* or in every case. That Oliver wants to position witnessing as something that has a stricter hold on us is clear; on what basis she might do so is not.

For both Beauvoir and Oliver, the other plays a foundational role in the possibility of my own subjectivity. Moreover, for both, the recognition—or perhaps just the fact—of this is supposed to be sufficient to generate an obligation: to will the freedom of others in Beauvoir and to witness to the impossibility of recognizing the other in Oliver. Thus, in a critical respect these two arguments come down to the same idea: there is something in the other that is beyond my grasp, even as my own subjectivity depends on it. Though the language of Beauvoir's and Oliver's accounts, themselves motivated by subtly different concerns, has only a partial overlap in each case with Levinas's, this idea squares quite neatly with the overall message of *Totality and Infinity*. This is the text, after all, in which the other's unknowability, his or her resistance to the appropriative grasp of representation, is pushed to the fore, and in which the ego's freedom is specifically said to be founded in the relation to alterity and not the reverse.

So, does Levinas's thought suffer from the same problem as Beauvoir's and Oliver's—namely, does it have universal aspirations when all it can legitimately claim is that we are called into question by some others or, more accurately, by *this* other who faces me here and now? Hilary Putnam has suggested that for Levinas "the irreducible foundation of ethics is *my* immediate recognition, when confronted with a suffering fellow human being, that *I* have an obligation to do something" (Putnam 2004, 23–24). Putnam characterizes Levinas's philosophy as a thought experiment in which I "imagine myself confronted with *one* single suffering human being" (26). So confronted, "I am supposed to feel the obligation to help *this* human being, an obligation which I am to experience not as the obligation to obey a *principle*, as a Kantian would, but as an obligation *to that human being*" (26–27). If Putnam is right, then Levinas's thought suffers from the same problem as Beauvoir's and Oliver's: it attempts to universalize a responsibility that must remain in every case particular. Now Putnam's characterization of Levinas may be fair as a description of *Totality and Infinity*, and even the language of thought-experiments may be less foreign to the general milieu of Levinas's thought than one might expect (e.g., the free variation of classical Husserlian phenomenology is also a kind of thought experiment). In any case, Putnam's characterization is plausible with respect to the 1961 work since it coincides with the suggestion in that text that we can put an end to ethical uncertainty. If we undertake the thought experiment, we arrive at a realization, recognition, and *feeling* of obligation that cannot be controverted by the skeptic. After all, one feels what one feels whether the feeling is rationally grounded or not. Putnam's characterization is thus in line with a tendency to see in Levinas's thought a kind of non-cognitivist ethics, at least to the extent that for Levinas responsibility is based at the level of affectivity. This reading must be given up in the case of *Otherwise Than Being*, however, since ethical certainty is precisely what the account there forgoes entirely. If *Totality and Infinity* seeks—covertly, perhaps, but recognizably—to answer the skeptic, *Otherwise Than Being* neither silences nor discredits skepticism, but sees in skepticism a figure of ethical life.

Skepticism and Reflective Endorsement

The argument given above shows why the skeptic's question—"What is the other to me?"—is out of place. It comes too late; asking it means one is already a reflective being, already in a world opened to one by the other. The other can never be only an object of value within the world, concerning which I might rightfully ask why she or her needs should matter to me. If I ask this question, it indicates that an other has already passed my way, already opened me to a world in which critical reflection is possible.

Put another way, we can say that the other introduces the ego into practices of reason-giving. From this vantage point, we can also reinterpret the motif, especially strong in *Totality and Infinity*, according to which the face of the other "calls me into question." *Totality and Infinity* repeatedly tells the reader that the face of the other calls the egoism of the ego into question and subsequently commits that ego to a path of infinite responsibility for the other. The reading proposed here has interpreted that moment not as an empirical, psychological event in the life of an adult ego, but as the moment in which the subject or ego is first constituted. This is consistent with Levinas's insistence that being called into question by the other is not equivalent to being conscious of having been called into question. By the time such consciousness has occurred—that is, by the time I am explicitly or consciously aware of being challenged by another—I have already become a subject with the ears to hear the other's demands. (Of course, as will be emphasized momentarily, by then I am also someone who can try and even succeed somewhat in turning a deaf ear to the other.) In either case, for the other's demand or question to be intelligible to me *as a demand or question,* for me to receive it as such, I already have to have been constituted—in a past I cannot assume or recuperate within memory—as a subject vulnerable to an other who makes demands and poses questions. The relations by virtue of which I have come to be constituted as a subject able to be addressed and capable of responding are not the product of my own will, even if I can make them "mine" in a subsequent intentional act. Subjectivity thus arises in the accusative before it achieves nominative status.[12]

Reflection here does not indicate simply that consciousness turns its "ray" back upon itself. Rather, to be capable of reflection means being susceptible to a demand for justification, which in turns means being susceptible to the other. Though a detailed reading of the sections of *Otherwise Than Being* on sensibility must be reserved for another work, the relation to the other is located at the level of sensibility, where the latter term is connected not to a theory about the reception or processing of sense-data, but to a view according to which susceptibility and exposure to the other—exposure, moreover, that is not a matter of exposing oneself, since it concerns the constitutive moment of subjectivity itself—are at the basis of all other intelligible experience.

In "Humanism and Anarchy," we read, "The subject is a responsibility before being an intentionality" (*CPP* 134). Formed or brought into being as a subject through its exposure to an other, responsibility—a fundamental social relation—both precedes subjectivity and is a condition for "concrete" or everyday moral responsibility. "Subjection [*asservissement*]" to the Good happens effectively "before" the subject is a subject, that is, before reflection has arrived or is possible. The Good "is not the object of a choice for it has taken possession of the subject before the subject had the time—that is, the distance—necessary for choice" (*CPP* 134). To be able to take a distance from one's object means being able to represent it and hence to have presented it in consciousness as an object of reflection. But the Good "seizes" the subject prior to the possibility of reflection. This does not mean that the Good sneaks up on an ego unawares; it means that the relation to the Good is prior to and facilitates the emergence of a subject. Since a relation to the Good—here synonymous with being for the other, with responsibility, with exposure to the other, and so on—precedes the very being of the subject, it is inescapable: "There is indeed no subjection more complete than this possession by the Good, this election" (*CPP* 134–35).

Is this a kind of servitude or enslavement to the good? Levinas denies the violence this suggests and maintains that "the subjecting character of responsibility . . . is nullified by the goodness of the Good that commands. The obeying one recovers his integrity on the hither side of subjection" (*CPP* 135). I am "formed" by social relations before I have the capacity to represent them to myself and thus to choose or reject them. Were it not for the other who opens the world to me, I would not become an I capable of reflection and judgment. But once I *am* an "I" and *am* capable of reflection, I can reflect critically on my being so and think it better to have been subjected to the other in this relation and to be capable of reflection rather than not. I reflect that it is better to be subject to the Good than not. Thus, according to Levinas, the ego recovers its "integrity" in the midst of its subjection.

The argumentative strategy Levinas employs here is not unlike the reflective endorsement found in Hume and other moral sense theorists. In brief, reflective endorsement acknowledges a basis for morality over which the subject has no control—in the Humean case because it is simply a matter of our human nature and our developed disposition. But this basis nonetheless survives the scrutiny and meets the approval of the moral faculty (which it also forms). Reflective endorsement asks, "All things considered, do we have reason to accept the claims of our moral nature?" (Korsgaard 1996, 19). Calling the mental operations that give rise to normative judgments in whatever field a "faculty" and the normative judgments themselves "verdicts," Christine Korsgaard explains that "a faculty's verdicts are normative if the faculty meets the following test: when the faculty takes itself and its operations for its objects, it gives a positive verdict" (62). As she points out, for Hume the faculty of understanding fails the test: "The harder we press the question whether we ought to believe our beliefs . . . the more the degree of our conviction—that is, the liveliness and vivacity of the ideas—will tend to diminish" (ibid.). The faculty of the moral sense, by contrast, passes the reflexivity test. "Reflection on the origin of our moral sentiments only serves to strengthen those sentiments. The moral sense approves of its own origins and workings and so approves itself" (63). While it is unclear how to distinguish this approval from the prejudiced approval of a prejudice, this is not necessarily a problem, since it only suggests that indeed "there is no place outside of our normative points of view from which normative questions can be asked" (65).

Levinas is not here being classed with moral sense theorists. To the extent that he rejects unequivocally the view that ethics is a matter of naturally arising moral feelings, he is far from the views of Shaftesbury, Hume, or others in this tradition. The similarity is limited to the *form* of the argument he employs to offset the heteronomous beginnings of ethical life. For Levinas, the relation to the other is the condition for reflection. Reflection, to say it again, is not a naturally occurring capacity, but the evidence and product of a prior social relationship—though it is a relationship which *brought forth* or which constitutes the subject who is then said to have been one of the terms of the relationship. It is by grace of the other, then, that rational critique or critical reflection—evaluation and the acceptance of responsibility—is possible for me. Once the other introduces me into the practice of critical reflection, I can reflect on reflection itself and endorse both its origin and its operation. To express this in Levinas's terms: sometimes people have been thankful for finding themselves able to thank. With reflection it is the same: I reflect on and approve reflection and the election that promotes it.

From this vantage point, the skeptic's question is put in a new light. The would-be amoralist asks for proof or evidence that the other is his concern: "What is my brother to me or I to him that I should concern myself with his welfare?" The skeptic effectively demands a *reason* that would justify the other's demand for care or concern. In so doing, the skeptic implicates herself in the very practices of reflection that indicate just the sort of relation she would like to deny. That is, the skeptic uses a faculty or practice granted to her by the social or ethical relationship in order to question whether such a relation could really be attributed to her. Her question thus involves her in a performative contradiction and is in this sense self-defeating or self-refuting.

Two further points need to be made in this connection. First, responsibility as it functions in Levinas's thought is never naturalized: "Nothing in this passivity of possession by the Good . . . becomes a natural tendency. The relation to the other is not convertible into a nature" (*CPP* 137). Specifically, Levinas seems to have in mind erotic relationships as the exemplar of a naturally occurring concern for the other, but his point can be generalized. Possession by the Good is not evidenced in nor does it result in natural sentiments of care, affection, love, or compassion. Levinas's is *not* an ethics of care and does not see a naturalized concern for the other as either the locus or the expression of pre-original responsibility. The "anarchical bond between the subject and the Good . . . is made without the subject having been a will. It is not the constitution of a 'divine instinct' of responsibility, an 'altruistic or generous nature,' or a 'natural goodness'" (*CPP* 137). Responsibility is a matter of a pre-subjective subjection to the Good and a posterior approval of it that does not and cannot amount to an experience of this Good or an assuming of it as my choice. It is only my election that I approve.

Second, reflection does not guarantee morality in the conventional sense, that is, subjection to the Good is not a guarantee of what we ordinarily call ethical goodness, moral character, or right action. The birth of an ego with a will and judgment—that is to say, the coming into being of a subject through its election by the Good—is certainly, on Levinas's view, the condition for moral responsibility in the non-Levinasian sense. But it is equally the condition for the "seductions of irresponsibility" (*CPP* 137). "This temptation to separate oneself from the Good is the very incarnation of the subject or his presence in being" (*CPP* 137). Levinas is careful to point out that incarnation is not the cause or source of such a temptation—his is not the tale of a fall from grace, nor does he view the body as that which impugns or corrupts an otherwise perfect or holy will. To be faced with "axiological bipolarity" or the choice between good and bad one has to have been constituted already as a subject, which means being constituted through an exposure to the other.

Sounding similar themes in *Otherwise Than Being*, Levinas denies that subjection to the Good is the "naïve unconditioned 'Yes' of submission" (*OB* 122). It is submission both before and after the fact, both in the original election and in the later endorsement, but it is not the unconditioned *yes* of "infantile spontaneity" (*OB* 122). It is, Levinas says, "the exposure to critique, the exposure prior to consent" (*OB* 122). The subject is constituted in a manner that makes it unable to be totally deaf to the other's demands, whether those be demands for reasons, a cry for compassion, an expression of pain, or the pangs of hunger. To be in a world as an ego means being exposed to the other in a manner that makes perfect indifference to her expressions impossible. I can harden my heart against the other, but I cannot claim literally that she is meaningless to me. Subjectivity is ever too late to say that the other in no way concerns it. This lateness signifies, as Levinas says, "the necessity that the Good choose me first before I can be in a position to choose" (*OB* 122).

We can return to the skeptic's question to see this more exactly. In demanding a justification, the moral skeptic is trapped in a performative contradiction between the content of her question and its practical conditions. The skeptic's question presumes a neutral, pre-social subject who has no constitutive relation to the other and thus must be provided with a reason to take the other into account. But the practices of reason-giving in which the skeptic's own question participates already belie her introduction into a socially or intersubjectively constituted world. When the skeptic asks "Why be moral?" or "What is the other to me?" she demands a reason for acting in one way rather than another. Far from casting doubt on the possibility of ethical life through such questions, skepticism is in fact its prolongation. It is the *enactment* of ethical life. If it were not for the other who opens the world to me, I would not be able meaningfully to ask the skeptic's question. Thus, being chosen before I can choose is the condition for all of my later choosing, for all my affirming or denying. I cannot without contradiction deny my ability to engage in the process of critical reflection, and, by extension, I cannot without contradiction deny my exposure to the other. This inability to turn a deaf ear, this non-indifference to the other, *is* the moment of normativity in Levinas's thought. What now remains to be examined is the relation of normativity in this sense to norms.

Getting Down to Cases: Can a Levinasian Ethics Generate Norms?

Writing of a responsibility that "commits me . . . before any truth and any certainty," Levinas says it makes of "the question of trust and norms an *idle* question" (*OB* 120). The formulation is provocative. Can we do without moral dispositions and norms once we have Levinasian responsibility? Are we to assume that Levinasian responsibility makes us morally good or virtuous, to the point where discussion of these is now unnecessary? If nothing else, Levinas's comment reinforces a supposed gap between his reflections on responsibility and our usual understanding of the term. A few lines later, he notes further that the "ethical language we have resorted to does not arise out of a special moral experience," and insists that "responsibility is not comprehensible on the basis of ethics [i.e., moral rules or norms]" (*OB* 120). None of this comes as a surprise, but what of the reverse? Can one derive moral norms from the condition of being bound to the other in an original responsibility? Here we arrive back at a consideration of the practical import of Levinas's thought—and back at the role of the skeptic.

Levinas writes of skepticism that it is the legitimate child of philosophy and the moment of the ethical saying *within* philosophy (*OB* 168–71). The full-grown, self-positing subject—the *ego* of Western philosophizing—thinks it is within its rights in demanding an account that shows that others must matter to it. But even as it thus attempts to chase off or dismiss the other's demands, the fact of its recognizing them *as demands* (that it may want to cast as illegitimate but that it nonetheless cannot claim are meaningless) means that it remains dogged by an ethical recognition enacted in its own discourse. Skepticism is both a figure for and an enactment of the fate of ethics: "It is as though skepticism were sensitive to the difference between my exposure without reserve to the other, which is saying, and the exposition or statement of the said in its equilibrium and justice" (*OB* 168). If the truth of ethical saying (exposure to the other that opens a world that can become intelligible and in which critical reflection is possible) is put on the same level as the truths made possible by it (the *logos,* or meanings, of that opened-up world), it no longer registers. The statement "You are infinitely responsible to the other" is always open to contestation. Why am I responsible? How so and to what extent? The skeptic is right to pose such questions, but in doing so she enacts the responsibility—the original election by the Good—that her words would like to consign to the ash heap. The skeptic can challenge individual moral statements, but she cannot, without contradiction, challenge her engagement (in the very act of posing her question) in an ethical relationship and by extension a form of ethical life. Or, as Levinas puts it, she cannot evade her election by the Good without denying herself and her own uniqueness (*OB* 122).

Norms belong to the class of particular moral statements and share their fate. Generated contingently (though not arbitrarily) in the history, culture, and material practices of a given society, norms belong to what Levinas calls "the said." They are a kind of thematization and sedimentation of the life of a people at a particular time in its history. As such, existing norms may always be contested in the name of new self-understandings, emerging or changing social and cultural practices, and ever varied forms of life. Each norm registers a demand, and each norm may be contested in the name of making another or a different demand heard. Whether I assent to the one demand or the other is a historical question, and the question of justice in such cases cannot be decided in abstraction from the given conditions and practices of a society. Indeed, particular conceptions of justice themselves have a history that intersects with the cases and norms that are the objects of their judgment. But whatever my position with respect to a given norm, what cannot be claimed without contradiction, from the Levinasian perspective, is that there is no normativity or that I am not bound to see or hear these demands *as* moral demands which demand my response. In effect, I cannot claim to be deaf to the fact that a demand has been registered. I can try to dismiss it as wrongheaded or pernicious, but I cannot claim that such demands are literally meaningless nonsense or none of my affair. And if I cannot do that, then I am already enmeshed in ethics. In short, for a Levinasian, every particular norm is contestable, but the *moment* of normativity—*that the other makes a claim on me to which I cannot be entirely indifferent*—is incontestable. To say "there is no normativity" or "there is no responsibility" is to make a claim that enacts the ethical relation even as it attempts to deny its existence.

Does this mean that Levinas's thought cannot be called on to help us adjudicate the moral and ethical controversies of our own time? Not exactly, but this much is clear: Levinas's thought will not function in relation to ethical controversies, as might Kantian or utilitarian ethics. It does not provide a principle or algorithm that could be used to determine the rightness or wrongness of some given action. Someone might object that by Levinas's own account the face provides at least one principle: thou shalt not kill. After all, Levinas attributes these words to the other on more than one occasion. To read this as a kind of categorical imperative prohibiting killing misunderstands the sort of thing Levinasian responsibility is. Levinas's account of responsibility, on the view of it developed here, can no more be used to argue against just-war theory than it can be used to intervene directly in debates on euthanasia, abortion, animal rights, ethical vegetarianism, capital punishment, or a right to self-defense. All of these cases involve the possibility of killing another—and they are only the tip of the iceberg—and in them we reflect on questions of the justice of taking another's life. To claim that killing is prohibited in any or all of these spheres is to propose a moral principle or norm. It is to make a demand. Levinas's thought does not give us a direct or indirect way to decide these cases. But it does tell us why we cannot walk away from them in utter indifference. Non-indifference to the other, as has been argued here, is not a matter of valuing the other or, by extension, of valuing what she values. It is rather a matter of a certain kind of vulnerability to the other being constitutive for my own possibility of being a subject. One is not an ego without being in relation to an other in such a way that one is already vulnerable to the other's demands at the very same moment in which one is first capable of making demands of one's own. My own demands, my "self-interest," have no priority, logically, chronologically, morally, or ethically on the Levinasian view. To be exposed to the other is constitutive for being myself. When it comes then to the other's demands—for rights, freedoms, benefits, opportunities, or whatever—Levinas's view explains why the infinite task of responding to those rights is incumbent on us, and why, though we can in fact act irresponsibly,[13] we can never argue that this is none of our own affair. Levinas would agree with Lyotard when he writes, "And so, when the question of what justice consists in is raised, the answer is: 'It remains to be seen in each case.'" But while justice must be taken case by case, our obligation to seek justice, to hear and weigh the other's demands and to weigh them against the demands of *all* the others (including also ourselves) is not just categorical, but constitutive of who we are—though without that moment being able to serve as a foundation or ground. Responsibility, in the Levinasian sense, is lived on permanently ambiguous ethical terrain.[14]

"Language is already skepticism," says Levinas, meaning that it always already betokens the intersubjective ethical relationship that makes critique possible (*OB* 170). And skepticism is already normative, we can add. Contrary then to those who would distance Levinas altogether from questions of normativity, the aim here has been to show that he has a powerful account of normative force. Having such an account does not mean that we can turn to his philosophy to be told how to act or what sorts of life goals to pursue: "The will is free to assume this responsibility in whatever sense it likes; it is not free to refuse this responsibility itself; it is not free to ignore the meaningful world into which the face of the Other has introduced it" (*TI* 219). By opening this world to me, the other does not demand that I fulfill her every need or that I do her exact bidding. The other does not give me rules or principles that will now constrain or guide my action. The discourse opened by a face only obliges me to more discourse (*TI* 201), to the practices of giving and weighing reasons and of doing so without taking my own "reason" to be the gold standard. The passage to rational social life that Levinas imagines, especially in *Totality and Infinity* but also later, "is not a dis-individuation"; it is not the movement to an abstract and universal reason. It is "a response to the being who . . . tolerates only a personal response, that is, an ethical act" (*TI* 219).

5

Scarce Resources? Levinas, Animals, and the Environment

But now ask the beasts, and let them teach you; And the birds of the heavens, and let them tell you.

—JOB 12:7

What haunts me is that in all the faces of all the bears that Treadwell ever filmed, I discover no kinship, no understanding, no mercy, I see only the overwhelming indifference of nature.

—WERNER HERZOG, IN THE 2005 DOCUMENTARY *Grizzly Man*

Readers have persistently noted the absence of animal others in Levinas's philosophy. They have worried about the humanism and anthropocentrism of his ethics. They have suggested that what concern for the environment is conveyed by his works is at most an interest in stewardship of the natural world for the sake of human ends rather than a direct ethical concern with nature or ecosystems. In effect, it seems to many that Levinas, that quintessential thinker of alterity and ethics, was relatively uninterested in the alterity of animals and of the possibility of ethical claims coming from the natural environment. His work, it would seem, provides us with but scarce resources for thinking ethical alterity outside of an anthropocentric framework. This essay does not challenge that suggestion outright. Indeed, a search of Levinas's writings and interviews uncovers neither an assurance that animals have a face nor the conviction that they do not. All one finds, again and again, is his uncertainty and hesitation on this issue. Taking into consideration, on the one side, those who criticize Levinas for failing to recognize non-human others and, on the other, those who find in his work positive (if still limited) resources for an ecological ethical stance, this paper argues *against both sides* that they rest on a shared misconception about the face of the other and the manner of its commands, and that they thus overlook the possibility that the best way to think about a Levinasian response to environmental issues is not to ask about an environmental or animal *ethics*, but to think about these issues in the register of what Levinas calls *politics*.

The question of how to understand the force of what Levinas calls the face is central to the issue of "Levinas and animals" or "Levinas and the environment." For example, some critics maintain that there is no way to extend the notion of the face to non-human animals or the environment, and they thus worry that there can be no obligation or responsibility in the Levinasian sense for animals or plant habitats. In accordance with this view is another that suspects Levinas's thought of being irredeemably humanist and anthropocentric and thus seriously limited for projects that want to extend moral consideration beyond the human. Other readers, even as they acknowledge the limitations of Levinas's own thinking on these issues, suggest that an extension of the notion of the face may indeed be possible, but only if we take Levinas's thought beyond the borders in which the author himself seems to have kept it. For both kinds of readers, however, the working premise is the same. Roughly put, they suggest that without an encounter with animals or the environment face-to-face, there can be no responsibility for the non-human other. For this reason, it is crucial for these accounts to know who can face me or with whom or what I can be face-to-face, and this is, indeed, the principal question they raise.

In what follows, the discussion turns first to a set of criticisms advanced by John Llewelyn, David Wood, Jacques Derrida, and others who worry about the humanism and anthropocentrism of Levinas's account, generally following the first path described above. The essay then looks to the work of Edward Casey and Alphonso Lingis for two accounts that, still deeply critical of Levinas, nonetheless appropriate a recognizably Levinasian ethics in the name of environmental concerns. Finally, I argue for viewing these same issues as political questions in Levinas's sense and suggest that they can be treated as ethical ones only so long as we cling to the misunderstanding that the face is a cause of obligation. Relying on the account of the face established in preceding chapters, I suggest that the face does not *create* value nor is it the *recognition* of a value. To think of the face as something that has value, or to think of the other who faces me as asserting his value or worth, is to paint Levinas as a substantive realist about ethics—a picture he would rightly oppose. On the reading developed here, the ethical mode in which the other faces me opens the possibility of valuing without itself existing *as* a value. Whatever does this work, I will suggest, can be or have a face. This interpretation has the advantage that it leaves room for animals to face us in some respects, but at the same time it avoids one particularly misleading way of understanding the face that lies beneath much of the current discussion of Levinas and questions of environmental ethics.

Animal Others

One of the first to raise the issue of Levinas and the animal other, John Llewelyn offers what is still its clearest expression. "Who is my neighbor?" Llewelyn asks. Does neighborliness, with all it implies of moral consideration, extend to every and any human being? Only to human beings? To God? To non-human animals? Llewelyn argues that the question of animal others must be a live one for anyone who eschews the climate of utilitarian calculation but is nonetheless attracted by utilitarianism's requirement that "consideration be given to the welfare of *any* sentient being" (Llewelyn 1991a, 234). With respect to animals, Llewelyn suggests that Bentham got it right when he wrote: "The question is not, Can they reason? nor Can they *talk?* but *Can they suffer?*"[1] And since they patently *do* suffer, Llewelyn is interested in the ethical significance that can be assigned to such suffering from a Levinasian perspective.

Dissatisfied with what he finds in Levinas's philosophy in this regard, Llewelyn comments: "In the metaphysical ethics of Levinas I can have direct responsibilities only toward beings that can speak, and this means beings that have a rationality that is presupposed by the universalizing reason fundamental in the metaphysics of ethics of Kant" (Llewelyn 1991a, 241).

On Llewelyn's reading of Levinas, since animals lack language, they are judged to lack reason. And as irrational or non-rational beings, they are outside the scope of our moral concern; or, at least, they do not make ethical demands on us in the same way as human beings.

Central to the establishment of this conclusion is Llewelyn's reading of the story of Bobby, a dog that strayed into the German camp for Jewish prisoners where Levinas was held during the war. In an essay originally written in tribute to Bram Van Velde, and later republished in *Difficult Freedom*, Levinas contrasts the behavior of this stray dog to the "free" men, women, and children who had dealings with the prisoners in the camp. The human beings, on Levinas's recounting, failed altogether to recognize the men in the camp as fellow human beings, and as such effectively "stripped" them of their "human skins" (*DF* 150–51). Bobby, meanwhile, greeted the prisoners with wagging tail and delighted bark when they appeared at morning assembly, and again as they returned from work details in the evening (*DF* 153). "For him," Levinas writes, "there was no doubt that we were men" (*DF* 153). Levinas adds, "This dog was the last Kantian in Nazi Germany, without the brain needed to universalize maxims and drives" (*DF* 153). Llewelyn concludes that though Levinas seems to be lauding the dog's behavior by calling him a Kantian, the implication, in fact, is that the dog is "too stupid, *trop bête*" (Llewelyn 1991a, 236; the French is Llewelyn's, not Levinas's) to be what he seems to be. "Bobby is without *logos* and that is why he is without ethics. Therefore he is without Kantian ethics; and so he is without Levinasian ethics, since the ethics of Emmanuel Levinas is analogous to the ethics of Immanuel Kant in that each is an ethics with a God within the limits of reason alone, but without a dog or any other beast except indirectly, if we are to judge by reason alone" (ibid.).

Now there is undoubtedly a Kantian stripe to Levinas's thought: Kant and Levinas both give ethics primacy within the overarching structure of philosophy, and each is centrally concerned with ethical life as the expression of human dignity.[2] But Levinas and Kant differ at just the point where Llewelyn credits them not only with similarity but identity. Even if both think that ethical life expresses the highest dignity possible for human beings, this dignity for Kant is a function of the capacity for reason and thus for a moral will, but, *contra* Llewelyn, Levinas's is not a philosophy in which some quality or capacity, no matter how important or distinctive, is that in virtue of which I am responsible to or for an other. Indeed, it is for this same reason that suffering—even though it has a role to play in Levinas's rethinking of the ethical—cannot have the *same* role that it would in a utilitarian moral theory. For Kantian moral theory, what matters about us is reason, that in virtue of which we are most godlike; for utilitarianism, what matters is that we are sentient and this puts us in ethical proximity to a whole range of non-human animals; for Levinas, what matters is not at all a *what* but a *who*: an absolutely incalculable other who cannot be reduced to some subset of properties and who is not worthy of ethical or moral consideration only in virtue of certain qualities or capacities—whether they be reason, language, a capacity to suffer, or anything else. Alterity is not a property on Levinas's view; nor is it something one has or enjoys by virtue of having other properties, such as a capacity for language. The line that Llewelyn reads as a claim about the dog's stupidity and consequent failure to meet the requirements for moral agency or moral worth may also be read as saying that the dog is a Kantian (which is to say, *is ethical*) *despite* Kant's own limited view of what could make one so. The human beings who ordered the prisoners to work, or who simply passed them coming and going in the streets, failed to be ethical and had no excuse for it since all possessed the modicum of reason that is a necessary condition of moral willing on Kant's view. The dog, even without reason, managed to do more and do better ethically speaking. The point of the story is then that reason may not be what makes you ethical, and that acknowledgment of the other *as such* or as a being who counts outside of every calculus and schema *is*.

Though I disagree with Llewelyn's reading of the case of Bobby, his essay ends with a question fundamental for any reader of Levinas. Going beyond the question of whether one can be face-to-face with a dog or other non-human animals, Llewelyn asks what it means to be "face-to-face" at all—that is, *What is it that the face says or does or requires of me?* In the absence of a criterion like sentience or a capacity to suffer, Llewelyn wonders what underwrites the authority of moral claims when they tell us that we *must* do this or must *cease* doing that. If the face is the moral authority *par excellence* in Levinas's thought, what stands behind this authority? Though Levinas explicitly denies that the God of the Jewish Bible stands in this relation to the face, Llewelyn is skeptical. He asks first how the other says anything at all, that is, how does the face command? But, just as crucially, Llewelyn asks, given the absence of constraints imported from positive religion (and he wonders what would justify our choosing one such religion over another), how can the face be prevented from saying "*anything whatsoever*" (244)? In other words, absent criteria that specify just what makes the other an obligatory object of my moral concern, it is difficult to discern what the substantive content of my obligation could be. If I must attend to the other because she suffers, then relieving suffering will be my task and responsibility. If the other commands me as a rational being with ends, then what is obligatory is that I treat humanity in myself and others always as an end and never only as a means. But if nothing and no one is that *by which* or *in virtue of which* a face commands, then how can the content of obligation be determined?

In an interview with Levinas roughly contemporaneous with Llewelyn's essay,[3] Tamra Wright, Peter Hughes, and Alison Ainley (at the time, graduate students at the University of Warwick) pursue a line of investigation similar to Llewelyn's and press Levinas on a number of similar points. Specifically, they want to know whether it is necessary to have the potential for language in order to be a face in Levinas's sense and whether it would be possible to "enlarge" the phenomenology of the face to include non-human faces. With respect to the latter, the interviewers explicitly raise a point akin to Llewelyn's and ask "where" obligations toward non-human animals might come from, on Levinas's view, if such animals are held to lack faces.

Levinas's reply to these questions is oddly hesitant and maddeningly indirect. Asked first about the distinctiveness of the human face, he responds, "One cannot entirely refuse the face of an animal. It is via the face that one understands, for example, a dog" (Wright, Hughes, and Ainley 1988, 169). This suggests that the dog *may* indeed have a face, but this suggestion is undercut moments later when Levinas remarks, "The priority is not found in the animal, but in the human face" (ibid.). Asked about language and the face—"Is it necessary to have the potential for language in order to be a 'face' in the ethical sense?"—Levinas responds that what is essential about the face in his view is its frailty, a frailty that is so superlatively weak that it becomes a demand, an "authority" (ibid.). An earlier response distinguishes this authority from a physical force, thus suggesting that he means a moral or ethical authority (169–70). The question about language returns when Levinas is asked a second time, "Is it necessary to possess the possibility of speech to be a 'face' in the ethical sense?" (171). The reply again is uncertain: "I cannot say at what moment you have the right to be called 'face'" (ibid.). He adds, a moment later, that in comparison to an animal the human face is "completely different and only afterward [i.e., after the encounter with a human face] do we discover the face of an animal" (ibid.). Yet another hesitation is expressed when he adds, "I don't know if a snake has a face" (ibid.). Asked about an enlarged phenomenology of the face, we hear more indecision: "I am not at all sure that the face is a phenomenon" (ibid.).

Though we might conclude from Levinas's remarks in this interview that the dog *does* have a face of some sort, it cannot be said whether that canine face expresses the moral commandment "Thou shalt not kill." Moreover, the snake is worse off, insofar as Levinas seems unsure whether it even *has* a face in any relevant sense. Moreover, he evinces hesitation about just what a "face" *is* or by what criteria it would be known.[4] Llewelyn's question—Who is my neighbor?—returns full force. How far and to whom can moral standing be attributed on a Levinasian view?

David Wood gives one possible answer to this question when he writes that Levinas, that "thinker of otherness, of the most radical alterity, of the unassimilability of the Other, can accommodate the animal only by analogy with the human being" (Wood 1999, 19). Wood's reading urges us to see Levinas's hesitation about the dog and his quandary about the snake as expressing an uncertainty about how far the analogy with human faces or human forms of life extends in these cases. Since the similarity to human beings is stronger in the case of the dog, Levinas is more certain that dogs have faces. When it comes to reptiles, the similarities are much less evident and Levinas becomes correspondingly unsure. I think Levinas's hesitation can be given a different reading, but let me first turn more fully to the charge of humanism.

Levinas's Humanism

Whereas Llewelyn and the Warwick graduate students are primarily concerned about the criteria governing ethical obligation and about the warrant behind the commandment "Thou shalt not kill," Wood's comment suggests that whatever the criterion might turn out to be, it will make sense only within the framework of a now discredited humanism. Derrida pursues a similar line in an interview with Jean-Luc Nancy, when he suggests that despite disrupting a "certain traditional humanism," Levinas's thought remains profoundly humanistic because it fails to "sacrifice sacrifice"; that is, it is never a question in Levinas's thought of forbidding an attempt on life in general, only on the life of another human being (Derrida says "another man") (Derrida 1991b, 113). Derrida's purpose is not to urge us to vegetarianism (which, he says, he might also want to do[5]) but to confront the manner in which dominant schemas of subjectivity and of the undoing or surpassing of subjectivity in Western philosophy, no matter how they have differed, have generally shared common ground in presupposing a discernible and untroubled distinction between the human and the non-human. Further, he suggests that they have shared a particular "sacrificial" structure in which subjects (even postmodern ones, even *Dasein* and its descendants) are idealized as masters with authority and autonomy over all that is conceived as non-subject (or non-human, sub-human, not fully human). Acknowledging that he is moving quickly in the somewhat informal context of an interview, Derrida makes the point this way:

Authority and autonomy . . . are, through this schema, attributed to the man (*homo* and *vir*) rather than to the woman, and to the woman rather than to the animal. And of course to the adult rather than to the child. The virile strength of the adult male, the father, husband, or brother . . . belongs to the schema that dominates the concept of subject. The subject does not want just to master and possess nature actively. In our cultures, he accepts sacrifice and eats flesh. (114)

Derrida's interest here might be described as an interest in the virility of modern Western subjects, and what no doubt attracts him to Levinas's thought is the way in which it introduces a certain passivity and end to virility into its conception of subjectivity.[6] Derrida's criticism, however, is that despite the emphasis on subjectivity as a relation to the other that puts an end to the subject's appropriative power, the other who enacts this relationship is never conceived as anything other than another human being. Human beings are still accorded not just a place of privilege but one of exclusive power to control the exercise of power. It is seemingly only the *human* other who has the power—even if it is inscribed as the "resistance of what has no resistance" (*TI* 199)—to put an end to the power claimed by the virile ego whose motto is "I can." This would be the lingering human-ism of Levinas's *humanisme de l'autre homme*.[7]

A second concern is tied to this. If it is the case that there can be no untroubled opposition between human and non-human, if this binary, like all the binarisms with which Derrida's work deals, can be continually deconstructed, then appropriation of the other—human and non-human alike—is inevitable. The ethical question is not do I or should I or have I eaten the other (for Derrida, one always *does*, one always *has,* and thus the question *should I* comes too late). The question, as Derrida puts it with characteristic rhetorical flair, is not *whether* to eat the other, but how to *eat well.* How to appropriate the other in a spirit of gift rather than sacrifice: "The moral question is thus not, nor has it ever been: should one eat or not eat, eat this and not that, the living or the nonliving, man or animal, but since *one must* eat in any case . . . *how* for goodness sake should one *eat well* (*bien manger*)?" (Derrida 1991b, 115). In an extended commentary on Derrida's recent writings on animal others, Carey Wolfe implies that what we learn from Derrida is that any ethics that depends on an unbridgeable distance or distinction between the human and the animal to accomplish its ethical aims does so at the risk of having this distinction come undone and its ethical position opened to a charge of speciesism (ibid.).[8] Wolfe contends that Levinas's philosophy is a case in point. In Levinas's thought, he argues, the emphasis on pure alterity ends up re-containing difference within identity, operating in a way that creates inclusion within an ethical community through exclusion: "The ethical status of the 'community at large' is purchased at the expense of the sacrifice of all forms of difference that are not human—most pointedly, of course, the animal" (ibid.).

The charges of humanism raised in Wood's and Derrida's work and the concomitant charge of speciesism raised by Wolfe are serious, but once again the charge that Levinas generates an obligation or responsibility to other humans *at the expense of* or through a sacrifice of animal others can be answered only if we know how the face generates obligations on the Levi-nasian account. That there is a shared misunderstanding on this point be-tween those who criticize Levinas's ethics as humanist or anthropocentric and those who see a way of moving beyond this limitation in his thought is a central thesis of this chapter. To see this, the discussion turns now to two approaches that appropriate important dimensions of Levinas's ethics in the name of environmentalism, but that also deliver serious criticism on the score of Levinas's own failure to extend his thought in this direction.

The Environing World

Edward Casey articulates the difficulty in extending Levinas's thought in an environmental direction in his "Taking a Glance at the Environing World":

It seems that either there is nothing like a face in the environment . . . or the face is all over the place: in which case, its meaning will be so diluted as to risk losing its ethical urgency. This is the kind of ethical dilemma into which Levinas, no less than Kant before him, puts us: either the face is strictly human (and then no ethics of the larger environment is possible) or it is part of a decidedly non-ethical totality called "life" or "nature." Otherwise put: ethics is human or does not exist at all. But this rigid choice gets us nowhere when we want to consider right and good action in the non-human world that includes us but much else of value besides. (Casey 2000, 11)

Casey seemingly overlooks a possible way around this dilemma, namely, that while there can be no ethics of the environment in Levinas, there may be political obligations in force in the environmental domain. Questions such as "Is it right to log old growth forests?" or "Would it be a good thing to build a water treatment plant here even if it eliminates a natural wetlands?" would be, I will argue below, *political* questions of the same order as others that require us to adjudicate between conflicting interests.

A revealing difficulty in Casey's presentation of the dilemma concerns the account of ethical force it implies. Casey worries that if the notion of a face is restricted to human faces, then we can have obligations only to human beings; this mirrors the Warwick students' question about where obligations to animals can come from if they are denied the status of faces or of beings who face me. Neither Casey nor Levinas's interviewers say explicitly that they understand the face as a *cause* of obligation or ethical responsibility, but their suggestion that without an animal face we are bereft of responsibilities to animals suggests a relationship that works very much as we tend to think causal relationships do. Where an antecedent cause is lacking, then so too is its effect (presuming a univocal cause).[9]

But the face simply does not work like this, and the picture of a one-to-one correspondence between the face as the source of normativity and our specific responsibilities needs to be challenged. To put it as plainly as possible, it simply is not the case that without an animal face we will have no responsibility to or for animals.

The search for a substitute for the face (though *not* a face analogue) is central to Casey's larger project. To be sure, the point is not to make of nature as a whole a kind of analogue for the face, since to do so is surely to anthropomorphize nature and thus fail precisely in the stated aim of respecting the alterity of the environment (Casey 2000, 12). Such a move also invites insoluble problems of "analogical apperception" in Husserl's sense (ibid.). Instead, Casey accords the *structural role* of face to the "place-world."[10] His idea is not that the place-world is a face, but that existing in a place-world is that which is fundamental to and equally shared by all entities and thus is that in virtue of which all are equally deserving of moral consideration. In effect, Casey changes the criteria for moral consideration from "a capacity to suffer" to "exists in a place-world." He writes, "There is . . . a long line of thought that ties together ethics and place in the West," citing the fact that the Greek word for ethics, *ethos*, has its origin in a word that in Homer's time meant "animal habitat," or "the place where animals such as wild horses characteristically settled down at night" (ibid.). But isn't Levinas's ethics meant precisely as an uprooting of this (Heideggerian) notion of ethos and place? of "my place in the sun"?

While we may grant the importance of the notion of habitat, or "place-worlds," for any consideration of our relation to the environment, is there a compelling reason to follow Casey in saying that place-worlds are *sources* of normative or ethical *force*? What is it about a place-world that commands me? Is a place-world *sufficient* to issue a command? Casey himself doubts that it is, and suggests that even if "place-worlds are the ultimate source of ethical force in the environmental field," the theory still needs "something more specific" to anchor an ethical imperative regarding the environment (13).[11] The worry is illuminating: it expresses the desire to discover an imperative that would make us have the right sort of sentiment about the environment.

Casey doesn't want us simply to care about the environment or to be obligated to protect place-worlds, he want us to care about them *for their own sakes* and not, for example, only for the sake of future generations of human beings whose lives will be healthier and richer for being lived on a planet with maximal biodiversity. This is perhaps one reason why Levinas matters to Casey's interest in the environment, and why, despite the residual humanism of Levinas's account, Casey is interested in developing a more or less recognizably *Levinasian* environmental ethics. Levinas wants us to care about other human beings, neither because it serves our interests to do so, nor because we recognize the other as being sufficiently like ourselves to merit equal treatment, nor because we have a natural sympathy for others. Rather, Levinas wants us to feel ourselves bound by responsibility for the other *because of the other,* or *for the sake of the other* in his or her irreducible alterity and singularity. It is the singularity of every creature and every specific habitat that an environmental ethics like Casey's urges upon our attention. Levinas is seemingly an ally for such views because he appears to want us not only to have the right obligations but to have them for the right reasons (a formal feature that his ethics shares with Kant's).

This is ultimately why Casey and others are tempted by the causal account of the face. When Levinas says that access to the face is *immediately* ethical, the assumption is that the face directly binds me to responsibility *for the other.* I will argue momentarily that this sort of directness is not necessarily there in Levinas's own account. Before doing so, it may be helpful to sketch the consequences of such a direct, causally produced response or responsibility as they unfold in Casey's essay.

Casey avers that the ethical significance of environmental place-worlds is obvious or discernible "in a glance." We are surrounded by surfaces and see our environment (as do animals) primarily as illuminated surfaces, says Casey, following the analyses of James J. Gibson. And "if vision plays a central role in ethics as I have argued earlier, then the perception of surfaces will be central in this life. We pick up distress . . . *directly from the surface*" (Casey 2000, 14). What spurs an ethics of the environment is "the direct presentation of environmental distress" (15). Casey gives the example of seeing a logged mountainside and taking in at a glance, or "sensing," the disorder and unethical character of what happened: "Nor did I need to have further evidence: the decisive and compelling evidence was before me, etched in the distress of the land. (Part of the distress was the loss of natural beauty; but the larger part was the elimination of whole groves of freestanding trees, the loss of their lives, their place in the biotic field.)" (17). Casey gives another example of taking in an ethical wrong "at a glance" when he describes the autobiographical experience of seeing a man beat a woman by repeatedly striking her head against a car (5). Acknowledging that he might have been risking his own safety and making the woman's situation worse rather than better by intervening, the theoretically salient point for Casey is that he saw *at a glance* and *in a glance* that something was wrong: "I saw injustice occurring; I saw immediately that things were not right in that street scene" (5).

It is hard to quibble with the example, but suppose that instead of a beating, Casey had seen a woman in a short skirt leaning against a doorway. And suppose he saw a car drive up and a man lean over from the driver's side to engage her in conversation. Suppose she gets in the car and they drive away. What would have been obvious then from his ethical standpoint? What would he have taken in "at a glance"? The examples Casey gives are tailor-made for his point, but if we complicate the example even slightly the theoretical outcome is much less obvious.

Certainly perception is a part of ethical life, and not only in the sense in which it is a part of life and action in general. But can we assume an untutored and naturalized vision that opens up a moral terrain? Can we assume that our glances and what they "take in" are not, in fact, shaped by social and political structures that often remain largely invisible to us? Isn't there an education or disciplining of vision every bit as effective at producing docile glances as it is at producing docile bodies? That there is seems undeniable when one gives even the most cursory consideration to changed attitudes about race and gender over the last hundred years. At the turn of the twentieth century, for example, interracial marriages *looked* unnatural and unethical to bigots and racists, much as the very sight of two women or two men standing up to be married seems obviously and *apparently* "wrong" to those on today's religious right. Casey's view risks thinking that we can know the difference between right and wrong or good and bad *at a glance*, thereby seemingly descending into a form of ethical intuitionism or naturalism that risks being nothing more than an uncritical affirmation of some heart's desire.

This has important implications for the question about the face. It is certainly true that Levinas says that the face appeals to me without the mediation of concepts, and that access to the face is immediately ethical. But is this to be understood as "makes my responsibility directly evident to me"? Do we read our responsibility off the surface of a face in just the way that Casey thinks we might read the wrongness of strip mining off the surface of the mountain? Patently not. The face is not a form; it doesn't give us anything we could read. Does it then directly address us? Again, Levinas says more than once that the face of the other *speaks* to me, and the words he most often puts in its mouth are "thou shalt not kill." The face seems directly to forbid us from killing it. It seems "evident" that this is what it requires of us. But can this be what Levinas means? How then do we reconcile this view with his claim, again made more than once, that the face of the other is not itself an evidence but is the evidence that makes evidence possible? In the same way, the face is not itself discourse but is the discourse that makes discourse possible. Below I will highlight the risks of reading Levinas too straightforwardly as a non-cognitivist about ethics— that is, I will suggest that if we read the face as something that tells us in a glance or in a word what to do or not do, we risk misunderstanding what is most fundamental about this key notion of Levinas's thought.

The Face and Practical Necessity

The question of the imperative force of the face is addressed even more directly by Alphonso Lingis as he considers Levinas's shortcomings as an environmental ethicist. In "Practical Necessity," Lingis, like Casey and others, takes Levinas to task for finding "the importance, urgency, and immediacy of a 'categorical' imperative only in the presence of another of [his own] species" (Lingis 1998, 76). Whereas Lingis wants to recognize the moral demands made on me by another human being as one specific case among others of practical necessity, Levinas, he says, sees such demands as the only possible kind of morally binding claim or ethical imperative. "And to find an imperative in the needs and wants of others of our species alone gravely misinterprets those needs and wants and that imperative itself" (ibid.).

Lingis's essay, like Casey's, relies heavily on selected examples to carry its point.[12] He imagines finding a lit cigarette in the forest or coming upon an animal in distress: "Strolling in the sequoia forest, I come upon a discarded, still smoldering, cigarette-butt in the dry leaves. I am here, and what has to be done has to be done right away. But also *I* must do it—because I can. Running as I do each day in the forest, I have the strength, which the old couple who stopped me do not have, to free the deer caught in the branches of a tree in the flooding river" (72). Practical necessities are not just material or hypothetical imperatives of the sort "If I want to do *x*, I must do *y*," where *y* is the means to *x*. Practical necessities, on Lingis's view, are imperatives *simpliciter*: they "impose themselves independently of our desires and projects" (71). Following Bernard Williams, Lingis describes such necessities as coming about "when something of intrinsic importance is seen to be fragile and threatened, and exhibits to me what has to be done, and does so with immediacy and urgency" (71).

Again there is the emphasis on *seeing* and on the immediacy of the ethical command. Ironically, in Lingis's imagined example, the deer's appeal is not in fact made directly, but by proxy through the elderly couple who want to help it but cannot. It is *their* faces, *their* words that command the runner to stop and help. Likewise, there may be a mediating moment in the case of the smoldering cigarette in the woods; it will present itself as an appeal only to those who are aware that a single cigarette is enough to start a forest fire. For those of us who grew up with "Smokey the Bear" saying "Only you can prevent forest fires," the cigarette cannot but present itself as a practical necessity. But presumably this connection was one that needed to be *made* or it would not have been the focus of a long-running national advertising campaign. There is the presumption in Lingis's work, as in Casey's, that the ethical appeal is made directly or immediately, and that what it commands is something immediately relevant to the situation at hand. The deer doesn't command me to activist work against the sport of hunting or against encroachment on its territory from suburban sprawl; it commands me to save it from the immediate peril of drowning. The cigarette is there to be put out (to say that it commands this or that the grove of trees commands this would surely be a case of anthropomorphizing nature).

The difference between a practical necessity in Lingis's sense and ethical demand in Levinas's is highlighted by returning to Levinas's remarks in the interview with the three graduate students at the University of Warwick: "There are two strange things in the face: [on the one hand,] its extreme frailty—the fact of being without means and, on the other hand, there is authority. It is as if God spoke through the face.[13] . . . For me, these two starting points are essential: the idea of extreme frailty, of demand, that the other is poor. It is worse than weakness, the superlative of weakness. He is so weak that he demands" (Wright, Hughes, and Ainley 1988, 169–70). This connection between frailty and height is crucial to Lingis's analysis, as he suggests that there is no reason to limit this fragility "so frail that it demands" to humans or even animals. The sequoia trees, on his view, are vulnerable and also have height (the pun being inevitable, even if unintended). The grove in which they stand is a unique environment, unable to be easily replicated elsewhere simply because of the time it takes for the trees to achieve their majestic canopy. This majesty (a gloss on Lingis's "intrinsic importance"), combined with the trees' inability to protect themselves from human logging, accidental destruction by fire, or from the (human) introduction of some other sort of imbalance to their ecosystem, makes the old grove sequoias seem exactly like the sorts of things in nature that could make an *appeal* or issue an imperative—that would be fragile and threatened in just the sense Lingis's notion of practical necessity spells out.[14]

Is this proposal to extend the Levinasian notion of the face or facing able to avoid the twin charges of humanism and anthropocentrism any better than Levinas's own? Lingis certainly goes further than Levinas in attributing alterity to non-human beings, but doesn't the determination of practical necessity in his account depend in every case on human perceptions, human needs, and human measurements? Isn't an ethics of practical necessities every bit as humanistic and anthropocentric as Levinas's?

The suggestion that alterity of any sort whatsoever is capable of commanding me ethically in just the way that human alterity commands me is problematic in several respects. First, it is unclear how Lingis's account avoids the charge that his, too, is an ethics based on analogy. Our ability to see or feel the deer's distress depends on our recognizing its bodily postures as similar to those of distressed humans and other animals. It is only because we can recognize the signs of its distress that we say that the deer makes some kind of appeal. In the case of dogs and cats, too, we tend to think that we have obligations to care for them and treat them lovingly, not only because we have accepted the responsibilities of being a pet owner but also because we are keenly aware of their need for care and love and of the care and love they are able to give in return. Their modes of indicating their needs and affection are not so different from our own, and especially those of young children. The case is somewhat different with pet turtles, snakes, spiders, and fish. Their fascination for us is not, I would venture, linked to reciprocally affective connections. Indeed, the lack of such connections may be one argument against keeping such animals as pets, since to do so is simply to maintain them in captivity for our own purposes and pleasures.

A perceived analogy between human responses and those of some animals is not necessarily a good basis for an animal or environmental ethics for numerous reasons. Analogy may simply be too weak to generate general obligations of the right kind and scope. Analogy gives an appearance of obviousness that may crumble upon reflection or due to a sustained attack over time on that way of "seeing" things. And as many have pointed out, seeing analogies between animal lives and our own does not prevent most people from eating animal flesh on a regular basis. An obligation fundamentally dependent on our capacity to see analogies will seem to some far too reliant on human good will and on established practices to be an adequate foundation for a critical environmental ethics (Benso 2000, xxxviii).

The analogical route also makes the question of the scope of responsibility difficult to answer. On such a view, I might be responsible to some life forms (e.g., large mammals, birds, some larger species of reptiles, perhaps) whose similarities to human beings I can perceive. (And even here the question will be what sorts of similarities I take to be relevant.) But where I can see no relevant similarity, only use-value (e.g., with insects or plants), an analogy-based ethics would have to admit that obligation here is of a different kind. To be sure, I might still care for insects or plants, either because they are useful to me or to other larger animals, and I may even think that I have moral obligations with regard to them on this account, but this was already true of the larger animals themselves in relation to human interests and lives, so it is hardly very compelling as a subsidiary argument and seems to leave large environmental populations at risk of being denied the status of being true ethical others. Moreover, if analogy is fundamental to moral considerability, responsibility would still be humanistic in orientation, since it gives priority to human modes of life in setting the relevant norms and, further, depends on human capacities to recognize relevant sorts of distress, need, etc.[15] This sort of account of moral obligation is at risk of raising the familiar specters of the skeptic and the moral monster, the former claiming to be unable to see signs of distress in enslaved fellow humans, in animals, in aquatic and plant habitats, and the latter actually unable to read them there.

To be fair, though Lingis's example of the deer may draw its rhetorical force from an analogy with human beings, the example of the sequoia grove seems designed to show that the appeal made by non-human ethical subjects would not be an appeal *by analogy*, and Lingis's invocation of Williams's notion of practical necessity is further support for a non-analogical reading. But, in fact, even if we can do away with an analogy to humans *per se*, it is not clear that the example of the sequoias does not still rely on a certain anthropocentrism. The sequoia grove appears majestic to us and seems to be "intrinsically important" because of the way it stands out in comparison to other groves of trees with which we (humans) are familiar. It may not be by analogy with human lives that we value such groves of trees, but their value has a distinct relation to human imagination and a human sense of the sublime. There are any number of unique habitats that are much less appealing to our aesthetic sense and that we might be less inclined or less likely to recognize when they appeal to us in their singularity and fragility. It is a truism in conservationist circles that it is easy to generate interest in and funds for programs that save mammals that are cute or cuddly, like baby harp seals, or those deemed to have human-like intelligence, in the way that dolphins and porpoises do. It is much harder to raise the required awareness and funds to save insects or small reptiles and the muggy, muddy swamps where they survive, even though they may be equally uniquely endangered. And even if we were able somehow to wean ourselves from human-centered modes of relating to the environment, the problem of scope—of how far to extend our responsibility to unique animals and habitats—would remain. Some kind of criteria would have to be developed. And even if we could develop such criteria and delimit the extension of those to whom we are responsible—and do so in a way that is self-aware about the possible humanism and speciesism of our criteria—won't there inevitably arise conflicts between the various beings and habitats to whom and to which I am responsible? How do I choose between the lion and its prey, or the deer and the natural environment it destroys? Since my every action draws on natural resources to some extent and impacts the environment in some fashion, how do I know where to draw the line and say that a certain action is impermissible?

These questions are reminiscent of those that Levinas raises as he imagines being confronted by two others, two faces that each demand of me an infinite responsibility. They also mirror his question "Is it righteous to be" when my life, my place in the sun inevitably involves denying this place to another? In the final sections of this chapter, I suggest that a Levinasian notion of *politics* may be a far more beneficial resource for thinking about environmental issues than an environmentalist extension of what Levinas says specifically about the *ethics* of the *face-to-face* relationship; and I want to consider what this means for how we should understand the *priority* that Levinas gives to human faces.

A Politics of the Environment

In *Otherwise Than Being, or Beyond Essence*, Levinas forges a close connection between the introduction of a third party (an other of the other who faces me) and the birth of politics as the critical adjudication of conflicting interests. He tells the following well-known story: if the ego and the other were alone in the world, the ethical relationship would have ordered the ego to a responsibility for the other alone and "there would not have been any problem, in even the most general sense of the term" (*OB* 157). The exclusive relation of infinite responsibility to and for the other "is troubled," however, "and becomes a problem" with the entrance of a third party (*OB* 157). The third is not just another other, one more of the same kind, but another uniquely singular being with a singular relation to the ego and also with a wholly different and singular relation to the first other. The third thus "becomes a problem" in the local or limited sense of presenting the ego with the dilemma of deciding whose claim to honor first. But, playing on the idea that there would not have been any problem without the third, Levinas contends that the "entrance" of the third is the entrance of *problems*, that is, of consciousness, self-consciousness, and conscience more generally, of the assessing, weighing, and judging that we associate with reflection and deliberation. The situation of the ego before multiple, unassimilable others who demand infinite responsibility is that it must begin to *think*, which is to say, to compare, order, assemble, thematize, make visible, represent as possible, desirable, impossible, undesirable, and so on. In a word, the third requires the ego to undertake the comparison of incomparables: "In the comparison of the incomparable there would be the latent birth of representation, logos, consciousness, work, the neutral notion *being*" (*OB* 158). And out of this representation, justice is born as the measuring of the relation of one to another, as the calculation that necessarily reduces the other to a quantum, to a weight or an interest that can be known and fairly assessed.

Levinas notes that the entry of third party is not an "empirical fact," and that responsibility for the other is thus not "constrained to a calculus by the 'force of things'" (*OB* 158). The third party or, as he says in *Totality and Infinity*, "the whole of humanity" (*TI* 213) already appeals to me or obsesses me in the face of the first other. As Adriaan Peperzak explains, "My responsibility for this other here and now who faces me is not confined to him or her; it does not have the clandestine and exclusive character of love and intimacy, but neither is it the application in this case of a general norm that would be valid for all the individual instances of the general class 'human beings,' whose equal rights would be due to their forming a community or having a common essence" (Peperzak 1993, 167). The ethical relationship, for Levinas, is constituted in such a way that I am already responsible to the other of my other, the other of my neighbor who is "another neighbor, and also a neighbor of the other, and not simply his fellow" (*OB* 157).

For Levinas, assessment and comparison is of the order of politics, not of the order of ethics. And with respect to environmental questions, it seems evident that they are calls to just this sort of activity. How, for example, do we compare the needs and interests of human beings against the needs and interests of non-human animals, of whole species of animals and plants, of habitats, and the like? Indeed, how do we determine what the relevant non-human sense of "need" and "interest" is when we begin to compare such true incomparables? On what basis and by what measure do we assess and weigh different courses of action, when any action to some extent depletes natural resources, displaces various animal, plant, and human populations, alters habitats, and, in short, has an effect on some environment? It seems to me that what Levinas describes under the heading of politics more exactly captures what we do when we begin to think about the complex relationship of human beings to the environment than anything he says about ethics per se.

Why then has the focus been on an environmental ethics? A tacit assumption of the positions canvassed above is that the ethical relation to a face is the direct source of specific obligations. This is why the question about the *priority* Levinas accords to the human face is an especially acute issue for his environmentally minded critics. If the link between the face and responsibility is direct, then it seems that a direct obligation to non-human animals or habitats can be produced only if one can show that there is something comparable to a face-to-face relation with such beings. This is also why readers like Wright, Hughes, and Ainley are so concerned with establishing the general criteria governing the application of the notion of a "face." If we can know what it is that makes something or someone a face, then we can reasonably ask whether that property is shared by other beings in a sufficient degree to consider them faces as well. (Alternately, we can challenge whether it is really *that* in virtue of which human beings command one another ethically—this is the strategy pursued by Casey and Lingis.) For Llewelyn and Lingis, Levinas appears to limit the application of the category "face" to animals who can *speak*, who have language, or *logos*. In another sense, this question of the criteria for establishing who is a "face" (i.e., who commands us or warrants our ethical attention) is also at issue for Derrida and Wolfe in their joint worry about Levinas's lingering humanism, though here the worry is as much about *what* the face commands as about *who* is doing the commanding. For all of these critics, the difficulty is that for Levinas it is seemingly *only* the human face that commands, and what it prohibits is *only* its own murder.

This is where I think it useful to return to Levinas's own hesitation about the face. How, we might ask, could Levinas *not know* whether the snake had a face? Why does he vacillate and say that the dog's face cannot be "entirely refused" but then suggest that it is nonetheless not the same as the human face or does not enjoy the same priority? What is the source, moreover, of his uncertainty, when he "cannot say" when someone has the "right" to be deemed a face, or when he is "not at all sure" that the face is a phenomenon? Is it that Levinas is unclear about the criteria for determining what (or who) counts as a face and what (or who) does not? Or is it that *the idea of criteria distinctly misses what is fundamental about the Levinasian notion of a face* in the first place?

It is not my aim to suggest that there are no criteria, no visible or discernible marks, by which we can tell a face from a non-face or one face from another. At times, Levinas's writing seems to suggest that this should be so—as, for example, when he says that the best way to see the face of the other is not even to notice the color of her eyes. Most often, however, Levinas suggests that the face is both perceptible and imperceptible, that it appears but is not reducible to its visual or perceptible form. It is a liminal figure, a structure that "undoes" its own form, "overflows" the determinate meaning that it nonetheless has, that is both open to my appropriating grasp and forever resisting that grasp with a "no" that has only "the resistance of what has no resistance." Levinas's account of the face suggests that ordinarily we are too ready to judge a book by its cover, or another human being by her face—that is, too quick to reduce the other to the various identity categories that we can "read" off of her face or glean from her biography. His philosophy contests this understanding which makes of the other one more object of knowledge—special perhaps in that this object has an "interior life" whose temporally extended structure makes it nigh-well impossible for us to follow along through all the twists and turns of its unfolding, but an object all the same that we could know in the same way as any other object given sufficient time and access. But while it is a mistake to think that his view is that the face of the other is entirely unknowable in the usual sense, as if we simply had no access to the other at all, it is equally problematic, however, to assimilate the exceptional presentation of the self in a face and the ethical commandment that translates this expression to something that we then *know* or that is incumbent on us or claims us in the same way as a belief or a knowledge claim.

Levinas speaks of the face as that which "can guarantee itself," and says that its manifestation (for which he commonly uses the very problematic term, "epiphany") "is somehow a word of honor" (*TI* 202). We have stressed in previous chapters the way in which his early writings emphasize that in the face the other is somehow given "in person" or in such a way as to be present but nothing else, as if one could be present without being graspable or presentable in general terms. These descriptions, which suggest a kind of immediacy, are often closely linked to others in which the face is portrayed as a kind of force, non-physical to be sure, but irresistible in its ethical appeal. Hence, the face is said to "impose itself," not as a kind of violence but as the promotion of my responsibility and freedom (*TI* 200); the expression of a face is the "discourse that obliges entering into discourse" (*TI* 201). It is that which "calls the ego into question"; what it commands—its "Thou shalt not kill"—is "ineluctable" (*TI* 200) and "leaves no logical place for its contradictory" (*TI* 201). In one of the densely textured passages in that crucial section of *Totality and Infinity* entitled "Ethics and the Face," we even read: "The face is the evidence that makes evidence possible—like the divine veracity that sustains Cartesian rationalism" (*TI* 204).[16]

Though it would be mistaken in my view to read Levinas as suggesting that language is a necessary precondition for an ethical relationship, or that it functions in Levinas's texts as a kind of litmus test picking out those to whom I am ethically responsible and cordoning them off from those to whom I am not,[17] Levinas's critics are right to press the question of whether Levinas presents the face as a kind of authority or guarantee. They are right, in other words, to press the questions of *how* I am faced by the other, of *who* can be an other, and of *what* responsibility demands of me. To bring together the lines of interpretation developed in preceding chapters and apply them to the question of animals and the environment is the task of the final section.

Command and Justification

What does it mean to be commanded by the "face of the other"? And can this face be an animal face or something in the environment that we do not ordinarily think of as a face at all? Consider again Levinas's response when pressed on just this question in the interview with the students from Warwick. The first thing he says is that "it is clear that, without considering animals as human beings, the ethical extends to all living beings" (Wright, Hughes, and Ainley 1988, 172). As he expands on this point, Levinas falls back onto a very ordinary view: animals can suffer; as human beings we know the torment of suffering; therefore, "We do not want to make an animal suffer needlessly and so on" (ibid.). Human ethics, he says, is the "prototype" for an extension of obligation to animals. This would seem to support the view that Levinas extends our *ethical responsibility* beyond the human only so far as he sees an analogy between human and animal suffering. But this view is inverted by the remainder of his answer, in which he argues that the human "breaks with pure being," thus breaks with a certain conception of nature as a systematic determination of beings in which each being strives only or primarily to maintain its own existence. "I do not know at what moment the human appears," Levinas says, "but what I want to emphasize is that the human breaks with pure being, which is always a persistence in being. This is my principal thesis" (ibid.). In relation to an animal world of instincts and interest, the human is "a new phenomenon" (ibid.).

In giving a more determinate and concrete sense of what is new in the advent of the human, Levinas speaks of saintliness:

With the appearance of the human—and this is my entire philosophy—there is something more important than my life, and that is the life of the other. That is unreasonable. Man is an unreasonable animal. Most of the time my life is dearer to me, most of the time one looks after oneself. But we cannot not admire saintliness. Not the sacred, but saintliness: that is, the person who in his being is more attached to the being of the other than to his own. I believe that it is in saintliness that the human begins; not in the accomplishment of saintliness, but in the value. It is the first value, an undeniable value. (Ibid.)

Saintliness is a manner of being which breaks with a supposedly natural desire to persist in one's being. It is the break with self-interest and self-regard in being more attached to the other than one is to oneself. The bearing of this text on the question of an environmental ethics initially seems to favor Levinas's critics. Put it this way: If a life like Sister Theresa's exhibits saintliness, why not also a life like that of Saint Francis of Assisi? Is the priority given to the human other in Levinas's account not just the last vestige of humanism and the same old speciesism decried by Singer and Wolfe alike? That is, is it not just as saintly to be more attached to the well-being of animals or place-worlds than to my own being? Couldn't we think of saintliness beyond the letter of Levinas's text as an ex-propriation of the self and its being in a being for *every* other, not just human others? This is what is urged by his critics (who are also, it must be acknowledged and remembered, some of his most sympathetic and long-standing readers).

What would it mean for the alterity of *every other* to command me? What sort of ethics would this be? There are two difficulties attendant on this reading of Levinas, neither of which may fully dissuade someone from this sort of reading, but both of which demand a response. Let me give the first worry the label *masochism*. What does it mean to be more attached to the singularity of dirt or a carrot than to one's own being? To the alterity of the other man when one is a woman? To the alterity of "whites" when one is "black"? If masochism has always threatened from the edges of Levinas's ethics, wouldn't this interpretation put it front and center? And as a result wouldn't this reading render Levinas's ethics a very exclusive and exclusionary ethics indeed, one that favors not just the human but only the most dominant humans at that? Wouldn't such an ethics be affordable only by the most dominant subjectivities, those whose egoism can be taken for granted? If Levinas's comments about saintliness are read in isolation, they do indeed tend to lead in this direction, and there may well be a danger for commentaries on Levinas that make much of this aspect of his thought without paying attention to the tension such a reading generates with other elements of his philosophy which are more decidedly interested in and of interest to marginalized, dispossessed, and oppressed peoples.

The second worry, already expressed in passing above, is a worry about *naturalism*. Why must we admire saintliness? If the only reason is that we naturally do, then Levinas's philosophy would be, like some caricatures of Hume, a philosophy that makes of ethics nothing more than a feeling (in Hume's case: sympathy). Levinas's philosophy would boil down to the claim that we simply do feel admiration for saintliness when we see it. But if this is the thrust of his work, and if admiration is simply to be regarded as a "fact" of our (human) moral life, then it seems that Levinas has abandoned the terrain of reason to offer us nothing but a biblically inspired non-cognitivism. The work of Lingis, Casey, Llewelyn, and others who want to expand the account of saintliness would then lie in a reeducation of our moral sentiments.[18] But, in effect, naturalism in ethics is as self-undermining as it is in logic. Naturalism as a moral theory says we ought to act in such and such a way simply because it is natural for us to do so. But this, in and of itself, is not a reason so long as it is possible to do otherwise than what our nature inclines us to do. And if we can do otherwise, then what is the purchase of saying something is natural? Indeed, strict ethical naturalism renounces the use of the term "ought" since it maintains that "questions of ethical justification can and should be replaced by questions about how in fact moral thinking works."[19] We need, perhaps, only mention the name of Foucault and the Nietzschean genealogical tradition to which he belongs to make the difficulties of any simple naturalism sufficiently apparent.[20] Levinas's thought becomes less vulnerable to the worries about masochism and naturalism if we understand him as committed to a humanism that is substantively different both from the humanism widely rejected in French thought from the late 1960s on and from the humanism *qua* speciesism that concerns Wolfe.

Why does Levinas give the human face priority? Not because he views humans as more intrinsically valuable than other beings, nor because he is simply accustomed to taking them and their concerns more seriously, but *because it is only in human society that it is possible to worry about justice for others*, human and animal others alike. The social relationship is, as Levinas's account of politics attests, the beginning of *problems*, that is, of questions that demand not just practical solutions but justifications that rise to the level of being reasons for the other as much as they are reasons for me. In addition to those passages where Levinas speaks of the value of saintliness, we need to remember those in which the face is quintessentially that which calls the ego into question and introduces into it both the demand for and the possibility of critique. This is the something "new" that the face of the other teaches me; this is the light that dawns in the face of the other. To respond to the face when it says "Thou shalt not kill" is not only not to kill the other but to put a check on my spontaneous freedom in the name of a world that is shared with others. It is to enter into a form of life in which practical necessities are not, in fact, the only sorts of necessities there are. This, I think, is where Levinas is truly a Kantian, because he sees our highest worth in the possibility of subordinating hypothetical and instrumental imperatives to something categorical. But this something, in his case, is not a principle or a faculty of Reason (or language-use), but the face-to-face relationship that makes rationality, understood as the demand to produce a justification, possible.

It may seem as if this reading attributes to the face a power—the ability to call the ego into question or to instigate critical reflection—and suggests that this power is uniquely human and uniquely valuable. Why is this alone uniquely valuable, we want to ask? And even more the issue for Levinas's environmentally minded readers (of which I hope I am also one), why is that which is uniquely valuable also held to be uniquely human? The answer to both questions is the same. What is distinctively human is the question itself. And what it means to say that the human face has priority is not to say that the human face is the highest good, but that the human face is that which demands anew that we justify and explain ourselves, that we give an account of our values and of how we apply them in practical situations. The priority of the face is not the priority of this "thing" (which, in any case, the face is *not*) but the priority of practices of critique understood as justification before the other and all the ever new others of the other.

If the dog or the snake or a place-world is secondary in terms of its role in opening up the critical dimension of human existing, this most certainly does not entail that such beings can only be secondary when it comes down to deciding what to save or whose interests to protect. Ethics opens up the world of politics, and opens it as a space in which we can be made aware of ever new others. These others cannot be given an ontological status in advance. It is because of scholars and activists, for example, that we become aware of the need to address the environment, aware that our current conceptual systems are too limited. It is in a *human* world that these things can matter and can matter *precisely for themselves* and not just because of their place in a system or because they serve a practical or instrumental purpose. To expropriate oneself from the center of one's own universe is to ask "Is it righteous to be?" and to worry about the way in which one's own use of natural resources depletes what is then available for others, whether they be plant or animal or human others, whether they be currently living or future generations. This question, Levinas wants to say, does not simply arise in the normal course of things, but is the meaning of what it means to be *in society*, to enter into a social relationship. It is in the political realm that there is justice for animal- and plant-worlds, and for the ego and for humans *tout court*. But it is the face that makes this questioning possible, that makes this demand for justice first intelligible and legible.

6

Failures of Recognition and the Recognition of Failure: Levinas and Identity Politics

The issue, then, is not who is or is not really whatever, but who can be counted on when they come for any one of us: The solid ground is not identity but . . . solidarity.

—NAOMI SCHEMAN

Levinas and the Failure of Recognition

In a recent essay, Sonia Sikka suggests that statements in Levinas's philosophy that betray a masculine and Eurocentric bias are more than regrettable lapses in judgment or unfortunate remnants of the times in which Levinas lived and wrote. She speculates "that an ethics emphasizing alterity and asymmetry, an ethics that deliberately refrains from imagining the Other as another like oneself, might contribute to a failure to recognize and respect [the] Other, and precisely in his or her very difference from oneself" (Sikka 2001, 115).

The problematic nature of Levinas's various descriptions of "the feminine" other are well known,[1] and presented succinctly by Sikka. Feminine alterities are invoked in Levinas's works almost exclusively in erotic, maternal, and domestic contexts. As homemaker (*TI* 155–57) and welcoming womb (*OB* 75), the feminine other is extolled as a paradigm of selfless being for others; as the beloved of a male lover, the feminine other is identified with an "incessant recommencement" of virginity (*TI* 258), but also with animality (*TI* 259), indecency (*TI* 260), wantonness (*TI* 261), and lasciviousness (*TI* 263). In early works, the feminine other is described as a "mystery" and an "enigma" who does not speak (*TO* 75); in later works, her speech is said to be equivocal, dissimulating, and nonsignifying (*TI* 264). In almost every instance where a feminine other appears in Levinas's thought, her existence seems defined in light of masculine needs, desires, and experiences. Reviewing this rather sorry state of affairs, Sikka is inclined to agree with Craig Vasey that Levinas's description of feminine alterity "seems fairly straightforwardly an expression of good old-fashioned masculine privilege and arrogance."[2]

Levinas fares no better when it comes to issues of multiculturalism, and Sikka's essay again provides a ready overview of his missteps on this terrain. Arguing that Levinas's thought evinces a "distinct failure genuinely to encounter the other," Sikka is understandably disappointed by both the substance and tone of Levinas's seemingly offhand remarks about non-Western traditions (Sikka 2001, 113). Citing his comment that "I always say—but privately—that in humanity the only serious things are the Greeks and the Bible; everything else is dancing," Sikka recounts Levinas's observation that the South African custom of dancing at the funerals of the dead "gives the impression of a dancing civilization."[3] Likewise, she cites his remark—paraphrasing an aggadic text, to be sure, but without distancing himself from the view expressed there—that "everything" that comes to us from India and China is "idolatry" (*NTR* 176). Though Sikka herself does not do so, others have noted similar failures to respond fully or adequately to questions about the Palestinian other.[4]

Sikka's critique draws its inspiration from Levinas's two most prominent feminist readers, Simone de Beauvoir and Luce Irigaray. Following Beauvoir, and conforming to the tradition of equality feminism, Sikka accuses Levinas of failing to accord woman the status of a fully equal subject. Levinas, she writes, "fails to imagine this [feminine] Other as another like himself. He fails to recognize her as a subject, and to constitute her alterity on the basis of this recognition" (Sikka 2001, 105). At a minimum, Sikka argues, feminism demands of men that they not "constitute women within the horizon projected by their own desires"; men should see women "more as they [men] see themselves and other men, at least to the point of acknowledging that women, too, look out at the world rather than merely being looked at, that they, too, desire rather than being merely desired, that they, too, speak rather than being merely spoken about, that they, too, are individuals with differing characteristics rather than a homogenous group possessing a simple and common essence" (104). Sikka insists that women are active, desiring, speaking subjects, and recognition of this must be the starting point for an ethics or politics committed to recognizing and validating the other. This principle is generalized beyond the case of women at the end of the essay, when Sikka writes, "Recognition will . . . begin by imagining the Other to be another like oneself—a subject, for instance— but can proceed, upon this basis, to take dissimilarity into account, and to respect it" (116).

In a second strand of the essay, following Irigaray rather than Beauvoir and emphasizing difference rather than equality, Sikka puzzles over the ironies of a philosophy that "claims to be based on difference, [but] is in another sense indifferent to difference" (115). Levinas famously says that the best way to "see" the face of the other is not even to notice the color of the other's eyes (*IR* 49, 135). Does this indicate an ethics indifferent to such specific differences as those of sexual difference, race, ethnicity, or nationality, Sikka wonders? It does, she concludes, and she faults Levinas for failing to encounter the other in her "genuine" difference (Sikka 2001, 114). Feminine and non-Western others tend to appear in Levinas's texts not as they are for themselves but as the phantasmatic projections of a masculine, Western ego: for Levinas, as already noted, women are imagined almost exclusively in the domains of sexuality, domesticity, and maternity;[5] Africans figure as dancing children who do not yet know the seriousness of adult pursuits or emotions. In the name of her own identity, "which includes being female, Asian, and Hindu," Sikka accuses Levinas of "the same old imperialism, the same old absence of hospitality towards the foreigner, lacking even the decency to suspend judgment when faced with one who is unknown" (114).

Sikka concludes with the reflection that projects seeking justice for those who have been rendered other by contemporary society will not be well served by the Levinasian notion of radical alterity which refuses to represent the other and thereby seemingly refuses that other representation within moral and civic life. Justice in such cases will be better served, she says, "by the grammar of 'recognition' (*reconnaissance*) even with all of its attendant difficulties" (116).

Now, Sikka is surely right that Levinas's record on these issues is not just spotty but amounts to a pattern of chauvinist and ethnocentric thinking. There can be little doubt that Levinas's others (women, non-Westerners, non-monotheists) are misrecognized and their lives distorted in fundamental ways by his remarks. Equally undeniable is the claim that these "others" most certainly experience themselves as subjects and have every right to demand that the validity of their self-conceptions be respected and recognized. But is Sikka right to link these attitudes directly to the notion of absolute alterity, and specifically to Levinas's claim that the other with whom one is in an ethical relationship defies representation? Moreover, need we follow her in preferring identity-based politics and the language of recognition to a Levinasian-inspired alterity politics?[6]

I begin with some reflections on the conflict between equality and difference in Sikka's criticism in order to move to a broader consideration of the compatibility between Levinas's philosophy and the concerns of New Left social movements. Where Sikka sees an incompatibility between Levinas's ethics of absolute alterity and twentieth-century struggles on behalf of particular subordinated or oppressed identities, I argue that if we understand his conception of alterity as a reference to the singularity rather than the difference of the other, his ethics is not only compatible with the emancipatory aims of progressive politics, but helps us move beyond the limitations of contemporary forms of identity-based politics.

The Equality/Difference Dilemma

It is not clear how to reconcile the discourses of equality and difference as they occur in Sikka's text. On the one hand, Sikka asserts that feminism requires men to view women as they (men) view themselves—that is, as universal subjects. On the other hand, she complains that Levinas's others are never encountered in their "genuine" difference. The call for a universally shared conception of subjectivity suggests that subjective experience can be theorized (and perhaps lived) in abstraction from cultural and historical contexts. By contrast, the insight about Levinas's specific misrecognition of various others is more in line with the view of standpoint theorists,[7] who argue that given subject positions cannot be rendered epistemologically or existentially transparent to those who stand elsewhere. If the latter claim has merit, then asking men to see women through the lens of masculine subjectivity will not only not correct for the kinds of distortions endemic in Levinas's writings on femininity, but may well increase their likelihood.

Relatedly, it is unclear how deep Sikka thinks differences go. Though her essay is ostensibly motivated by the desire for an ethics and politics capable of doing justice to difference, and though the differences she writes about are above all those that have been the concern of multiculturalist identity politics, her ultimate plea appears to be for a politics that begins from a recognition of sameness. Though she does not put it quite this way herself, Sikka appears to be saying that because Levinas fails to accord to the other the same sort of subjectivity that he claims or assumes for himself, he fails to recognize that the other's cultural and religious traditions are meaningful for her in the same sense and to the same degree as his own are for him. In effect, because Levinas fails to see the other as the same, he also fails to respect the other in her difference. For Sikka—and she explicitly acknowledges the irony of this position (105)—ethical and political recognition of difference depend on a prior representation of the other as the same. But it must be asked, if representation of the other as a subject *like* oneself is the condition for recognizing the other's difference, in what sense does the other's difference remain ethically or politically salient? Suppose I give the other all due recognition as a subject, need I do anything more? Specifically, need I take the further step of recognizing her *difference,* or is any difference between us now construed effectively as that which must be put aside in order for our equal status as subjects to come to the fore? To be sure, I might have to leave the other enough room, literally and figuratively, to express or realize her difference, but it does not seem that I would be obliged to embrace her difference as such any more than she would have to embrace mine. Sikka's plaint for recognition of sameness effectively runs the risk of depoliticizing precisely those differences which, at least some of the time, she seems interested to bring into the political sphere.

Finally, the subjectivity Sikka claims on behalf of women is notable in being active rather than passive, self-determining rather than determined by its relationships to others, master of its own identity and in control of the production of that identity. This conception of subjectivity mirrors precisely the classically masculine subject that has been a target of critiques within both European and Anglo-American feminisms.[8] Not incidentally, this virile subject is equally the target of Levinas's own nascent critique of Western political theory from Plato to Hobbes.[9] Indeed, Levinas is surely closest to feminism when he is exposing the ways in which conceptions of the unencumbered, autonomous subject fail to do justice to the ethical significance of human interdependence and to the moral necessity (rather than mere desirability) of social cooperation in political as well as economic and social contexts.[10]

The conflicting claims made on behalf of equality and difference in Sikka's account reflect a general dilemma increasingly noted in contemporary feminist discussions. Legal scholar Martha Minnow has called it the sameness and difference conundrum:

if women claim they are the same as men in order to secure the rights of man, any sign of difference can be used to deny those rights; and if women claim they are different from men in order to secure special rights, those very differences can be cited to exclude women from the rights that men enjoy. (Minnow 1990, 152)

In an earlier essay, Minnow refers to much the same difficulty as the "dilemma of difference," arguing that if ignoring difference is problematic, focusing on it may be equally so (Minnow 1984). Where difference is ignored, it "leaves in place a false neutrality" that is harmful to socially subordinated groups. However, insisting on group difference can lead to re-stigmatization and lend support to existing forms of prejudice and disadvantage (Minnow 1984, 160; see also Ford 2004; Williams 1997).

This dilemma is echoed by Amarpal Dhaliwal, who argues that "while oppositional identities are necessary, they are, in and of themselves, insufficient to achieve radical sociopolitical transformations" (Dhaliwal 1994, 23). On the one hand, appeals to identity have been an effective strategy for mobilizing resistance to the kinds of injustices and oppressions which are not necessarily the result of overt forms of discrimination or exclusion but which result from the unreflective practices of dominant groups (hooks 1989; Young 1990; Mohanty 1991; Alcoff 1997, inter alia). Ethnic, linguistic, and national minorities, for example, may work consciously to cultivate a strong sense of group identity as a means to gaining a voice and fair representation in various networks of power. If such groups are capable of voting or consuming as a bloc, they are more likely to find themselves with a seat at the proverbial bargaining table. There is also much to be said, of course, for the benefits of a strong, positive sense of identity within groups whose members otherwise face widespread, institutionalized patterns of cultural and social devaluation. As Dhaliwal explains, "The naming of experience, the critical reading of this experience (consciousness), and the construction of politicized selves that are aware of structures of domination are all processes implicated as essential in and for resistance" (Dhaliwal 1994, 23). On the other hand, these same oppositional identities which provide a means of access to cultural, social, and political institutions and which are a source of group strength and pride also function in less appealing ways. Claims to special treatment—whether advanced to counter the legacy of past injustices (e.g., in some cases of affirmative action) or in recognition of "natural" or "essential" differences (e.g., in special protections for pregnant workers)—have produced a backlash that sustains rather than diminishes hierarchical relations between majority and minority, dominant and subordinate groups. Claims that seek to preserve "traditional" cultures and ways of life may implicitly or explicitly be a means of preserving patriarchal family and social structures as well as other forms of subgroup or caste subordination *within* a marginalized culture (Narayan 1997; Okin 1999; Shachar 2000; Benhabib 2002). Moreover, identity politics are as likely to be mobilized in the name of conservative and reactionary political agendas as they are on behalf of progressive policies and points of view. As Axel Honneth points out, identity claims are as likely to be militant assertions of particularity made in the name of violently exclusive, non-democratic aims (e.g., those of white supremacy) as they are to be the sort of demands for cultural recognition that are consistent with the values of peaceful anti-racist or anti-sexist social movements.[11]

The rub of much identity-based politics is that even as such a politics seeks recognition for a given group in virtue of the oppression and marginalization experienced by its members, it re-marks those same subjects precisely in terms of the categories through which social and economic subordination operates. This suggests that the affirmation of difference (where the latter is conceived in terms of social identities) is not necessarily emancipatory nor always in the interest of marginalized groups or individual members of those groups. This is one of the lessons of Wendy Brown's work: "Without recourse to a white masculine middle-class ideal, politicized identities would forfeit a good deal of their claims to injury and exclusion, their claims to the political significance of their difference" (Brown 1993, 395). Much of the "potency and poignancy" of the claims to social misrecognition and economic mistreatment made by various politicized identities is thus directly dependent on the unfavorable comparison between their lot and that of white middle-class men, which means that the lives and experiences of such men continue to be maintained as an ideal to which others aspire. Rather than dismantling the privileges of the dominant position, identity politics can have the unintended consequence of upholding the larger systematic structures that produce social and economic inequities and that, indeed, naturalize and depoliticize them. This does not mean that we should ignore difference, but it alerts us to one set of risks in basing political agendas on a primary recognition of difference.

Nancy Fraser details a similar dynamic, in which policies meant to redress the injuries caused by the imbricated forces of inequitable social and economic arrangements in fact deepen the stigma attached to certain subject positions, increase antagonism between advantaged and disadvantaged groups, and render the latter more vulnerable than ever. As she wryly remarks, "Public assistance programs 'target' the poor, not only for aid but for hostility" (Fraser 1997, 25). Fraser suggests that efforts to extend full inclusion in social and economic goods to marginalized or subordinated groups are less likely to be successful if inclusion comes at the price of assimilation into the system that generated the inequity in the first place. In her view, the sort of difference-recognizing inclusion that should be sought is not one that simply permits historically disadvantaged groups a voice in *already existing* sociopolitical structures or procedures, but one for which inclusion entails a *transformation* of the structures and procedures by which that disadvantage has been incurred.

In effect, the positions taken by Brown, Fraser, and others locate a central problem for discourses focused on recognition of difference: there is no sure route from difference to recognition that precludes the kinds of backlash which have become all too familiar in contemporary identity politics. Indeed, there is good reason to think that recognition, at least where it is understood as the affirmation of difference within existing economic and political structures, may not be capable of bringing about a transformative political culture. Brown and Fraser both effectively challenge the claim that positive recognition of group differences necessarily dismantles the privilege of dominant identities.[12] Jeffrey Nealon does likewise when he indicates that we need a discourse that understands difference positively, but non-essentially. Echoing Brown, and with an explicit eye toward Levinas's work, Nealon argues that despite its gains, contemporary identity politics "remains unable to deal with the other *as* other; it continues to thematize difference among persons, groups, and discourses in terms of (the impossibility of their) sameness" (Nealon 1998, 6–7). Whether this impossibility is nostalgically mourned or prematurely celebrated as a realm of creative possibility, the conceptualization of difference in terms of the lack of sameness is responsible, on Nealon's view, for "the recriminatory politics of resentment that has plagued and continues to plague identity politics" (7). Nealon applauds the move from subject-based to intersubjectively based models of political relation, but suggests that theories that "argue that we *need* each other for recognition and happiness . . . continue to harbor a regulatory ideal of complete subjective freedom, which is actually *freedom from recognition, freedom from difference itself*" (ibid.). If recognition is granted because each of us sees that we need the others in order to complete ourselves or realize our potential for self-creation, then it should be no surprise to anyone that recognition is more often than not granted only grudgingly and resentfully.

The conflict in Sikka's essay between the call to base politics on respect for individuals as universal subjects and the call to recognize group differences replicates the horns of Minnow's sameness/difference dilemma and lands us in the problematic terrain so well mapped by Dhaliwal, Brown, Fraser, Nealon, and others. It is the contention here, *contra* Sikka and *pace* Nealon, that rather than abandoning Levinas at this juncture, the dilemma gives us a reason to embrace his thought. In the remainder of the essay I defend Levinas's refusal to represent the other, showing that far from necessitating a chauvinistic indifference to particular differences, his view supports a conception of ethics and politics that demands institutional recognition (or, as appropriate, elimination) of group differences, *not* in the name of difference itself but in the name of the singularity of each human being. My contention is that when Levinas's conception of alterity is understood as a concern for singularity rather than difference, we see that his philosophy reflects in important ways our concern to do justice both to the uniqueness of individual lives and to the ways in which those lives are embedded, for better and worse, within social, cultural, and religious communities and within social categories such as race, gender, class, and disability.

From Difference to Singularity

As they function in contemporary political discussions, *identity* and *difference* are relative terms. As William Connolly explains, a given identity "is established in relation to a series of differences that have become socially recognized. These differences are essential to its being. If they did not coexist as differences, it would not exist in its distinctness and solidity. . . . Identity requires difference in order to be, and it converts difference into otherness in order to secure its own self-certainty" (Connolly 2002, 64). Connolly's analysis, exemplary in this respect as in others, emphasizes the mutual interconnection of identities, making visible the construction of both dominant and minority identities through active processes of exclusion and social subordination. Moreover, making such processes visible has been a valuable strategy in combating the perception that hierarchically organized social relations—e.g., those between Westerners and non-Westerners, men and women, whites and blacks, hetero- and homosexuals—are the product of natural and inevitable differences between members of these groups.

Levinas's work is increasingly invoked in such discussions, and understandably so, given the central place of alterity in his thought and his ethical concern for the vulnerability of the other. Nonetheless, one of Levinas's foremost interpreters is right to call for caution before we too readily assimilate Levinas's notion of an *absolute* alterity to the subject-*relative* alterity that dominates current social and political discourses (Bernasconi 2006, 246). The latter owe a debt to Hegel in conceiving "identity" as structured by "difference" (Connolly's remarks make this explicit), and tend to view the self and the other as locked in an agonistic struggle for mutual recognition. In contrast, Levinas is explicit in wanting to break with the Hegelian dialectic to develop a form of alterity no longer structured by negation and dialectical mediation.[13]

In *Totality and Infinity*, as in earlier works, Levinas distinguishes between the *relative* alterity of objects and the *absolute* alterity of the other person. The things in the subject's surrounding environment—whether small items like a pencil or an apple, or larger, less tangible "things" like a cityscape or concerto—have only a relative alterity because their otherness is determined in relation to the subject (rather than being a proper determination of the objects themselves), and this alterity can be suspended as the subject appropriates these things for her own use and enjoyment. Of the food I eat or the landscape I view outside my window, Levinas says, "I can 'feed' on these realities and to a very great extent satisfy myself, as though I had simply been lacking them. Their *alterity* is thereby reabsorbed into my own identity as a thinker or possessor" (*TI* 33). This is difference or alterity in its familiar, logical meaning.

In contrast to this understanding of alterity as a relative difference that is subjectively determined, Levinas claims that the other (*Autrui*) is infinitely and absolutely other: "The metaphysical other is other with an alterity that is not formal, is not the simple reverse of identity, and is not formed out of resistance to the same, but is prior to every initiative, to all imperialism of the same. It is other with an alterity constitutive of the very content of the Other" (*TI* 38–39). Levinas famously claims that it is only the other person, the personal other (*Autrui*), who is a metaphysical other in this sense, and he imagines a relation to the other in which "neither possession nor the unity of number nor the unity of concepts link me to the Other. Absence of a common homeland which makes the other a Stranger; a Stranger who disturbs my being at home with oneself" (*TI* 39; translation modified).[14] This passage suggests that the other is the stranger, the one who comes from a different nation, family, or culture. But it also suggests the possibility of an "I" and an "Other" so foreign to one another that they do not share even the *lack* of a common community that makes two people strangers to one another: neither the unity of number, nor the unity of a concept, nor even the *absence* of a common fatherland binds the I and the Other together. For Levinas, the "I" and the "Other" are terms which share no border, since every such common frontier would serve as a medium by which the otherness of the other would be made relative to the ego's position as the same.

It should be clear from even this cursory overview that "alterity" in Levinas's sense is not a synonym for "difference," at least where the latter could be understood as relative or oppositional difference. As has been argued above, a more appropriate understanding of alterity makes it synonymous with singularity. The other is not an absolutely *different* being, but is an absolutely *singular* being. Singularity expresses the idea that each human being is a unique, irreplaceable self, irreducible to any of the attributes or qualities that could be used to describe her and that would inevitably reduce her to what she has in common with others. In addition, it expresses the idea that the other has ethical standing. As such, singularity contains within it the idea of persons as having moral worth and dignity, though these terms are too attached to the horizon of Enlightenment thinking to be an adequate translation of Levinas's thought. In his early writings, alterity expresses the idea that the other concerns the ego not in view of some shared or universal property (a capacity for reason or pain, e.g.) but *simply as such*. The relation to the other is a relation to someone who "does not affect us in terms of a concept. He is a being (*étant*) and counts as such" (*BPW* 6).[15] This locution marks Levinas's attempt to differentiate between the way in which objects appear to consciousness and the manner in which I am engaged by someone who faces me.

There is a similar distinction in Hannah Arendt's work between persons viewed as objects (reducible to a set of social roles or descriptions) and persons viewed as agents or actors. The discussion of political action in *The Human Condition* is predicated on the idea that *who* one is as a unique human being is not equivalent to *what* one is, and cannot be revealed or known in the same way. Though who I am is implicit in everything I say and do, this "who" is strangely intangible, Arendt notes, and "confounds all efforts toward unequivocal verbal expression" (Arendt 1958, 181). The generality of every conceptual determination makes it impossible to produce an unequivocal definition or articulation of *who* someone is: "The moment we want to say *who* somebody is, our very vocabulary leads us astray into saying *what* he is; we get entangled in a description of qualities he necessarily shares with others like him" (ibid.). Even a list of qualities that uniquely identifies some person will be insufficient to render *who* she is. To borrow an example from Adriana Cavarero, Virginia Woolf may be a white, bourgeois, Eurocentric, lesbian, feminist writer, but this is not all she ever was or will be, nor is she alone in meeting this description (Cavarero 2002, 92). What Woolf is or was does not exhaust who she was and it does not and cannot convey the sense in which she was a singular being. Even a proper name fails to convey the singularity of the other, since though it identifies a *particular* person, it identifies her in terms of family and kinship affiliations, religious and national identities, rather than in her irreducibility to these categories.

Levinas's discussion of the other as a "face" parallels Arendt's view of the *who*, in that the face "counts" outside of every use-value and every specification of *what* one is:

> To be sure, most of the time the *who* is a *what*. We ask "Who is Mr. X?" and we answer: "He is President of the State Council," or "He is Mr. So-and-so." The answer presents itself as a quiddity; it refers to a system of relations. To the question *Who?* answers the non-qualifiable presence of an existent who *presents himself* without reference to anything, and yet distinguishes himself from every other existent. The question *Who?* envisages a face. (*TI* 177)

The face is not a face because it meets some determinate set of criteria, for example, those for rational agency, sentience, language-use, membership in the species *Homo sapiens*, or anything else conveyable in terms of a *quid*. (And here, to some extent, Levinas's account parts company with Arendt's, since for the latter singularity is conferred on subjects in view of their capacity for action, which functions as a sort of criteria.) Being a face in Levinas's sense is not some*thing* that one *is*. If it were, singularity or alterity would become one more property of the ego, an ineffable core of personality (or whatever) that *makes* each of us unique. In contrast to this view, which ontologizes that which is supposed to contest the primacy of ontology, Levinas's later work makes clear that the singularity of the face is *enacted* in the I-Other relationship. Singularity is not what this relationship *recognizes*, but what it *produces*.

If singularity were a quality or attribute of the other, then we could say that it is in virtue of this property that the other deserves or is owed respect. But singularity is no such thing on Levinas's account. Uniqueness as it figures in his notion of alterity is not the source of obligation; it does not confer a special moral status or ethical standing. If it did, we would be oddly obligated to every particular being—bits of mud and snowflakes no less than the widow, the orphan, and the stranger that Levinas's texts so often invoke. The alterity and singularity of the other is not the origin or cause of the ethical relationship. It neither makes us responsible, nor is it the evidence or proof of our responsibility. Rather, the singularity of the face is the *trace* of our being already in an ethical relationship. It marks my relation to the other as an ethical one or as a relationship in which I have been called to responsibility. But this trace and this call are thoroughly ambiguous.[16] The call to responsibility that "comes" from the face is such that one can never be sure one has heard it. The only way to know that one has been called is to find the response—acknowledging the other's singularity—forming in one's own mouth.

Levinas consistently turns to the interlocutive dimension of language to isolate the possibility of a relation to the other that does not pass through knowledge and representation and that thus preserves the *who* in addition to the *what.* In discourse, Levinas says, the other person is never only an object of knowledge, because in the very same moment which constitutes her as an object for consciousness she is also the addressee of the speech act. The gap that opens up here between the other as my theme and the other as my interlocutor suggests, for Levinas, the possibility of a relationship that is not structured only or exclusively in terms of knowledge. "Sociality is . . . irreducible to *knowledge* of the other; it is delineated in language after an entirely different model than intentionality" (*OS* 142). To be in relation to the other is not reducible to knowing the other; nor, for Levinas, is the social relation predicated on a prior moment in which the other is known and is an object for thought. This attempt to distinguish the relation to the other from the relation to things is repeated in Levinas's ban on representation.[17] Moreover, when Levinas rejects representation or denies that the other can be known, this is not the statement of a fact or a state of affairs. The statement itself is an ethical act. If one likes, it is simultaneously the creation and reflection of the ethical relationship.

Refusing to Represent the Other

Representation belongs intrinsically to the sphere of objects and to the practice of enumerating *what* someone is. To represent the other is to begin the process that reduces her from a *who* to a *what*. It is a way of getting hold of the other, of exercising social control over her. This is especially evident in the sorts of representations that are at issue in identity-based politics. Representation of the other in terms of her race, class, gender, or sexuality cannot be neutral (i.e., *merely* or innocently descriptive) so long as the representation is made within a racist, classist, sexist, or homophobic society.[18] Though Levinas rarely addresses contemporary ideas about identity directly, what he says about *works* can be applied to social and political identities.

As Levinas uses it, the term "works" encompasses everything from artworks, music, and literary texts, to furniture, food, and other fungible goods. Moreover, his interest in works is an interest in the way they become alienated from their makers and become the means for the worker's alienation from his or her own will. Levinas notes that the creative control exercised by the one who makes or does the work does not extend to the meanings the work will have for those who appreciate, consume, or use it. Though I intend one thing by my painting, it is constitutively open to multiple interpretations in my own time and to further variation as it travels through different social and historical contexts. In being delivered over to others, moreover, the work delivers the worker over to market forces and effectively inscribes the agent's will within a foreign will: "Inscription in a foreign will is produced through the mediation of the work, which separates itself from its author, his intentions, his possession, and which another will lays hold of" (*TI* 227). Though brief, Levinas's analysis makes plain that willing is never entirely in the agent's command: willing is always "in a certain sense . . . abortive. I am not entirely what I want to do" (*TI* 228). This situation, in which the will is not self-contained or entirely self-controlled, "amounts to the possibility the others have of laying hold of the work, alienating, acquiring, buying, stealing it. The will itself thus takes on a meaning for the other, as though it were a thing" (*TI* 228).

All that Levinas says here of the work and will can be applied to social and cultural identities. Whatever a given identity means to me, whatever control I exercise in affirming it as my own, I nonetheless do not completely control what it betokens to others. Identities are no more in the control of those who inhabit them than works are in the control of their makers. If I affirm that I am a woman or a man, Jewish or Christian, disabled or able-bodied, I do not fully control the meanings that will be attached to or derived from this identity by others. Having identity x, y, or z exposes me to a veritable economy of expectations, opportunities, and obstacles which may have little to do with anything intrinsic to being x, y, or z. Identities can be a source of power and comfort; they can help me feel at home or be expressions of the social locations and contexts in which I am most comfortable, most "myself." But they can also serve to alienate me from myself, since though I affirm that I am such-and-such, I do not control the social meanings attached to given identity categories. That the agent is never without some power is clear: as the reappropriation of such identity-terms as "black" or "queer" suggests, labels that are meant to be pejorative and stigmatizing can become sources of individual and group pride and power. But that I never fully control this power is equally evident. Identities, or representations of the self or other by identity terms, thus reflect inherently ambiguous operations of power (see *TI* 230).

Thus, when Levinas says that the face of the other cannot be represented, and when we identify the face with the singularity of the other, these ideas express ethical resistance to the misappropriations that become possible with representation. This resistance is not mounted in the name of the rationality or autonomy of the subject, since these are effectively no more that a different way of establishing identities that become the basis for inclusion in or exclusion from the community of those with moral standing. Nor is this ethical resistance mounted in the name of the sheer uniqueness of the individual, since uniqueness itself does not confer ethical standing but reflects it. To become aware of this resistance is not like becoming aware of a fact. It is itself an enactment of the ethical relationship.

Sikka concludes that because Levinas "obstinately refuses"[19] to represent the other, those identities rendered "other" in contemporary society are better served by standard forms of identity politics and by a politics of recognition than they are by a Levinasian ethics of radical alterity. This is where she gets Levinas most wrong: Levinas's problematic depictions of femininity do not stem from his failure to represent the other (as either the same or different), but precisely from his ceding to the temptation to representation. Here, contrary to the strictures of his own writing on the face, Levinas does not refuse to represent the other, and it is precisely the stereotypical images of women and other others that he dishes up that cause his readers such consternation and pain.

From Identity to Alterity Politics, or, the Importance of Recognizing Failure

From a Levinasian perspective, the problem with claims for recognition of difference is that they cast the agents or subjects of those claims as a *what*—female, black, gay, or Jewish, for example—while arguably claiming recognition for those subjects as, each of them, singular faces or *whos*.

The paradoxical figure of the face, in representing the unrepresentability of the other, thereby represents the manner in which a *who* stands irreducibly outside of every identity category. No social identity exhausts the whole of who one is, nor is who I am a matter of adding up or combining a set of overlapping and interwoven identities. Socially ascribed identities fail to capture who I am for at least three reasons. First, to think that one can fully inhabit a given identity is to mistakenly think that identities are static and self-contained. They are not.[20] What it means to be Croatian, atheist, or a woman changes with changes in time and place and will be experienced in radically different ways by subjects in different historical, social, and geographic locations. Second, identities are multiple and their borders fluid *within* the individual (or, to borrow a term from Donna Haraway, within each *dividual*). Context will determine which identities matter to me most in a given situation or at some particular time in my life. In the fight against sexism, gender may be the most salient aspect of my identity, whereas in the fight to protect against the erosion of civil rights, national identity may take center stage. That identities intersect (and that forms of oppression do so as well) has long been recognized by feminists, among others. Further, having multiple, shifting, and intersecting identities means that who I am is no more conveyed by the whole assemblage or constellation of my identities than it is by any single identity. Third, and perhaps most importantly from the point of view of Levinas's thought, every identity category—every representation of identity—is potentially alienating since socially ascribed meanings shape and misshape my self-understanding, open up but also limit my possibilities, and fundamentally make of me something that can be laid hold of by others.

The face exceeds any and every representation of what one is and every representation of the groups with which one identifies or can be identified. Singularity prescribes that I cannot be reduced to any one identity or aspect of my life, nor to some exhaustive list of the identities attributable to me. But at the same time, singularity is not meant to convey some merely abstract otherness or formal alterity. As has been argued at length in the preceding chapters, it refers to the concrete life lived by this here and now being. This produces a further paradox to which Levinas's account must respond. If being a *who* means that I resist and reject any characterization that reduces me to some particular category, it also means that characterizations that do not include my socially salient identities or those identities that matter to me also miss *who* I am and cannot explain key aspects of what it is to live my life and not another's. Falsely universalizing approaches (that subsume my experience into everyone's experience or the neutral experience of "the" subject) are as distorting as falsely particularizing approaches (e.g., "You think that only because you are a woman"). As an excess with respect to what can be represented, as the paradoxical representation of an unrepresentable singularity, the face of the other signals the other's refusal to be contained in an image or description. "I am this," the face says, "but not only this." And even as it refuses representation in one sense, the face demands it in another! Singularity *must* be said—it demands its due—and yet it cannot be said. The singularity "represented" by the face cannot appear in language as such, or it appears only at the price of losing its singularity. This is not an incidental feature of Levinas's thought, a peculiarity or a strange liability that one works around. Rather, it expresses a fundamental tension characteristic of our ethical situation: the whole of singularity's desire and demand is that it be affirmed, and yet every affirmation of it is the beginning of its betrayal.

In the preface to the second edition of *Gender Trouble*, Judith Butler speaks in a similar manner of the ways in which an identity may be culturally unintelligible and thus rendered invisible within the dominant modes of social discourse (Butler 1999, xix–xxi). Before the bearers of such identities can even claim to have suffered injury, they must attain a certain visibility and intelligibility; they must achieve representation. But representation, as Butler's more recent work in *Precarious Life* makes evident, and as the criticisms of identity politics canvassed here have emphasized, is not a guarantee of social justice or the acknowledgment of one's humanity or singularity. Employing Levinas's sense of the face, but reflecting on the ironic manner in which the previously veiled faces of Afghani women were unveiled to American viewers as "a symbol of successfully exported American cultural progress," Butler remarks: "We were, as it were, in possession of the face; not only did our cameras capture it, but we arranged for the face to capture our triumph, and act as the rationale for our violence, the incursion on sovereignty, the deaths of civilians. . . . Indeed, the photographed face seemed to conceal or displace the face in the Levinasian sense, since we saw and heard through that face no vocalization of grief or agony, no sense of the precariousness of life" (Butler 2004, 142).

In light of this dilemma, where the precariousness of life or the singularity of the other *demands* representation but where no representation can succeed since representation is precisely the means for the cooptation and appropriation of the other, Butler proposes that the only sort of representation that will do is one which marks its own failures. In a sense, this would be representation with a conscience, though Butler doesn't use this phrase. The face is not identical to what is represented, but neither is it rightly identified with the unrepresentable as such. It is neither representable nor unrepresentable. To affirm the latter would prevent such faces from ever reaching the screen of the visible, and this erasure would constitute one more ethical injury. But at the same time, as Levinas emphasizes over and over, representation of the face can never succeed without also instituting the conditions for injury.

For Levinas, then, the human is not *represented by* the face. Rather, the human is indirectly affirmed in that very disjunction that makes representation impossible, and this disjunction is conveyed in the impossible representation. For representation to convey the human, then, representation must not only fail, but it must *show* its failure. There is something unrepresentable [*someone* singular] that [who] we nevertheless seek to represent, and that paradox must be retained in the representation we give. (144)

Butler's strategy does not leave representation behind, even as it insists that representation alone cannot succeed. Nor is the answer to think that there is some mode of bearing witness to the other that is something *other than* a recognition or representation, as if one could place oneself outside the system of representation to relate to the other through some purer means somehow protected from the ambivalence and recuperations of recognition. What Butler demands are recognitions that *bear the visible marks of their own failure*. It is only through this trace, this disjunction between success and failure, that the relation to singularity finds expression, and it is for the sake of this singularity that recognition and acknowledgment, even as they fail, must be attempted.

This strategy is no doubt one way to understand the relation between ethics and politics in Levinas's thought—a relationship which Derrida, too, characterizes as disjunctive (Derrida 1999). Levinas describes politics as the need to compare incomparables and to develop a political calculus that somehow includes each singular face:

In the comparison of the incomparable there would be the latent birth of representation, logos, consciousness, work, the neutral notion [of] *being*. . . . Out of representation is produced the order of justice moderating or measuring the substitution of me for the other, and giving the self over to calculus. Justice requires contemporaneousness of representation. It is thus that the neighbor becomes visible, and, looked at, presents himself, and there is also justice for me. (*OB* 158–59)

Justice requires representation. Levinas may well have been thinking of representation in this passage only in the sense of the presentation of an object in consciousness—that is, as the representation of persons in the abstract. But it is clear that political representation, as the right and actuality of having an effective voice in civil society and government, is equally necessary for justice. The other whose identity is rendered unintelligible or unrepresentable is thus done an injustice—an ethical as well as a political injustice. In this we can come to a point of agreement with some of the concerns that motivate Sikka's essays, if not the conclusions she draws from them.

The relation of ethics to politics as Levinas describes it in the final chapter of *Otherwise Than Being, or Beyond Essence* is structurally parallel to the figure of transcendence in immanence that is so important to his work elsewhere.[21] In both cases, terms that initially seem opposed to one another or that appear to belong to different, perhaps mutually exclusive, orders are shown to bear an internal reference to one another such that to understand the one term is to be sent significantly to its polar opposite, and vice versa. This means that ethics, or the ethical relationship, is never present without referring us directly to politics, and politics likewise contains an internal reference to ethical proximity. In the ethical relationship of infinite responsibility for *this* singular other, this *face*, "all the others than the other obsess me," Levinas writes (*OB* 158). The ethical relationship "already . . . cries out for justice" (*OB* 158). Considered from this perspective of a co-referential relation between the ethical and the political, the face is "both comparable and incomparable, a unique face and in relationship with faces" (*OB* 158). Likewise from this perspective, justice cannot be viewed as a calculus to which I am constrained by practical necessity or strictly prudential considerations. Justice, for Levinas, is not (as it has been for a contractarian tradition originating with Hobbes) a "technique of social equilibrium," nor a procedure for "harmonizing antagonistic forces" (*OB* 159). Justice arises "in the midst of" an ethical proximity to the other. Justice remains just, in other words, only if it is a consideration for the equal standing of all which simultaneously does not forget the incomparable singularity of the one: "Justice remains justice only in a society where there is no distinction between those close and those far off, but in which there also remains the impossibility of passing by the closest" (*OB* 159). What calls for "recognition" or "representation" within a Levinasian-informed politics is thus precisely the limits of recognition and representation in the name *both* of the singularity of the one closest by, the one whom I meet in ethical proximity, *and* the one farthest off whose difference I am least likely to understand.

The constitutive tension in Levinas's notion of singularity is instructive for the sameness/difference dilemma with which we began. The problem with a discourse of sameness or equality is that it risks reinstating a falsely universal subject and returning us, in Joan Scott's words, "to the days when 'Man's' story was supposed to be everyone's story" (Scott 1990, 143). But at the same time, recognition of difference does not give rise in any straightforward way to a progressive political agenda, since the representation of differences it demands is the means by which those differences are maintained and often naturalized as socially relevant categories. The notion of singularity and the failures of the face—a failure to coincide with either its representation or unrepresentability—does not merely reflect the difficulties in which this dilemma leaves us (which would already be something), it *mobilizes* these difficulties in a manner that refuses moral complacency. Confronted by claims to universality—claims which necessarily cover over or distort the manner in which hierarchically differentiated social locations render subjects unequal—singularity drives discourse toward the particular and the concrete, in other words, toward differences. But arriving at the concrete, singularity again leaves us with no place to rest. The face refuses to be identified with or constrained by a particular representation: I am *that*, it says, *but not only that.* I am, like every other, a unique and singular *who.* Singularity shuttles between the demand to be represented and the refusal of representation. It is the driving force of an ethics that demands politics—laws, institutions, formal mechanisms of representation, justice—but also the sting of conscience that calls those same mechanisms into question in the name of one more other who has yet to be heard, yet to be made visible. This is perhaps just one more way to understand what Levinas means by an *infinite* responsibility in which I am never quite with the other, never done with the demands of ethical and political life. Thus, rather than dismissing Levinas's thought simply as a refusal to represent the other and thus as a failure of recognition, we can see in his thought both a demand for representation and a critique of the way in which representation objectifies and instrumentalizes the other. This politics allows us to condemn Levinas's own statements about particular others but still see in his work the promise of an alterity politics which strives for justice for each singular face, each and every other—even those, or maybe especially those, who have not yet achieved visibility.

Notes

INTRODUCTION

1. The phrase "ethics as first philosophy" has become so closely associated with Levinas that it serves as the title of two collections of essays devoted to his work, one in French (Greisch and Rolland 1993), the other in English (Peperzak 1995). It is also the title of a late essay by Levinas summarizing his intellectual path. The claim is also found in *Totality and Infinity*, where Levinas writes, "Morality is not a branch of philosophy, but first philosophy" (*TI* 304), and can likewise be found in *Ethics and Infinity* (*EI* 75).

2. Bernard Williams framed the history of ethics this way in his now classic *Ethics and the Limits of Philosophy*.

3. Jacques Rolland (2000, 20) points out that this language of "first philosophy" largely disappears from Levinas's writings between the publication of *Totality and Infinity* (1961) and that of *Otherwise Than Being, or Beyond Essence* (1974).

4. Levinas himself, of course, makes these claims at *CPP* 56 and *EI* 90, among others. This way of presenting Levinas's thought can be found in a fairly straightforward form in Ciaramelli (1991, 85), Peperzak (1993, 123–24), and Davis (1996, 3). It is worth noting that the last two texts are explicitly introductory in nature. I would hazard that it is in such contexts above all that this way of introducing Levinas's thought has become standard. A quite subtle version of this story, and one with which the present work is often in agreement, is found in Simon Critchley's *The Ethics of Deconstruction* (1992, especially 3–9).

5. Simon Critchley concurs with this description of Levinas in his introduction to *The Cambridge Companion to Levinas* (Critchley and Bernasconi 2002, 28).

6. Whether class and gender are meant to stand for a whole range of socially imposed and maintained differences is unclear. After this mention, Putnam's text remains virtually silent on such topics.

7. For an account of Nietzsche's influence on French critiques of universal normative ethics, see Peter Baker, *Deconstruction and the Ethical Turn* (1995). While there are many texts dealing with the influence of the "Letter on Humanism" on French thought, an especially good introduction is found in Descombes (1981).

8. Levinas, *Autrement que Savoir* (Paris: Osiris, 1987), 28, cited in Critchley 1992, 17.

9. See Levinas and Kearney 1986, 29. Levinas does not maintain this terminological difference with any precision.

10. It is no more the aim of this book to distinguish Levinas's thought from various forms of post-structuralism than it is the intention to show the continuing relation of his work to themes and issues within Enlightenment moral philosophy. Suffice it to say, I take his work to be situated somewhat uncomfortably at the intersection of modern and postmodern discourses and to illuminate the point of their unresolved and irresolvable tension.

CHAPTER I

1. The bulk of these titles have appeared since 1999 and reflect a broad spectrum of disciplines in the humanities and social sciences. A similar search for titles in English nets about 25 books with "alterity" in the title since 1994, with almost half of them devoted to Levinas or phenomenology. However, in a search simply for "alterity," Amazon.com generated 2,645 results for books that contained the word in the body of the text or in promotional materials. As one would expect, there was an astonishing range of genres and disciplines represented and most such titles were from university presses. Even accounting for multiple listings of the same work, this number leads one to believe that if alterity is an obsession in France, it is a mania in the English-speaking academy.

2. Among others, see Derrida 1978; Manning 1993; Peperzak 1993; Peperzak 1997; Greisch 1998; Marion 1998; and Bernet 2002.

3. Husserl did not see this point as clearly or consistently as did Heidegger and, later, Levinas. Levinas's presentation of these ideas in *The Theory of Intuition in Husserl's Phenomenology* clearly draws on Heidegger's formulation of this issue.

4. Although Husserl brands this version of the problem a pseudo-problem, our relation to transcendent objects (the nature of which must now be clarified by a phenomenological philosophy) does not thereby become unproblematic; rather, it is only the task regarding such objects that changes. Robert Sokolowski emphasizes that Husserl intends neither to "solve" nor to "dissolve" the problem of transcendent knowledge, preserving the idea that there is an enigma or mystery in the fact that "what reality is in itself can be reached by consciousness even though it must remain, in principle, radically distinct from and transcendent to consciousness" (Sokolowski 1964, 135). Unlike the dominant approaches to this problem in the philosophical tradition, Husserl neither absorbs reality into consciousness (idealism) nor consciousness into reality (reductive realism), but maintains "both terms of the paradox: consciousness on one hand, and transcendent reality on the other" (ibid.). While Sokolowski is right that Husserl continues to see cognition

as an enigma that needs analysis, the characterization of his view in terms of consciousness on one side opposed to reality on the other mirrors Husserl's own tendency to slide back into the language of the metaphysical picture he is otherwise out to discredit.

5. Levinas's discussion of this point is clearly indebted to Heidegger, whose influence, he says, "will often be felt" in his presentation of Husserl's philosophy (*TIHP*, xxxiii).

6. See *HCT* 27. In *The Basic Problems of Phenomenology*, Heidegger explains that he will no longer use the term "subject," because it remains inextricably connected to false conceptions of intentionality: "Because the usual separation between a subject with its immanent sphere and an object with its transcendent sphere—because, in general, the distinction between an inner and an outer is constructive and continually gives occasion for further constructions, we shall in the future no longer speak of a subject, of a subjective sphere, but shall understand the being to whom intentional comportments belong as the *Dasein*, and indeed in such a way that it is precisely with the aid of *intentional comportment*, properly understood, that we attempt to characterize suitably the being of the Dasein" (*BPP* 64).

7. In lecture courses given between 1925 and 1928, Heidegger suggests that intentionality suffers from unclarified assumptions that leave it open to misinterpretation, and argues that this notion has yet to be raised to the level of a genuine phenomenological problem. *The Metaphysical Foundations of Logic* (1928) suggests that in neither Brentano nor Husserl does the insight into intentionality "go far enough to see that grasping this structure as the essential structure of Dasein must revolutionize the whole concept of human being" (*MFL* 133). Commenting on the disappearance of the word "intentionality" from Heidegger's vocabulary in *Being and Time*, Frederick Olafson rightly notes, "It thus looks very much as though in the case of intentionality Heidegger made a terminological decision like the one he made in the case of 'consciousness' and abandoned the term on the grounds that the subjectivistic connotations it had taken on through its use by Husserl especially had made it unsuitable for employment in the very different context of Heidegger's own thought" (Olafson 1987, 26–27).

8. In the same introductory discussion, Dreyfus speaks of Heidegger as countering Husserl's philosophy with the identification of "a more basic form of intentionality than that of a self-sufficient individual subject directed at the world by means of its mental content" (Dreyfus 1991, 2–3). While it is certainly true that Heidegger claims that the transcendence of Dasein is more fundamental as a structure and as a problem than that of intentionality alone (see especially *MFL* 133–35), it is a mistake to speak of transcendence as a form of intentionality at all. Heidegger, for example, maintains that the "problem of transcendence as such is

not at all identical with the problem of intentionality," even if the latter prepares the way to the former (*MFL* 135).

9. Although the point cannot be elaborated here, it is worth noting that in *Basic Problems* the discussion moves on to a consideration of temporality as the ground of transcendence (*BPP* 301ff.).

10. The section in *Totality and Infinity* entitled "Transcendence and Fecundity" describes the problem this way (*TI* 274–77). This section reprises material published in 1949 under the title "Transcendence and Plurality."

11. For two different accounts of transcendence in Levinas's thought, see Francois Guibal's "La Transcendence" (in Marion 2000, 209–38) and chapter 9 of Rudi Visker's *Truth and Singularity* (1999).

12. One way to read Levinas's critique of Husserl and Heidegger is to see that despite the laicization or secularization of their respective discourses on transcendence, both still fall prey to the underlying valuation of being (*Sein*) predominant within the tradition.

13. The reference here is most likely to Rimbaud, whom Levinas quotes in the opening pages of *Totality and Infinity*.

14. The text goes on at this point to argue that Bergson's notions of "creative evolution" and the "vital impulse" may break with the present in a way that is suggestive for the motif of escape or transcendence, but that this philosophy, in reinterpreting the vital urge in terms of creation, nonetheless remains on the side of the philosophy of being and ontologism (*OE* 53–54).

15. The source of this phrase is a seminar on "Transcendence and Immanence" given by Bernasconi at the 2003 Collegium Phaenomenologicum in Città di Castello.

16. See note 10 above.

17. Derrida takes issue with this point in *Violence and Metaphysics* (VM 125). I discuss this point further in Chapter 2.

18. While the sexist ramifications of this discourse on the son have been widely discussed, the messianic resonances of Levinas's language here have gone relatively unremarked. The figure of a son who both *exists* and effects a *transcendence* of being, in relation to whom the ego both is and is not finite or mortal, etc., needs to be considered in light of both Judaic and Christian treatments of messianism.

19. This absolute separation of erotic relationships from power relationships is, of course, thoroughly contested in the work of Michel Foucault, Judith Butler, Eve Sedgwick, and others. Our aim here is not to endorse Levinas's view, which in any case he does not maintain for very long. What remains essential for his account is the way in which the relation to alterity is a relation in which the subject's power as a power of appropriation is brought up short not by a physical challenge or obstacle but by the *ethical* resistance—the "no"—of the other.

20. Both the sexism and the potential biologism of Levinas's account of paternity need to be addressed before it can be made palatable as any sort of free-standing account of the relationship of parent to child. However, since my interest here is in a structural feature of the relationship, rather than in its content *per se*, I leave aside further exploration of these problematic aspects of Levinas's view.

21. A second stab at characterizing Levinas's critique of Husserl and Heidegger would thus say that he does not necessarily disagree with their conceptualization of being, but rather that he disagrees with the original valuation out of which or in relation to which this conceptualization is developed. This is precisely why, despite the rich innovations of phenomenology (particularly in Heidegger's works), Levinas can nonetheless see it as part and parcel of a traditional manner of treating the notion of being.

22. An important consequence of this is that for Levinas there is no totality *per se*. There may well be a drive to totality and, indeed, the egoism of the ego is often described in these terms, but totality in and of itself is not achievable if being is, from the first, always and already plural.

23. Recognizing that Heidegger argues that *Mitsein* is a mode of being-in-the-world that is different from but no less originary than Dasein's relation to things within the world, Levinas nonetheless dismisses this argument as a possible interpretation of the sort of relationship he is interested in articulating and that he finds impossible in the terms of Heidegger's fundamental ontology. He suggests that *Mitsein*, in Heidegger's thought, is always community around a third term—common interests, work, leisure pursuits—and it is not the unmediated relationship to the alterity of the other that Levinas will eventually designate as the face-to-face relationship. Why not? Because in being-with-others in the world, the other is not encountered in his or her singularity; the other does not count or signify *as such*, but only through those shared projects that give the *mit* its particular consistency or pattern.

24. An excellent discussion of this aspect of Rosenzweig's thought and its relation to the notion of responsibility in Levinas may be found in Bernhard Casper's "Responsibility Rescued," in *The Philosophy of Franz Rosenzweig*, ed. Paul Mendes-Flohr (Hanover, NH: University Press of New England, 1988), 89–106. For more extensive treatments of Levinas's relation to Rosenzweig, see Cohen (1994) and Gibbs (1992).

25. In a short essay on "The Roots of Existentialism," Jean Wahl summarizes Hegel's philosophy and Kierkegaard's opposition to it in terms that clearly influenced Levinas's interpretation of both figures. Wahl writes that Hegel "tells us that our thoughts and feelings have meaning solely because each thought, each feeling, is bound to our personality, which itself has meaning only because it takes place in a history and a state, at a specific epoch in the evolution of the universal Idea. To understand anything that happens in our inner life we must go to the to-

tality which is our self, thence to the larger totality which is the human species, and finally to the totality which is the absolute Idea. This is the conception which Kierkegaard . . . came forward to contradict" ("Roots of Existentialism" 1993, 5). Wahl's view of Hegel clearly informs Levinas's polemic with the notion of history as the final arbiter of the meaning of individual lives. In an early essay, Levinas writes: "The human world is a world in which one can judge history. . . . What is inhuman is to be judged without there being anyone who judges" (*CPP* 40). And in *Totality and Infinity*: "The idea of a being overflowing history makes possible *existents* both involved in being and personal, called upon to answer at their trial and consequently already adult—but, for that very reason, *existents* that can speak rather than lending their lips to an anonymous utterance of history" (*TI* 23).

26. The importance of the second issue has been widely acknowledged in the secondary literature, though often with the caveat that Levinas was not fully cognizant of this problem before Derrida's critique in "Violence and Metaphysics." Putting aside the question of whether he treats the issue adequately prior to the late 1960s, there can be no mistaking the fact that Levinas was aware of the problem from very early on. It would not even be going too far to suggest that this problem was the catalyst for his positive project from its inception.

27. I am hesitant to call the aspect of language under consideration here "performative," even though the claim is that in *stating* something, language also *does* something, namely, invokes the other as an interlocutor. Since the doing in question is not a special feature of some particular class of sentences but of all linguistic utterances, it seems wiser to leave "performative" to designate that special class of examples, like "I christen thee . . . " or "I promise . . . ," that have been identified by J. L. Austin and ordinary language philosophers. In the latter cases, to say, in the right circumstances, "I promise . . . " or "I christen thee . . . ," *is* to promise or christen, and nothing else counts as having done so. This is not quite the same for the sort of *doing* at issue in Levinasian invocation.

28. In "Is Ontology Fundamental?" we find the idea of the face as signifying independently of a meaning-giving context, but this structure is not given a technical name (*BPW* 10).

29. In an interview in *The Provocation of Levinas* (Bernasconi and Wood 1988), Levinas himself gives a similar account of the difference between *Totality and Infinity* and *Otherwise Than Being*.

CHAPTER 2

1. The situation of the ego before the face is thus likened to that of the people of Israel at the foot of Mount Sinai, who receive the Torah saying, "We will do and we will hear" (see Levinas, "The Temptation of Temptation," *NTR* 30–50). "Do-

ing before hearing" becomes the principal trope in Levinas's very late works for an event that is "straightaway ethical."

2. This approach to Levinas is not unique. Quoting Lyotard, Jill Robbins remarks that to welcome the other when the other is Levinas's text requires that we "take care not to flatten the alterity of his work" (Robbins 1999, 13; the original may be found in Lyotard's essay, in Cohen 1986). A reading that adequately captures or faithfully re-presents Levinas's thought attempts to master it, to reduce its alterity. Hence, Robbins avers, "if the reader does not want 'to flatten the alterity' of Levinas's work, he *has* to flatten the alterity of the work. . . . From here it is only a short step to realizing that the best way for the commentator to respect Levinas's work is not a straightforward exposition. The best way to respect the work is to read it deviously, to misunderstand it entirely" (Robbins 1999, 13). What follows is an exercise in productive misunderstanding that insists on the legitimacy and centrality of a set of questions about the face that are, strictly speaking, unanswerable and, at times, consciously excluded by the terms of Levinas's account.

3. It must be noted with respect to the idea of infinity that the formal structure and its theological content are, in fact, no easier to separate in Levinas's employment of the idea than in Descartes', since for both the idea of infinity is not a mathematical idea but an idea of God's perfection. Levinas no longer hesitates before certain religious commitments connected with the idea of infinity in the foreword to *Of God Who Comes to Mind.* Similar connections can be found in a late essay on "The Idea of Infinity in Us," in *Entre Nous* (*EN* 219–22).

4. It would be interesting to compare Levinas's rather informal use of the term *concretization* with Roman Ingarden's technical use of the term throughout *The Cognition of the Literary Work of Art* (1973a) and in chapter 13 of *The Literary Work of Art* (1973b).

5. A fuller discussion of the positive and explicitly ethical dimension of Levinas's account of the face is undertaken in Chapter 3.

6. The target of these remarks could be Heidegger's discussion of *Stimmung,* or mood, as preceding and guiding objectifying intentions, and likewise his articulation of a system of practical comportments as our basic, everyday mode of relating to objects in the world. As such, Levinas could be read as making the case for seeing Husserl's work as philosophically more radical that Heidegger's (which would reverse the position he takes in *The Theory of Intuition in Husserl's Phenomenology*). It is just as likely, however, that the target of the remarks is the dissertation reading of Husserl itself, which extolled as a significant philosophical advance those aspects of the theory of intuition that allowed it to admit of practical and axiological truths that were not merely subjective overlays (even if Husserl himself paradoxically claims the priority of representation even in such acts) (*TIHP* 132–34), and that criticized Husserl's thought for abstracting itself from the historical situation of human existence (*TIHP* 155–58). The reappraisal undertaken in 1959 is thus, in

any case, one which credits Husserl's transcendental philosophy with opening the way for Levinas's own rethinking of transcendence.

7. This concern has been articulated most effectively by Bernard Waldenfels, who argues for a "responsivity" (*Responsivität*) that precedes responsibility. See his magnum opus, *Antwortregister* (1994), and also his essay and my response in *Interrogating Ethics* (Hatley 2006).

8. Derrida raises both questions at VM 112. It is worth noting that the same set of challenges will recur in relation to the term "proximity," which in Levinas's later work is privileged in relation to the I-Other encounter and which, again, we are told must be read non-spatially.

9. See also "The White Mythology" (Derrida 1982).

10. The tradition of negative theology, as Derrida and his readers well know, characteristically arrives at this impasse but has little trouble over the idea that the infinite cannot be stated. Words can be viewed as inevitably inadequate to the task of stating positive infinity or God's perfection. Levinas cannot avail himself of this solution when it comes to the face, not only because he rejects an instrumentalist view of language when he follows Merleau-Ponty in identifying thought and language, but because he insists from 1951 on that the relation to alterity is accomplished only *in* language: "Absolute difference, inconceivable in terms of formal logic, is established only by language. Language accomplishes a relation between terms that . . . absolve themselves from the relation, or remain absolute within relationship" (*TI* 195). The best account of Levinas and apophatic theology is found in de Vries (2005).

11. For example, he criticizes Michel Leiris's *Biffures* for doing so, despite an otherwise appreciative reading of that extraordinary text (*LR* 149).

12. This is argued in more detail in Chapter 5, which takes up the problem of whether animals can have a face and whether having language is a criterion of having a face, in the Levinasian sense.

13. Mark Rothko's explanation of why he gave up painting human figures is suggestive of a Levinasian turn of mind: "I belonged to a generation that was preoccupied with the human figure and I studied it. . . . It was with utmost reluctance that I found that it did not meet my needs. Whoever used it mutilated it. No one could paint the figure as it was and feel that he could produce something that could express the world. I refuse to mutilate and had to find another way of expression" (quoted in Breslin 1993, 395; and in Marion 2002, 75).

14. Here I am thinking of the work of John Caputo in *Against Ethics* (1993), which in certain moments or in one of its voices seems to me altogether too certain of the impossibility of ethics.

CHAPTER 3

1. The idea that responsibility is a theme of the late works is common in the secondary literature on Levinas and can be found fairly explicitly in Philippe Nemo's interviews with Levinas in *Ethics and Infinity*. In these interviews, which are often chosen as a classroom introduction to Levinas's thought, the seventh session begins: "In *Totality and Infinity* you speak at great length of the face. It is one of your frequent themes" (*EI* 85). The eighth session opens in parallel fashion: "In your last great book published, *Otherwise Than Being, or Beyond Essence*, you speak of responsibility" (*EI* 95). To be sure, responsibility is used far more frequently in the later work, but this approach mistakenly implies that the notion developed there can be understood without knowing its roots in the problematic of *Totality and Infinity*. Though it is beyond the scope of the present chapter to argue the thesis directly, it is maintained indirectly here that the account of responsibility in *Otherwise Than Being* is not intelligible without the failed account of responsibility in the work that precedes it. The *Totality and Infinity* account is not just a precursor, then, or a ladder that can be done away with once one has climbed to the higher reaches of Levinas's thought. It is present in the later thought in a fundamental way. On the early uses of responsibility in Levinas's work, see especially the 1954 essay "The Ego and the Totality," where Levinas characterizes subjective existence in terms of a "responsibility that extends beyond the scope of the intention" (*CPP* 33). In a passage anticipating the most complex formulations of his later thought, he writes of a relation "where the *other* [*l'autre*] does not weigh on the same, but only places it under an obligation, makes it responsible, that is, makes it speak" (*CPP* 41). The same essay states baldly, "Ethics is language, that is, responsibility" (*CPP* 43). In these comments, characteristic connections between language and ethics, response and responsibility are already plainly in evidence.

2. Commenting on a passage in *Otherwise Than Being* that ends with the sentence "A subject is a hostage," Ricoeur writes: "This expression, the most excessive of all, is thrown out here in order to prevent the insidious return of the self-affirmation of some 'clandestine and hidden freedom' maintained even within the passivity of the self summoned to responsibility. The paroxysm of the hyperbole seems to me to result from the extreme—even scandalous—hypothesis that the Other is no longer the master of justice here, as is the case in *Totality and Infinity*, but the offender, who, as offender, no less requires the gesture of pardon and expiation" (Ricoeur 1992, 338).

3. This exact passage does not occur in the Hebrew text; however, there is a discussion at 104b from which one could draw a conclusion along these lines. My thanks to Joseph Stern for this observation.

4. Both views are implied in Thomas Nagel's *The Possibility of Altruism* (1970).

5. Joe Campisi discusses these similarities in detail in his dissertation, "The Morals of Language: Habermas, Levinas, and Discourse Ethics" (Duquesne University, 2005).

6. Levinas makes it clear that this language of priority and posteriority is at odds with what he is trying to express: "The term welcome of the Other expresses a simultaneity of activity and passivity which places the relation with the other outside of the dichotomies valid for things: the a priori and the a posteriori, activity and passivity" (*TI* 89).

7. In this respect, the narrative Levinas constructs has an odd similarity to classical social contract theories, in which the individual is presented as initially outside of society in a state of nature and the problem is to explain and justify his entering into the social field. The comparison with social contract theory is both invoked and inverted in *Ethics and Infinity* when Levinas says: "It is extremely important to know if society in the current sense of the term is the result of a limitation of the principle that men are predators of one another, or if to the contrary it results from the limitation of the principle that men are *for* one another" (*EI* 80). On the comparison with social contract theory, see also Bernasconi (2002, 246).

8. The quotation from Wittgenstein occurs in paragraph 145 of Lyotard's *The Differend* (1988, 83). De Vries gives a remarkable analysis of the similarities between Lyotard's and Levinas's notion of obligation, as well as a subtle reading of the difference, or *differend,* between them.

9. Rabelais writes, "Do you believe . . . that fire is the great Master of the Arts, i.e., the source of everything? If so you are wrong . . . Messer Gaster [is] the first Master of Arts in the world" (1944, 652). See also Levinas's discussion of Messer Gaster in "Secularization and Hunger" (Levinas 1998). Thanks are due to Paul Jacobs for initially tracking down this reference.

10. Tina Chanter makes a similar suggestion about Antigone, as Levinas reads the figure, in "Hands that Give and Hands that Take: A Consumptive Ethics of Exclusion, Conditionality, Abjection" (paper presented at Loyola College in Maryland, April 1, 2005).

11. VM 128 and passim. Part of Derrida's argument is that violence is a meaningful category only from *within* an ethical life. In nature, there can be no murder, that is, no ethically or morally blameworthy or proscribed action. Hence, violence belongs to the phrasing of ethics, and to speak of a pre-ethical violence (as Levinas sometimes seems to suggest in respect of the violence of conceptuality) is, strictly speaking, non-sensical.

12. See, for example, Derrida 1999, 58.

13. Levinas described the method of his work this way in 1961: "The method practiced here does indeed consist in seeking the condition of empirical situations, but it leaves to the developments called empirical, in which the conditioning possibility is accomplished—it leaves to the *concretization*—an ontological role that

specifies the meaning of the fundamental possibility, a meaning invisible in that condition" (*TI* 173). In the sentence just preceding this one, Levinas distances his own thinking from the ontic/ontological distinction so prevalent in Heidegger. This is no doubt of a piece with his very earliest critique of Heidegger as attending to existence at the expense of the existent—that is, of the unique and singular beings in whom Being is realized. Heidegger, in Levinas's view, dismisses empirical events as ontic and accords weight only to the ontological. Levinas's own method, as the quotation above states, allows to singular beings the possibility of determining fundamental aspects of human existing.

14. That Rolland's own analyses do not fall prey to these interpretations is obvious. That he is more than familiar with the entirety of Levinas's *oeuvre* is equally evident.

15. The second half of "Meaning and Sense," beginning roughly with section 6, incorporates the essay on the trace almost word for word, omitting only a few paragraphs and isolated sentences and adding a transition or change of wording here or there. Where a sentence occurs in both texts, I will cite "Meaning and Sense." The publication information given for "Phenomena and Enigma" in the *Collected Philosophical Papers* is mistaken. The essay first appeared in *Esprit* 33, no. 6 (June): 1128–42.

16. Though he still tends to think of the advent of the infinite in terms suggested by moral awakening. In "God and Philosophy," written after *Otherwise Than Being*, he speaks of the relation to the infinite as "the breakup of consciousness, which is not a repression into the unconscious but a sobering or a waking up that shakes the 'dogmatic slumber' that sleeps at the bottom of all consciousness resting upon the object" (*GCM* 63).

CHAPTER 4

1. These categories, which are standard within Anglo-American approaches to ethics, are not the predominant lenses through which ethics is viewed in French philosophical contexts; hence, the attempt to distance Levinas's thought from this schema in particular is not such a fixture in French commentaries, though it can be found there (see Rey 2001).

2. For an excellent discussion of the ambiguity of obligation, see de Vries 1998.

3. When he uses this phrase again, at *OB* 150, a footnote gives the reference as Job 4:12 (see *OB* 199n19).

4. For a fuller discussion of this idea, see Wyschogrod 1980.

5. That Levinas imagines the skeptic in this way is evident in the opening lines of *Totality and Infinity* where he writes: "Everyone will readily agree that it is of the highest importance to know whether we are not duped by morality" (*TI* 21).

6. To avoid misunderstanding, it needs to be emphasized that "valuing" in the ordinary sense in which it is used here is not in any way a synonym for "responsibility" in the Levinasian sense. The skeptic's question is "Why need I value the other's demands?" and the account of responsibility is, in a certain sense, the answer to this sort of question. However, as will be shown, to be responsible to and for the other person is not a matter of *valuing* the other; it is a matter of owing him or her an accounting of oneself.

7. That this is not Levinas's own way of going about the question of responsibility will be clear to even the most casual reader of his texts. Nonetheless, the proposal here follows the structure of his thought, even if it illuminates his position from a different perspective and in a different idiom.

8. It is worth noting that Heidegger, too, recognizes something like this structure when he makes the self a secondary formation not identical to the mode of being of *Dasein*. However, to the extent that *Dasein* is either an individuated being or the abstract mode of being of all beings such as we are, the role of others is left ambiguous at best.

9. The human being, he notes in an early text, is not a rational animal in the sense of being an animal who *in addition* to sensing and other instinctual behaviors is also capable of reason. If we use the term "rational animal," it must indicate "an original structure" (*CPP* 27).

10. A detailed account of the notion of reflection in *Totality and Infinity* is found in de Bauw (1997).

11. Oliver develops the notion of witnessing in express opposition to recent theories that have made recognition central to subjectivity. "With critical theorists," she writes, "the other is usually either the one who confers recognition on us (à la Honneth and Jürgen Habermas) or the one on whom we confer recognition (à la Taylor and Nancy Fraser)" (Oliver 2001, 6). For such theories, and equally in those where the focus has been on *misrecognition* as the basis of social relations (e.g., Lacan, Kristeva, or Butler), the intersubjective dimension of subject-formation is conceived in an essentially Hegelian fashion, as an agonistic struggle to dominate, overcome domination, or achieve a standoff between subjects. Though Oliver has a number of cogent criticisms of theories of recognition, the most salient for the comparison with Levinas is her suggestion that theories of recognition privilege sameness over alterity, since what is recognized has to be something familiar to the subject: "The subject and what is known to him and his experience are once again privileged. Any real contact with difference or otherness becomes impossible because recognition requires the assimilation of difference into something familiar" (9).

12. The case being attributed to Levinas in this respect is structurally similar to Jane Gallop's reading of Lacan's mirror stage (though the similarity will be limited to a single feature). Before the child sees itself in the mirror, it is a fragment-

ed body, or a body in bits and pieces (*corps morcelé*). The reflected image that the infant assumes and identifies as his own—the *imago*—is not preceded by a subjectivity who recognizes itself (as if it had already grasped itself or known itself). Rather, the recognition *is* the birth of subjectivity and not the act of a pre-existing subject. But, as Gallop emphasizes, we can have little confidence in this story which purports to say how each of us goes from the condition of a *corps morcelé* to that of a fully imaged ego. After all, the fragmented and unorganized body cannot be the object of an experience, since experience is possible only for one who has achieved subjectivity. Following Laplanche and Pontalis, Gallop writes, "The mirror stage would *seem to come after* 'the body in bits and pieces' and organize them into a unified image. But actually, *that* violently unorganized *image only comes after* the mirror stage so as to *represent what came before*" (Gallop 1985, 80). What came before cannot be represented except retroactively. Levinas might speak here of a dis-integrated body that belongs to an immemorial or anarchic past, one that cannot be made present except in a trace structure. So, too, with the pre-history of subjectivity itself in the Levinasian account. To have undergone without there being a subject who undergoes is possible because the locus of subjectivity is in sensibility and corporeality.

13. For a discussion of irresponsibility in Levinas, see Visker 2003.

14. Agata Zielinski (2004) thus calls it a responsibility *sans pourquoi*.

CHAPTER 5

1. Jeremy Bentham, *An Introduction to the Principles of Morals and Legislation* (Oxford: Clarendon Press, 1907), 311, quoted in Llewelyn 1991a, 234.

2. On Levinas's relation to Kant, see Chalier 1998 and Perpich 2001.

3. Llewelyn takes account of Levinas's remarks on animals in an expanded version of his original essay published in his study *The Middle Voice of Ecological Conscience* (1991b).

4. As we remarked in Chapter 2, Levinas gives the same sort of reply to Philippe Nemo when the latter proposes that Levinas is engaged in a "phenomenology of the face": "*I do not know* if one can speak of a 'phenomenology of the face,' since phenomenology describes what appears" (*EI* 85; emphasis added).

5. And, interestingly, the essay in which Levinas describes the dog Bobby also suggests that something can happen in the course of plunging one's fork into a roast at the dinner table that would be "enough . . . to make you a vegetarian again" (*DF* 151).

6. See *TO* 72, 81–84; and also *OB* inter alia 72, 91–92, 121.

7. A similar point is made by Silvia Benso (2000). A central question for the middle chapters of Benso's work is, "Does Levinas's ethics remain, along with the very tradition other aspects of which he so successfully contributes to disrupt, an

anthropocentric humanism?" (xxxiii). The central thesis of Benso's book is that in order to be an ethics of the other, Levinas's account of ethical relationships between human beings needs to be supplemented (in the Derridean sense in which supplementation fundamentally disturbs the logic of that which it supplements) by an ethics of things (44).

8. Wolfe takes the term "speciesism" largely in the meaning given to it in the work of Peter Singer. For Singer, as for Wolfe, speciesism works like racism or sexism in that it "involves systematic discrimination against an other based solely on a generic characteristic—in this case, species" (Wolfe 2003, 1).

9. It is worth noting, perhaps, that even if the face *were* analogous to a cause, the lack of non-human faces would not necessarily entail Casey's conclusion that no larger ethics of the environment is possible. Why couldn't the command for this sort of ethics come from a human face? Why would it be less compelling if it did so? I will return to this question below.

10. A fuller discussion of this idea is found in Casey 1993.

11. Again, why isn't a Kantian categorical imperative enough here? If I am setting the forest on fire or acting in a negligent way that risks setting the forest on fire, I can determine my maxim, universalize it, and already have reason enough not to act as I am currently acting: I endanger other human beings, I endanger myself, I destroy something beautiful, I destroy a natural resource, etc.

12. In and of itself, of course, a reliance on examples need not be philosophically or epistemically suspect. After all, Socrates carries off most of his arguments by employing examples and analogies. In the two cases under consideration here, the difficulty is that the examples are inevitably of clear-cut cases—or, at any rate, of cases that are supposed to seem clear-cut to us. Further consideration suggests, however, that not even these cases can do the work they are meant to do. Casey's example of the woman being beaten is supposed to show clearly how the glance opens up a moral terrain for our action and reflection, but insofar as it raises the question of how we "see" gendered relationships, it even more clearly and persuasively calls our attention to the way in which vision is disciplined. Likewise, Lingis's examples may show his account to be caught in the same humanism that he claims damages Levinas's thought.

13. When Levinas says "It is as if God spoke through the face," I find myself wondering, *pace* Llewelyn: If God speaks through a human face, why not an ungulate face, or a bovine or feline one? Moreover, I find myself sharing Llewelyn's worry that this is nothing but a covert appeal to religious authority—the "as if" notwithstanding. And, if God is not being appealed to here as an authority, Llewelyn is again right to press for a clarification of how a face can say "anything at all" that is not "anything whatsoever."

14. In a further move that abjures some of the *pathétique* of Levinas's account, Lingis remarks that suffering should not be privileged in our accounts of ethical

life, since as Nietzsche pointed out there are sufferings that do not seek to be consoled and others that it might be arrogance to think we can assuage. Moreover, Lingis wants to consider that joy might also have an imperative force. His work encourages us to imagine an ethical world that is pan-affective: open to the imperatives exerted by any number of unique, fragile events provoking all manner of affective responses.

15. Our ability to "read" the moods and desires of animals like cats, dogs, and horses is vastly greater because of our familiarity with them. It seems legitimate to conclude that we could become better "readers" of less familiar species and habitats if we were to devote the time to it.

16. This statement occurs in the context of Levinas's attempt to guard against a reading that would make his conception of ethics a kind of mysticism, or that would otherwise see it as complicit with an anti-rationalist stance. Levinas claims that his thought "breaks" with the Platonic prejudice (which he feels is widely shared in philosophy, though it takes many different guises) that all knowledge comes from the subject itself through a kind of remembering, aided perhaps by a teacher but in a way that restricts this teaching to midwifery. The other, he says, introduces into me something *new*. To suggest this, however, is not to break with rationalism, but to affirm an understanding of rationality as a product of inter-subjective relationships.

17. Such a view would take Levinas's argument down the well-known slippery slope of how much language counts as "enough" to warrant the attribution of a face, and of what we mean by language anyway. I think when Levinas refuses to say just when one has a right to be deemed a face, it is exactly because he is very wary of this slope and of all ethical systems based on criteria of inclusion (which are thus also the means for exclusion).

18. Incidentally, such a reading invites us to revisit the criticism that Levinas's ethics is in some way "religious" or "theological." The views of his critics may or may not be inspired by or equivalent to existing positive religions (though Llewelyn's position and that of Lingis both have resonances with certain elements of Buddhism), but insofar as they are sentiment-based, they are potentially far more dogmatic than a view that bases itself in the Bible and Talmud where these latter are understood not as the "true" word of God but as the prophetic revelation of a community.

19. Timmons 1997, 534. Timmons points out that most philosophers today, himself included, find this view implausible, and that what currently goes by the name of ethical naturalism is actually the much weaker view that "empirical results in psychology are relevant to questions in moral epistemology" (ibid.).

20. An ethical naturalism like John McDowell's that develops a broadly Aristotelian notion of human character as a "second nature" is not as vulnerable to this charge (McDowell 1995). However, as sophisticated as the account is that Mc-

Dowell gives, it does not deal sufficiently with the social and political aspects of moral formation.

CHAPTER 6

1. For critical responses to Levinas's notion of the feminine, see the essay by Luce Irigaray in Cohen 1986, and the essays by Irigaray and Tina Chanter in Bernasconi and Critchley 1991. See also Sanford 2000, Kayser 2000, and the edited collection, *Feminist Interpretations of Emmanuel Levinas* (Chanter 2001). For a positive reappraisal of Levinas's view of the feminine, see Chalier 1982 and Katz 2003.

2. Craig Vasey, "Faceless Women and Serious Others: Levinas, Misogyny, and Feminism," in *Ethics and Danger: Essays on Heidegger and Continental Thought,* ed. Arleen B. Dallery and Charles E. Scott, with P. Holley Roberts (Albany: State University of New York Press, 1992), 324–25, quoted in Sikka 2001, 103.

3. Quoted in Sikka 2001, 113, from an interview with Christoph von Wolzogen.

4. The most often-cited example is Levinas's puzzling failure to condemn the loss of innocent human life in the massacres at Sabra and Chatila. See his interview with Shlomo Malka and Alain Finkielkraut (*LR* 289–97).

5. It has been suggested to me that the figure of the widow as she appears in the oft-cited biblical phrase "the widow, the orphan, and the stranger," is perhaps an exception to this rule. While the widow, the orphan, and the stranger represent quintessential figures of those with whom one is in an ethical relationship, they are also presumably figures to whom one owes special consideration because they fall outside the networks of kinship that incorporate individuals into society and provide them with economic, civil, political, and cultural protections. Of course, a system that normatively presumes that women and children will be provided such protections primarily in the instance of their being subsumed within a male-headed household cannot exactly be said to be feminist-friendly, nor can it be said to convey a conception of feminine alterity that sees that alterity apart from stereotypical assumptions about women's roles as mothers and wives.

6. The term "alterity politics" is borrowed from Jeffrey Nealon (1998).

7. Among others, see the essays in Alcoff and Potter 1993, and Collins 2000.

8. The literature here is vast. Among others, see Jaggar 1983, Lloyd 1984, Irigaray 1985, Gould 1988, Benhabib 1992, Gatens 1996, and Friedman 2003.

9. This critique is not worked out explicitly or fully in Levinas's *oeuvre*, but the general tenor of his position can be found in "Freedom and Command" (*CPP* 15–23), *EI* (especially chapter 6), and *TI* (especially the section entitled "Truth and Justice," 82–101). See also Chalier 1993.

10. For a fuller treatment of this point in the feminist literature, see especially Gould 1998 and Benhabib 1992.

11. Fraser and Honneth 2004, 21. In a similar vein, Craig Calhoun (1995, 215; quoted in Fraser and Honneth 2004, 121) notes that theorists sympathetic to identity politics have tended to group together "relatively 'attractive' movements, vaguely on the left," while leaving out, without much theoretical rationale, other contemporary movements, such as the new religious right or white supremacists.

12. A similar point is made by George Yúdice: "Precisely because straight white men are perceived by progressives within identity politics and multiculturalism as the center of the dominant culture, they are not permitted to claim their own difference. There is an irony here, for the very objective of progressive politics to-day—to dismantle privilege—ends up keeping in place in our imaginary an even greater monolith of power" (1995, 280; quoted in Nealon 1998, 146).

13. For a fuller discussion of this point, see Nealon 1998, 4–5ff.

14. In French, the full passage reads: "Ni la possession, ni l'unité du nombre, ni l'unité de concept, ne me rattachent à autrui. Absence de patrie commune qui fait de l'Autre—L'Etranger; l'Etranger qui trouble le chez soi" (*Totalité et Infini* [Vrin: Editions du Poche, 28]).

15. This point is discussed in detail in Chapter 1.

16. See our discussion of responsibility and the trace in Chapter 3.

17. For a concise summary of Levinas's ban on representation (and its relation to the question of human rights), see *AT* 129–37.

18. I agree with Fanon that a society is either racist or it is not, either sexist or not, and so on. This need not mean that every member of the society harbors the view that whites are superior to blacks, or men to women, but it suggests that the policies and practices that shape the public and private lives of the society's members are ones that reflect a history of institutionalized racism and sexism, and that maintain, whether knowingly or unknowingly, the unearned and unjust privilege of some groups to the distinct detriment and disadvantage of others (see Fanon 1967, 85).

19. Sikka never explains why Levinas rejects representation as the basis for the relation to the other, and, in fact, she only cites this information secondhand, twice relying on Ewa Ziarek's characterization of the originality of Levinas's ethics as residing in its "obstinate refusal to think the other" (quoted in Sikka 2001, 105, 115). The citation is taken from Ziarek's essay, "Kristeva and Levinas: Mourning, Ethics, and the Feminine," in *Ethics, Politics, and Difference in Julia Kristeva's Writing*, ed. Kelly Oliver (New York: Routledge, 1993). For a more extended reading of Levinas's politics, see Ziarek 2001.

20. See Benhabib 2002 for a detailed critique of the assumption that cultures and cultural identities are static.

21. For an interesting and detailed reading of Levinas's politics, see Caygill 2000.

Works Cited

Abensour, Miguel. 1998. "To Think Utopia Otherwise." *Graduate Faculty Philosophy Journal* 20/21, no. 2/1: 251–79.

Agamben, Giorgio. 1999. *Potentialities*. Stanford, CA: Stanford University Press.

Ajzenstat, Oona. 2001. *Driven Back to the Text: The Premodern Sources of Levinas's Postmodernism*. Pittsburgh: Duquesne University Press.

Alcoff, Linda. 1997. "Cultural Feminism versus Post-Structuralism: The Identity Crisis in Feminist Theory." In *The Second Wave*, edited by Linda Nicholson, 330-55. New York: Routledge.

Alcoff, Linda, and Elizabeth Potter, eds. 1993. *Feminist Epistemologies*. New York: Routledge.

Arendt, Hannah. 1958. *The Human Condition*. Chicago: University of Chicago Press.

Bailhache, Gérard. 1994. *Le sujet chez Emmanuel Levinas: Fragilité et subjectivité*. Paris: Presses Universitaire de France.

Baker, Peter. 1995. *Deconstruction and the Ethical Turn*. Gainesville: University of Florida Press.

Baudrillard, Jean, and Marc Guillaume. 1994. *Figures de l'altérité*. Paris: Descartes et Cie.

Bauman, Zygmunt. 1989. *Modernity and the Holocaust*. Ithaca, NY: Cornell University Press.

Bauw, Christine de. 1997. *L'Envers du sujet: Lire autrement Emmanuel Levinas*. Brussels: Editions Ousia.

Beauvoir, Simone de. 1994. *The Ethics of Ambiguity*. Translated by Bernard Frechtman. New York: Citadel Press.

Benhabib, Seyla. 1992. *Situating the Self: Gender, Community, and Postmodernism in Contemporary Ethics*. New York: Routledge.

———. 2002. *The Claims of Culture: Equality and Diversity in the Global Era*. Princeton, NJ: Princeton University Press.

Benso, Silvia. 2000. *The Face of Things: A Different Side of Ethics*. Albany: State University of New York.

Bernasconi, Robert. 2002. "What is the Question to Which 'Substitution' is the Answer?" In *The Cambridge Companion to Levinas,* edited by Simon Critchley and Robert Bernasconi, 234–51. Cambridge: Cambridge University Press.

———. 2006. "Strangers and Slaves in the Land of Egypt: Levinas and the Politics of Otherness." In *Difficult Justice: Commentaries on Levinas and Politics,* edited by Asher Horowitz and Gad Horowitz, 246–61. Toronto: University of Toronto Press.

Bernasconi, Robert, and Simon Critchley, eds. 1991. *Re-reading Levinas.* Bloomington: Indiana University Press.

Bernasconi, Robert, and David Wood, eds. 1988. *The Provocation of Levinas: Rethinking the Other.* London: Routledge.

Blum, Roland Paul. 1983. "Emmanuel Levinas' Theory of Commitment." *Philosophy and Phenomenological Research* 44, no. 2 (December): 148–68.

Breslin, James. 1993. *Mark Rothko: A Biography.* Chicago: University of Chicago Press.

Brown, Wendy. 1993. "Wounded Attachments." *Political Theory* 21, no. 3 (August): 390–410.

Butler, Judith. 1993. "Kierkegaard's Speculative Despair." In *The Age of German Idealism,* edited by Robert C. Solomon and Kathleen M. Higgins, 363–95. New York: Routledge.

———. 1999. *Gender Trouble: Feminism and the Subversion of Identity.* 2nd ed. London: Routledge.

———. 2004. *Precarious Life: The Powers of Mourning and Violence.* London: Verso.

Calhoun, Craig. 1995. *Critical Social Theory: Culture, History, and the Challenge of Difference.* Cambridge, MA: Blackwell Press.

Caputo, John. 1993. *Against Ethics: Contributions to a Poetics of Obligation with Constant Reference to Deconstruction.* Bloomington: Indiana University Press.

Casey, Edward. 1993. *Getting Back Into Place: Toward a Renewed Understanding of the Place-World.* Bloomington: Indiana University Press.

———. 2000. "Taking a Glance at the Environing World." In *Confluences: Phenomenology and Postmodernity, Environment, Race, Gender,* edited by Daniel J. Martino, 3–38. Pittsburgh: Duquesne University Simon Silverman Phenomenology Center.

Cavarero, Adriana. 2002. "Who Engenders Politics?" In *Italian Feminist Theory and Practice: Equality and Sexual Difference,* edited by Graziella Parati and Rebecca J. West, 88–103. Madison, NJ: Fairleigh Dickinson University Press.

Caygill, Howard. 2002. *Levinas and the Political.* London: Routledge.

Chalier, Catherine. 1982. *Figures du féminin: Lecture d'Emmanuel Lévinas.* Paris: La Nuit Surveillée.

————. 1993. *Lévinas: L'utopie de l'humain.* Paris: Albin Michel.

————. 1998. *Pour une morale au-delà du savoir: Kant et Levinas.* Paris: Albin Michel.

Chanter, Tina, ed. 2001. *Feminist Interpretations of Emmanuel Levinas.* University Park: Pennsylvania State University Press.

Ciaramelli, Fabio. 1989. *Transcendance et éthique: Essai sur Lévinas.* Brussels: Ousia.

————. 1991. "Levinas's Ethical Discourse between Individuation and Universality." In *Re-reading Levinas,* edited by Robert Bernasconi and Simon Critchley, 81–105. Bloomington: Indiana University Press.

Cohen, Richard. 1994. *Elevations: The Height of the Good in Rosenzweig and Levinas.* Chicago: University of Chicago Press.

————, ed. 1986. *Face to Face with Levinas.* Albany: State University of New York Press.

Collins, Patricia Hill. 2000. *Black Feminist Thought: Knowledge, Consciousness, and the Politics of Empowerment.* 2nd ed. New York: Routledge.

Connolly, William. 2002. *Identity/Difference: Democratic Negotiations of Political Paradox.* Minneapolis: University of Minnesota Press.

Critchley, Simon. 1992. *The Ethics of Deconstruction.* Cambridge, MA: Blackwell Publishers.

————. 1999. *Ethics—Politics—Subjectivity: Essays on Derrida, Levinas, and Contemporary French Thought.* London: Verso Books.

Critchley, Simon, and Robert Bernasconi, eds. 2002. *The Cambridge Companion to Levinas.* Cambridge: Cambridge University Press.

Davis, Colin. 1996. *Levinas: An Introduction.* Cambridge: Polity Press.

Derrida, Jacques. 1982. *Margins of Philosophy.* Translated by Alan Bass. Chicago: University of Chicago Press.

————. 1986. "Débats." In *Altérités: Jacques Derrida et Pierre-Jean Labarrière,* 69–94. Paris: Osiris.

————. 1991a. "At This Moment in This Text Here I Am." In *Re-Reading Levinas,* edited by Robert Bernasconi and Simon Critchley, 1–48. Bloomington: Indiana University Press.

————. 1991b. "'Eating Well,' or the Calculation of the Subject: An Interview with Jacques Derrida." In *Who Comes After the Subject?* edited by Eduardo Cadava, Peter Connor, and Jean-Luc Nancy, 96–119. New York: Routledge.

————. 1999. *Adieu: To Emmanuel Levinas.* Translated by Pascale-Anne Brault and Michael Naas. Stanford, CA: Stanford University Press.

Descartes, Rene. 1983. *The Philosophical Works of Descartes,* vol. 1. Translated by Elizabeth S. Haldane and G. R. T. Ross. Cambridge: Cambridge University Press.

Descombes, Vincent. 1981. *Modern French Philosophy.* Cambridge: Cambridge University Press.

de Vries, Hent. 1998. "On Obligation: Lyotard and Levinas." *Graduate Faculty Philosophy Journal* 20/21, no. 2/1: 83–112.

———. 2005. *Minimal Theologies: Critiques of Secular Reason in Adorno and Levinas.* Translated by Geoffrey Hale. Baltimore: Johns Hopkins University Press.

Dhaliwal, Amarpal. 1994. "Responses." *Radical Society* 23, no. 3: 81–98.

Dreyfus, Hubert L. 1991. *Being-in-the-world: A Commentary on Heidegger's "Being and Time, Division I."* Cambridge MA: MIT Press.

Dostoyevsky, Fyodor. 1957. *The Brothers Karamazov.* Translated by Constance Garnett. New York: New American Library.

Fanon, Frantz. 1967. *Black Skin, White Masks.* New York: Grove Press.

Feron, Etienne. 1992. *De l'idée de transcendance à la question du langage.* Grenoble: Editions Jérôme Millon.

Fischer, John M., ed. 1986. *Moral Responsibility.* Ithaca, NY: Cornell University Press.

Ford, Richard T. 2006. *Racial Culture: A Critique.* Princeton, NJ: Princeton University Press.

Fraser, Nancy. 1997. *Justice Interruptus: Critical Reflections on the "Postsocialist" Condition.* New York: Routledge.

Fraser, Nancy, and Axel Honneth. 2004. *Redistribution or Recognition? A Political–Philosophical Exchange.* London: Verso.

Friedman, Marilyn. 2003. *Autonomy, Gender, Politics.* Oxford: Oxford University Press.

Gallop, Jane. 1985. *Reading Lacan.* Ithaca, NY: Cornell University Press.

Gatens, Moira. 1996. *Imaginary Bodies: Ethics, Power, and Corporeality.* London: Routledge.

Gibbs, Robert. 1992. *Correlations in Rosenzweig and Levinas.* Princeton, NJ: Princeton University Press.

Gould, Carol. 1988. *Rethinking Democracy: Freedom and Social Cooperation in Politics, Economy, and Society.* Cambridge: Cambridge University Press.

Greisch, Jean. 1998. "Ethics and Ontology: Some 'Hypocritical' Considerations." *Graduate Faculty Philosophy Journal* 20/21, no. 2/1: 41–70.

Greisch, Jean, and Jacques Rolland, eds. 1993. *Emmanuel Levinas: L'éthique comme philosophie première.* Colloque de Cerisy-la-Salle. Paris: Cerf.

Hatley, James. 2000. *Suffering Witness: The Quandary of Responsibility after the Irreparable.* Albany: State University of New York Press.

Held, Virginia. 1989. "Birth and Death." *Ethics* 99, no. 2 (January 1989): 362–88.

hooks, bell. 1989. *talking back: thinking feminist, thinking black.* Boston: South End Press.

Ingarden, Roman. 1973a. *The Cognition of the Literary Work of Art.* Translated by Ruth Ann Crowley and Kenneth R. Olson. Evanston, IL: Northwestern University Press.

———. 1973b. *The Literary Work of Art.* Translated by George G. Grabowicz. Evanston, IL: Northwestern University Press.

Irigaray, Luce. 1985. *This Sex Which Is Not One.* Cornell, NY: Cornell University Press.

Jacob, André, ed. 1989. *Encyclopédie philosophiques universelle.* Paris: Presses Universitaires de France.

Jaggar, Alison. 1983. *Feminist Politics and Human Nature.* Totowa, NJ: Rowman and Allanheld.

Janicaud, Dominique. 1991. *Le tournant théologique de la phénoménologie française.* Combas: Editions de l'Éclat. (English translation in Dominique Janicaud et al., *Phenomenology and the Theological Turn: The French Debate* [New York: Fordham University Press, 2001]).

Kagan, Shelley. 1989. *The Limits of Morality.* Oxford: Oxford University Press.

Kayser, Paulette. 2000. *Emmanuel Levinas: La trace du feminine.* Paris: Presses Universitaire de France.

Katz, Claire. 2003. *Levinas, Judaism, and the Feminine: The Silent Footsteps of Rebecca.* Indianapolis: University of Indiana Press.

Kittay, Eva. 1998. "Welfare, Dependency, and a Public Ethic of Care." *Social Justice* 25, no. 1 (Spring): 82–94.

Korsgaard, Christine M. 1996. *The Sources of Normativity.* Cambridge: Cambridge University Press.

Le Doeuff, Michèle. 1989. *The Philosophical Imaginary.* Translated by Colin Gordon. Stanford, CA: Stanford University Press.

Levinas, Emmanuel. 1989. "Entretien." In *Répondre d'Autrui: Emmanuel Levinas,* edited by Jean-Christophe Aeschlimann, 9–16. Boudry-Neuchâtel: Editions de la Baconnière.

———. 1998. "Secularization and Hunger." *Graduate Faculty Philosophy Journal* 20/21, no. 2/1: 3–12.

Levinas, Emmanuel, and Richard Kearney. 1986. "Dialogue with Emmanuel Levinas." In *Face to Face with Levinas,* edited by Richard Cohen, 13–33. Albany: State University of New York Press.

Lingis, Alphonso. 1998. "Practical Necessity." *Graduate Faculty Philosophy Journal* 20/21, no. 2/1: 71–82.

Llewelyn, John. 1991a. "Am I Obsessed by Bobby?" In *Re-reading Levinas,* edited by Robert Bernasconi and Simon Critchley, 234–45. Bloomington: Indiana University Press.

————. 1991b. *The Middle Voice of Ecological Conscience.* New York: St. Martin's Press.

————. 1995. *Emmanuel Levinas: The Genealogy of Ethics.* New York: Routledge.

————. 2000. *The HypoCritical Imagination: Between Kant and Levinas.* New York: Routledge.

Lloyd, Genevieve. 1984, 1993. *The Man of Reason: "Male" and "Female" in Western Philosophy.* Minneapolis: University of Minnesota Press.

————. 1988. *The Differend: Phrases in Dispute.* Translated by Georges Van Den Abbeele. Minneapolis: University of Minnesota Press.

Manning, Robert J. S. 1993. *Interpreting Otherwise Than Heidegger.* Pittsburgh: Duquesne University Press.

Marion, Jean-Luc. 1998. "A Note Concerning the Ontological Indifference." *Graduate Faculty Philosophy Journal* 20/21, no. 2/1: 25–40.

————. 2002. *In Excess: Studies of Saturated Phenomena.* Translated by Robyn Horner and Vincent Berraud. New York: Fordham University Press.

————, ed. 2000. *Emmanuel Lévinas: Positivité et transcendence.* Paris: Presses Universitaires de France.

May, Todd. 1997. *Reconsidering Difference.* University Park: Pennsylvania State University Press.

McDowell, John. 1995. "Two Sorts of Naturalism." In *Virtues and Reasons: Philippa Foot and Moral Theory,* edited by Rosalind Hursthouse, Gavin Lawrence, and Warren Quinn, 149–79. Oxford: Clarendon Press.

Mies, Françoise. 1994. *De l'autre: Essai de typologie.* Namur: Presses Universitaires de Namur.

Minnow, Martha. 1990. "Adjudicating Differences: Conflicts Among Feminist Lawyers." In *Conflicts in Feminism,* edited by Marianne Hirsch and Evelyn Fox Keller, 149–63. New York: Routledge.

————. 1985. "Learning to Live with the Dilemma of Difference: Bilingual and Special Education." *Law and Contemporary Problems* 48, no. 2 (Spring): 157–211.

Mohanty, Chandra. 1991. "Under Western Eyes: Feminist Scholarship and Colonial Discourses." In *Third World Women and the Politics of Feminism,* edited by Chandra Talpade Mohanty, Ann Russo, and Lourdes Torres, 58–80. Bloomington: Indiana University Press.

Mouffe, Chantal, ed. 1996. *Deconstruction and Pragmatism.* London: Routledge.

Nagel, Thomas. 1970. *The Possibility of Altruism.* Princeton, NJ: Princeton University Press.

Nancy, Jean-Luc. 2000. *Being Singular Plural.* Translated by Robert D. Richardson and Anne E. O'Byrne. Stanford, CA: Stanford University Press.

Narayan, Uma. 1997. *Dislocating Cultures: Identities, Traditions, and Third World Feminism.* New York: Routledge.

Nealon, Jeffrey T. 1998. *Alterity Politics: Ethics and Performative Subjectivity.* Durham, NC: Duke University Press.

Newman, Michael. 2000. "Sensibility, Trauma, and the Trace: Levinas from Phenomenology to the Immemorial." In *The Face of the Other and the Trace of God: Essays on the Philosophy of Emmanuel Levinas,* edited by Jeffrey Bloechl, 90–129. New York: Fordham University Press.

Okin, Susan. 1999. *Is Multiculturalism Bad for Women?* Princeton, NJ: Princeton University Press.

Olafson, Frederick. 1987. *Heidegger and the Philosophy of Mind.* New Haven, CT: Yale University Press.

Oliver, Kelly. 2001. *Witnessing: Beyond Recognition.* Minneapolis: University of Minnesota Press.

Peperzak, Adriaan. 1993. *To the Other: An Introduction to the Philosophy of Emmanuel Levinas.* West Lafayette, IN: Purdue University Press.

———. 1997. *Beyond: The Philosophy of Emmanuel Levinas.* Evanston, IL: Northwestern University Press.

———, ed. 1995. *Ethics as First Philosophy: The Significance of Emmanuel Levinas for Philosophy, Literature, and Religion.* New York: Routledge.

Perpich, Diane. 2001. "Freedom Called into Question: Levinas's Defense of Heteronomy." In *In Proximity: Emmanuel Levinas and the Eighteenth Century,* edited by Melvyn New, with Robert Bernasconi and Richard A. Cohen, 303–25. Lubbock: Texas Tech University Press.

Poirié, François. 1987. *Emmanuel Lévinas: Qui êtes vous?* Paris: La Manufacture.

Putnam, Hilary. 2004. *Ethics without Ontology.* Cambridge, MA: Harvard University Press.

Rabelais. 1944. *Gargantua and Pantagruel.* Translated by Jacques Le Clercq. New York: Modern Library.

Rey, Jean-François. 2001. *La Mesure de l'homme: L'idée d'humanité dans la philosophie d'Emmanuel Lévinas.* Paris: Éditions Michalon.

Ricoeur, Paul. 1992. *Oneself as Another.* Translated by Kathleen Blamey. Chicago: University of Chicago Press.

———. 1997. *Autrement: Lecture d'autrement qu'être ou au-delà de l'essence d'Emmanuel Lévinas.* Paris: PUF.

Robbins, Jill. 1999. *Altered Reading: Levinas and Literature.* Chicago: University of Chicago Press.

Rolland, Jacques. 2000. *Parcours de l'autrement.* Paris: Presses Universitaire de France.

Rosenzweig, Franz. 1937. "Urzelle des Stern der Erlösung." In *Kleinere Schriften.* Berlin: Schocken Verlag.

Sandford, Stella. 2000. *The Metaphysics of Love: Gender and Transcendence in Levinas.* London: Athlone Press.

Scheman, Noami. 1997. "Queering the Center by Centering the Queer." In *Feminists Rethink the Self,* edited by Diana Tietjens Meyers, 124–62. Boulder, CO: Westview Press.

Scott, Charles. 1995. "A People's Witness Beyond Politics." In *Ethics as First Philosophy,* edited by Adriaan T. Peperzak, 25–35. New York: Routledge.

Scott, Joan. 1990. "Deconstructing Equality-versus-Difference." In *Conflicts in Feminism,* edited by Marianne Hirsch and Evelyn Fox Keller, 134–48. New York: Routledge.

Shachar, Ayelet. 2000. "The Puzzle of Interlocking Power Hierarchies: Sharing the Pieces of Jurisdictional Authority." *Harvard Civil Rights–Civil Liberties Law Review* 35, no. 2 (Summer): 387–426.

Sikka, Sonia. 2001. "The Delightful Other: Portraits of the Feminine in Kierkegaard, Nietzsche, and Levinas." In *Feminist Interpretations of Emmanuel Levinas,* edited by Tina Chanter, 96–118. University Park: Pennsylvania State University Press.

Sokolowski, Robert. 1964. *The Formation of Husserl's Concept of Constitution.* The Hague: Martinus Nijhoff.

Timmons, Mark. 1997. "Will Cognitive Science Change Ethics?: Review Essay of Larry May, Marilyn Friedman and Andy Clark (eds.), *Mind and Morals: Essays on Ethics and Cognitive Science.*" *Philosophical Psychology* 10, no. 4 (December): 531–40.

Visker, Rudi. 1997. "The Core of My Opposition to Levinas: A Clarification for Richard Rorty." *Ethical Perspectives: The Journal of the European Ethics Network* 3, no. 4 (October): 154–70.

———. 1999. *Truth and Singularity: Taking Foucault into Phenomenology.* Dordrecht: Kluwer Academic Publishers.

———. 2003. "Is Ethics Fundamental? Questioning Levinas on Irresponsibility." *Continental Philosophy Review* 36, no. 3 (July): 263–302.

Wahl, Jean. 1944. *Existence Humaine et Transcendance.* Neuchatel: Editions de la Baconnière.

———. 1993. "The Roots of Existentialism." In *Essays in Existentialism,* by Jean-Paul Sartre; edited, with a foreword by Wade Baskin, 3–28. New York: Citadel.

Waldenfels, Bernhard. 1994. *Antwortregister.* Frankfurt am Main: Suhrkamp Verlag.

Williams, Wendy W. 1997. "The Equality Crisis: Some Reflections on Culture, Courts, and Feminism." In *The Second Wave: A Reader in Feminist Theory,* edited by Linda Nicholson, 71–91. New York: Routledge.

Wolfe, Cary. 2003. *Animal Rites: American Culture, the Discourse of Species, and Posthumanist Theory.* Chicago: University of Chicago Press.

Wood, David. 1999. "*Comment ne pas manger*—Deconstruction and Humanism." In *Animal Others: On Ethics, Ontology, and Animal Life,* edited by H. Peter Steeves, 15–35. Albany: State University of New York Press.

Wright, Tamra, Peter Hughes, and Alison Ainley. 1988. "The Paradox of Morality: An Interview with Emmanuel Levinas." In *The Provocation of Levinas: Rethinking the Other,* edited by Robert Bernasconi and David Wood, 168–80. London: Routledge.

Wyschogrod, Edith. 1980. "Doing Before Hearing." In *Textes pour Emmanuel Lévinas,* edited by François Laruelle, 179–203. Paris: J.-M. Place.

Young, Iris Marion. 1990. *Justice and the Politics of Difference.* Princeton, NJ: Princeton University Press.

Yúdice, George. 1995. "What's a Straight White Man to Do?" In *Constructing Masculinity,* edited by Maurice Berger, Brian Wallis, and Simon Watson. New York: Routledge.

Ziarek, Ewa. 2001. *An Ethics of Dissensus: Postmodernity, Feminism, and the Politics of Radical Democracy.* Stanford, CA: Stanford University Press.

Zielinski, Agata. 2004. *Levinas: La responsabilité est sans pourquoi.* Paris: PUF.

Index

Cultural Memory | in the Present

Kaja Silverman, *World Spectators*

Samuel Weber, *Institution and Interpretation: Expanded Edition*

Jeffrey S. Librett, *The Rhetoric of Cultural Dialogue: Jews and Germans in the Epoch of Emancipation*

Ulrich Baer, *Remnants of Song: Trauma and the Experience of Modernity in Charles Baudelaire and Paul Celan*

Samuel C. Wheeler III, *Deconstruction as Analytic Philosophy*

David S. Ferris, *Silent Urns: Romanticism, Hellenism, Modernity*

Rodolphe Gasché, *Of Minimal Things: Studies on the Notion of Relation*

Sarah Winter, *Freud and the Institution of Psychoanalytic Knowledge*

Samuel Weber, *The Legend of Freud: Expanded Edition*

Aris Fioretos, ed., *The Solid Letter: Readings of Friedrich Hölderlin*

J. Hillis Miller / Manuel Asensi, *Black Holes / J. Hillis Miller; or, Boustrophedonic Reading*

Miryam Sas, *Fault Lines: Cultural Memory and Japanese Surrealism*

Peter Schwenger, *Fantasm and Fiction: On Textual Envisioning*

Didier Maleuvre, *Museum Memories: History, Technology, Art*

Jacques Derrida, *Monolingualism of the Other; or, The Prosthesis of Origin*

Andrew Baruch Wachtel, *Making a Nation, Breaking a Nation: Literature and Cultural Politics in Yugoslavia*

Niklas Luhmann, *Love as Passion: The Codification of Intimacy*

Mieke Bal, ed., *The Practice of Cultural Analysis: Exposing Interdisciplinary Interpretation*

Jacques Derrida and Gianni Vattimo, eds., *Religion*